'Powell and Pressburger made beautiful, deviant and mongrel films that are famously un-pindownable. Moor's book challenges this belief in their rootlessness and shows how they fit into the movie genres, social history, empire, gender, nation, literature and iconography. He's particularly good on the postwar films, and brilliant on David Niven.'

Mark Cousins

'At last, an in-depth account of the Powell-Pressburger partnership. Andrew Moor does full justice to the richness of their great films of the 1940s, and relates them in fascinating ways to the events of this pivotal decade in twentieth-century British history.'

Charles Barr

'Moor's sustained and coherent investigation of the films ... meaningfully explores the central importance of the construction of "magic spaces" within an aesthetic which is often seen to sit uncomfortably within prevailing notions of British cinematic realism. The critical commentaries are exceptionally sensitive and illuminating, a riposte to those contemporary critics who found the films "baffling", and a lifeline to students encountering them for the first time today. Moor's ability to relate these films to cultural dynamics, not least emergent postwar masculinities and femininities, and to the quest for idealism which he sees as central to Powell and Pressburger's films, is powerfully cogent.'

Screen

'In the Introduction almost every sentence has something important to say without being dense or difficult to read. Moor's style is accessible, communicating complex ideas in a compact and comprehensible way. ... [H]e combines a lightness of touch with an intellectual gravitas... Moor is passionate about his subject and has researched and read widely.'

Historical Journal of Film and Television

'Moor delivers a strong auteurist reading of Powell and Pressburger's work, taking care not to neglect the larger framework of cultural references and filmic reception. In unearthing a series of narrative spaces that blend the boundaries between the individual and environment and illustrating the extent to which identity can be "performed" and is a fluid negotiated concept, Moor provides a valuable text.'

Journal of Popular Film and Television

Cinema and Society series
GENERAL EDITOR: JEFFREY RICHARDS

Best of British: Cinema and Society from 1930 to the Present
  Anthony Aldgate and Jeffrey Richards

Brigadoon, Braveheart and the Scots: Distortions of Scotland in Hollywood Cinema
  Colin McArthur

The British at War: Cinema, State and Propaganda, 1939–1945
  James Chapman

British Cinema and the Cold War
  Tony Shaw

Children, Cinema and Censorship: From Dracula *to the* Dead End Kids
  Sarah J. Smith

The Crowded Prairie: American National Identity in the Hollywood Western
  Michael Coyne

An Everyday Magic: Cinema and Cultural Memory
  Annette Kuhn

Femininity in the Frame: Women and 1950s British Popular Cinema
  Melanie Bell

Film and Community in Britain and France: From La Règle du Jeu *to* Room at the Top
  Margaret Butler

Film Propaganda: Soviet Russia and Nazi Germany
  Richard Taylor

From Moscow to Madrid: Postmodern Cities, European Cinema
  Ewa Mazierska and Laura Rascaroli

Hollywood Genres and Post-War America: Masculinity, Family and Nation in Popular Movies and Film Noir
  Mike Chopra-Gant

Hollywood's History Films
  David Eldridge

Licence to Thrill: A Cultural History of the James Bond Films
  James Chapman

Past and Present: National Identity and the British Historical Film
  James Chapman

Powell and Pressburger: A Cinema of Magic Spaces
  Andrew Moor

Propaganda and the German Cinema, 1933–1945
  David Welch

Spaghetti Westerns: Cowboys and Europeans from Karl May to Sergio Leone
  Christopher Frayling

Spectacular Narratives: Hollywood in the Age of the Blockbuster
  Geoff King

Typical Men: The Representation of Masculinity in Popular British Cinema
  Andrew Spicer

The Unknown 1930s: An Alternative History of the British Cinema, 1929–1939
  Edited by Jeffrey Richards

POWELL
A Cinema of Magic Spaces
PRESSBURGER

Andrew Moor

I.B. TAURIS
LONDON · NEW YORK

New paperback edition published in 2012 by I.B.Tauris & Co Ltd
6 Salem Road, London W2 4BU
175 Fifth Avenue, New York NY 10010
www.ibtauris.com

Distributed in the United States and Canada
Exclusively by Palgrave Macmillan
175 Fifth Avenue, New York NY 10010

First published in hardback in 2005 by I.B.Tauris & Co Ltd

Copyright © Andrew Moor, 2005, 2012

The right of Andrew Moor to be identified as the author of this work has been asserted by him in accordance with the Copyright, Designs and Patent Act 1988.

All rights reserved. Except for brief quotations in a review, this book, or any part thereof, may not be reproduced, stored in or introduced into a retrieval system, or transmitted, in any form or by any means, electronic, mechanical, photocopying, recording or otherwise, without the prior written permission of the publisher.

ISBN: 978 1 78076 377 4

A full CIP record for this book is available from the British Library
A full CIP record is available from the Library of Congress

Library of Congress Catalog Card Number: available

Typeset in Garamond by Dexter Haven Associates Ltd, London
Printed and bound by CPI Group (UK) Ltd, Croydon, CR0 4YY

For Mam,
and
in memory of Dad

Contents

	Illustrations	viii
	General Editor's Introduction	ix
	Acknowledgements	xi
	Introduction – Magic Spaces: Migration, Home and the National	1
1	Alien Territories and Enemy Lines – *The Spy in Black, Contraband, 49th Parallel, '…one of our aircraft is missing'*	27
2	Satire, Epic and Memory – *The Life and Death of Colonel Blimp*	54
3	Two Pastorals – *A Canterbury Tale, I Know Where I'm Going!*	85
4	Post-war Masculinities: The Pilot and the Back-room Boy – *A Matter of Life and Death, The Small Back Room*	126
5	Post-war Femininities: Mopu, Madness and Melodrama – *Black Narcissus*	168
6	Art and Artists – *The Red Shoes, The Tales of Hoffmann*	197
	Notes	229
	Bibliography	239
	Index	245

Illustrations

1. Gender boundaries: Conrad Veidt hesitates as Valerie Hobson draws the line in *Contraband*. (BFI Stills) — 44
2. The Great War: Paul Nash, *The Menin Road* (1918). (Courtesy of The Imperial War Museum, London) — 77
3. The Great War remembered: Roger Livesey on Alfred Junge's set in *The Life and Death of Colonel Blimp*. (BFI Stills, © Carlton International Media Ltd) — 77
4. Ludic spaces: Sgt John Sweet and village children find pastoral release in *A Canterbury Tale*. (BFI Stills, © Carlton International Media Ltd) — 100
5. Post-war, post-op reparations: David Niven and Kim Hunter embrace the future in *A Matter of Life and Death*. (BFI Stills, © Carlton International Media Ltd) — 149
6. Kathleen Byron crosses the threshold into psychosis in *Black Narcissus*. (BFI Stills, © Carlton International Media Ltd) — 186
7. Robert Helpmann contemplates his fragmented, de-centred self. (BFI Stills) — 222

General Editor's Introduction

Few film-makers have been as controversial, as innovative, as adventurous, as visionary or as deeply romantic as Michael Powell and Emeric Pressburger. Working within mainstream commercial cinema, they produced a succession of films that were distinctively and recognisably personal, yet said something profound about England and the English. They were without question the most remarkable of several film-making teams who made major contributions to British cinema. It was Alexander Korda who first teamed Powell and Pressburger to make *The Spy in Black* in 1939. Pressburger, a Hungarian Jewish writer and refugee from Nazi Germany, and Powell, the Kentish director who had gained critical recognition with *Edge of the World* (1937), worked so well together that in 1942 they formed the Archers, one of a number of independent production units working under the overall umbrella of Rank. They signed their films jointly – produced, directed and written by Michael Powell and Emeric Pressburger – though it was generally recognised that Pressburger provided the scripts and Powell directed. The films which the Archers produced read like a roll call of Britain's finest – *The Life and Death of Colonel Blimp, A Canterbury Tale, Black Narcissus, The Red Shoes* and *I Know Where I'm Going!*, to name but a few. In his absorbing and insightful new study, Andrew Moor analyses the key films of Powell and Pressburger from a variety of revealing perspectives: space and place, myth and magic, masculinity and femininity, the exotic and the pastoral, art and ideology. Wide-ranging, scholarly, enthusiastic and readable, the book makes a major contribution to our understanding of a unique body of work.

Jeffrey Richards

Acknowledgements

During this book's elephantine gestation I received advice and general midwifery from seasoned practitioners. Bruce Babington, Peter Evans, Chris Perriam, Phil Powrie and John Saunders provided insight, encouragement and films to watch. Particular thanks to Bruce, for wise counsel. Ian Christie encountered a rough-hewn first draft of this work, and has been on hand with good advice since. I'm indebted to him for his valuable assistance. Any defects in this final product are down to me, and bear no resemblance to help given.

Thelma Schoonmaker kindly granted me access to Michael Powell's archive at the British Film Institute's Special Collections Department, where Janet Moat was her helpful, hospitable self. The staff in the BFI library often leapt to my aid too. I'm grateful to the Imperial War Museum, London, for permission to reproduce the image of Paul Nash's *The Menin Road*. I've tried to locate copyright for all material used; and inquiries regarding this should be directed to the publishers.

Philippa Brewster at I. B. Tauris and Jeffrey Richards both had confidence in this project and lent some of it to me. Emails, videos and web pages from Steve Crook were appreciated, and seminar discussions with film students at the University of Wales, Bangor, helped to clarify some of my muddier thought patterns. The University of Wales granted study leave, the Arts and Humanities Research Board (AHRB) supplemented it, and the British Academy Small Grants scheme subsidised trips to London: this assistance smoothed the book to its conclusion. I'm also grateful to colleagues at Bangor for helping to fill whatever breach was left by my absence. Particular thanks to Linda Jones for help with references and formatting.

Blimp makes me reflect on friendship. David Alderson, Robin Beaumont, David Clarke, Tony Claydon, Stephen Emms, Jerome de Groot, David Robinson, Matthew Rothery, Sharon Ruston, Ceri Sullivan and Simon Tibbs have been priceless, and their support (nutritional, emotional, intellectual, residential and otherwise) kept things chugging along.

Greg Thorpe makes things fun and gladly gets special mention – for thoroughbred support on the home straight, for tolerating the wayward irregularities of my schedules (and causing some), for his keen proof-reader's eye, for pithy marginal scribbles, and for lots more.

Introduction
Magic Spaces: Migration, Home and the National

In my films, miracles occur on screen.

Michael Powell, *A Life in Movies*

MAGIC SPACES

What is the relationship between migrant film-makers and the domestic cinema of their new homeland? Can they assume vital positions in the culture of their host nation while still speaking 'from the margins'? Does the experience of deterritorialisation and reterritorialisation register in their films? What differences are there between cosmopolitan experiences of travel and tourism, and the the condition of exile? Do representations of journeys, border crossings and other geographical shifts relate to, or tell us anything about, more interior, psychological 'journeys' and changes in identity? What is the link between the subject and the space s/he occupies? Topical questions like these, central to post-colonial studies, to postmodernism and to cultural geography, can also be asked about British and European cinema of the 1930s and 1940s, a time and a place of massive political upheaval and migration which also saw notions of 'national cinema' begin to solidify. The cinema of Michael Powell and Emeric Pressburger cannot be reduced to these lines of inquiry, but their long collaboration saw them develop an aesthetic which speaks of their own trans-national status and yet simultaneously strikes a chord with older European Romantic cultures. Powell was, from early on, open to European

1

and global influences, but he still expressed a deep fascination with and affection for Britishness. As a young man he took himself to the French Riviera to work in his father's hotel at Cap-Ferrat, an experience which brought him into contact with the Dublin-born Hollywood director Rex Ingram at the Victorine Studios in Nice and thereafter into film-making himself. Powell is cosmopolitan and international, and his formative exposure to the cinematic spectacle of the silent period from France, Germany and America places him in a tradition oblivious to the narrow realist concerns which would become more central to British cinema by the 1940s. Returning to Britain in 1928, a prolific career on low-budget quota films then led to *The Edge of the World* (1937), which he wrote and directed. Powell's imagination was kindled by the evacuation of St Kilda, and the film was shot in the spectacular, remote landscape of Foula in the Shetlands. It trails with it clouds of mythic grandeur from the silent era, telling an epic saga of love, death, tribal continuity and enforced exile, while Robert Flaherty's *Nanook of the North* (1922) and *Man of Aran* (1934) showed Powell how grand narratives and a sense of geography could be coupled to a sense of 'documentary' truthfulness. The film won Powell respect and led him to producer-director Alexander Korda.

Pressburger, three years Powell's senior, was born into a Jewish Hungarian background in 1902, and after a migrant childhood his home town of Temesvar in Transylvania was incorporated into Romania in the wake of the First World War. This initiated a lifetime of exile from his language and homeland. Spells in Prague, Stuttgart and Budapest followed before he arrived in Berlin in the late 1920s. He sold stories to the UFA studios and worked on scripts in their 'Dramaturgie' department before leaving for France in 1933 when working conditions for Jews became more difficult. He left the French film industry in 1935 to come to London, probably to work up his English in order to cross to America. Many of his relatives in Europe perished under Nazism, including his mother, deported to Auschwitz. He was working for fellow Hungarian Alexander Korda when he scored his first British success, his original screenplay for *The Challenge* (co-directed by Milton Rosmer and Luis Trenker, 1938). This tells the story of the first ascent of the Matterhorn, and like Powell's *The Edge of the World* it has signs of what was to come later in his career. It was made in English and German, and studio footage from London was spliced together with Trenker's location material from the Matterhorn. 'Magic' geography like this would also knit genuine Canadian and Scottish images with British studio work in Powell and Pressburger's *49th Parallel* (1941) and *I Know*

Where I'm Going! (1945). The Matterhorn lies between Switzerland and Italy and the race to conquer it was a tale of international rivalry. Edward Whymper's British expedition from Zermatt competes with the Italian guide Carrel's attempt from Breuil. They are separated by nationhood, but united in common endeavour, and the cross-border friendship between them rehearses the love between Clive and Theo in *The Life and Death of Colonel Blimp* (1943). The snow-covered mountain symbolises utopian values that ultimately transcend national boundaries. In a curious biographical coincidence, Michael Powell's maternal grandfather, Frederick Corbett, had climbed the Matterhorn with Whymper, and told a rapt infant Michael about its first ascent. His uncle founded the Himalaya Club. Even in the Kent-bound world of the wartime parable *A Canterbury Tale* (1944), mountaineering tales are used to bring out themes of idealism and high vaulting ambition.

Powell and Pressburger's cinema betrays their oblique relationship to accepted, national models of 'British cinema'. The style of their films varies enormously, from black-and-white 'noir', travelogue location footage, artificial studio staging, Technicolor epics and sustained sequences of pure cinematic fantasy. Their narratives range from thrillers, pastorals, propaganda works, melodramas, metaphysical explorations, back-stage drama, ballet films, operas and battle films. Taken as a whole, their output is notably experimental and thematically complex. Ideas recur throughout this work: journeys are undertaken or arrested; 'quest' narratives are imbued with a sense of fairy-tale; drama and spectacle interact in a constructive dialogue between the picaresque and the picturesque. The impact of place on character is explored, as landscapes imprint their effect on protagonists, or as concrete places become externally projected renditions of subjective states. The boundaries between individuals and their environments are made porous. While Powell and Pressburger's films often use real locations, this is never just a matter of naturalistic detail, but is for *effect*, for the cultural, poetic or pictorial connotations of the landscape, for a 'spirit of place'. Where topographical space is abandoned in favour of a more controlled studio-based aesthetic, the inner terrain of the unconscious is presented, or pure, sustained fantasy worlds unfurl. Reality is banished. They escape the empirical to lodge in the sequestered territory of the artistic imagination.

What we repeatedly find in Powell and Pressburger's films, as Charles Barr has noted repeatedly, is the presentation of 'alternative' areas and entrances into different places.[1] These new worlds are given a sense of magic – sometimes utopian, sometimes threatening, sometimes surreal. There are enforced expeditions across enemy lines in *The Spy in Black* (1939), *Contraband* (1940), *49th Parallel* and *'...one of our aircraft is missing'* (1942). In *Blimp*, a young Englishman ventures to Berlin, and later a Prussian émigré seeks asylum in Britain. This film marks a transition by presenting memory, biography, history and romance as magic spaces too. The earlier films have their ideal spaces – usually connected to homeland. In *Blimp*, home is important, but it is treated more imaginatively, and the three roles played by Deborah Kerr are symbolically invested with a sense of magic. The triple casting transforms her into a collective, subjective dream-site of romantic longing, unconsciously removed from history by Clive, the unreliable male narrator to whom she is an 'ideal'. Then there is the theatre-space in *The Volunteer* (1943). In this drama-documentary Ralph Richardson is shown transforming himself back-stage, 'blacking up' to play Othello, and this transformation is connected to the equally amazing metamorphosis which recruitment to the armed services brings to Richardson's dresser, Fred. Imbued with Richardson's inimitable, eccentric personality, military training is made a matter of Puckish alchemy. Theatre-space is presented again in *The Red Shoes* (1948), although, here, the stage on which Vicky dances is explicitly inscribed as her subconscious. Motifs deriving from English pastoral drama, especially *A Midsummer Night's Dream*, figure in *A Matter of Life and Death* (1946), which moves between heaven and earth, and the same play gives Powell and Pressburger the title to their last true collaboration, *Ill Met by Moonlight* (1957). The pastoral as a ludic space, as a place of potential, of development, of magic, is found again in the Kentish countryside of *A Canterbury Tale*, and it is given a more sexual, sensual meaning in the Celtic spaces of *I Know Where I'm Going!* and *Gone to Earth* (1950). *Black Narcissus* (1947) takes a group of Anglican nuns to the remote Himalayas, although its more pertinent relocations and disruptions are subjective and generic, as it shifts from melodrama towards gothic horror, and as its two female protagonists begin to display the psychological disturbance, discontinuity and paranoid irrationality which typify the geographically displaced. In their 'art films', *The Red Shoes*, *The Tales of Hoffmann* (1951) and *Oh...Rosalinda!!* (1955), ballet and opera (and, by extension, cinema itself) become magic spaces, where anti-naturalistic designs, trick photography and the eradication of any sense of realism turn the screen into a new, imaginative space. The same self-reflexive fetishisation of cinematic illusion had featured in *The Red Shoes*. Finally, the late, genre war films, *The Battle of the River Plate* (1956) and *Ill Met by Moonlight* echo the interest in borders and neutral territory which underpinned the first collaborations, but they are now robbed of the sense of anxiety and try to excite us with *Boy's Own* adventure instead. Hence, a cinema of transition, alternatives, journeys, borders and flights of fancy, constructing a multiplicity of spaces: an alien or exilic sensibility.

These magic spaces form a running motif, but it is important not to become too fixed on them as abstract structures, to adhere too strictly to pure auteurism, or to lose sight of the various authors' historical and cultural frameworks. It is vital, also, to be alert to ambiguities in the films, to the possibility of resistant readings, and to the importance of reception. The stress Powell and Pressburger laid on their own creative freedom invites us to detach their work from its industrial context and to consider its uniqueness. Paradoxically, though, they emphasise collaboration, and the famous credit 'Written, Produced and Directed by Michael Powell and Emeric Pressburger' slaps a gauntlet at the feet of the auteur-critic. It also promotes the role of the writer. Under the banner of their production company, 'the Archers', the pair occupy a place within British cinema, and a place within that cinema's historiography. This study moves through and round the Archers' films, seeking to situate them within that culture, but also to write them into a wider historical context.

As John Ellis has shown, the dominant critical discourse surrounding British cinema in the 1940s often found Powell and Pressburger's films troubling because the critically endorsed aesthetic was bound to a form of 'quality realism' which intertwined moral, nationalist and class-bound imperatives.[2] If I am reluctant to revisit this well-covered discussion, it is partly because the job has already been admirably done. It is also because the repetition of a handful of salaciously disgruntled reviews from the 1940s (and the temptation to run on to the notorious attack on Powell's own *Peeping Tom* (1960), dangling ominously over his career) can only serve to fix the idea that Powell and Pressburger were and remain misunderstood outsiders, and to romanticise them because of it. Ellis's analysis of the discourse of 'quality realism' is important, for it provides us with one model of British national cinema against which the Archers' oeuvre can be measured. Truly 'British National Cinema', according to the model, is understated, unsensational, 'true', anti-fantastic, restrained, un-Hollywood: a set of qualities which echo ideas about the national character. The model is, though, just one discourse among many. Its proscriptions and its endorsements are fascinating, and as the basis for a model of national cinema its shortcomings and its blind spots are many. Powell and Pressburger's work stands as a test case, for its existence interrogates not only the boundaries of the 'quality realist' model, but also the broader idea of what 'British Cinema' is, and even the problem of what 'British Film Studies' might be. As a discipline, British Film Studies has often taken its object of study for granted, and has been premised upon a common-sense acceptance of borders (and even those of us who think and write about the hybridity and permeability of the topic in universities usually teach it under the banner of modules called 'British Cinema').

When thinking how the historical facts of Powell and Pressburger's careers relate to the dominant national cinema, migrant thoughts return. The Hungarian Alexander Korda, the industry's most flamboyant and important exile, exemplifies one strain of émigré culture: assimilation. By directing a film like *The Private Life of Henry VIII* (1933) or producing Imperial epics such as *The Four Feathers* (1939) he is grasping his new nation's indigenous culture as enthusiastically as he grasped his new British passport. This kind of self-fashioning, which is reflected in the experience of many émigrés to the USA in the 1930s, is a performative strategy, and Korda instinctively felt bolstered by his proximity to the centre, building up his studio and setting his sights on international markets. Powell's travelling was as a tourist-adventurer, and was facilitated by his comfortable class position. In notes he made in 1979, in answer to questions from William Johnson of *Film Quarterly* magazine, he sketches himself as a 'loner' and admits he likes 'mountain-walking, jungle exploring, breaking trails' – a culture of *Boy's Own* adventure. He has a keen eye, too, for national characteristics and personal traits: '[T]he middle-class self-styled educated Englishman is frivolous and a snob,' he suggests in his memoirs, and he guiltily admits, 'I am one of them.'[3]

Pressburger's situation was more critical. Denied the stable national identity within which Powell matured, and experiencing an enforced vagrancy from childhood, his works recurrently search for an idealised home and for a condition of stasis. As his grandson Kevin Macdonald points out, 'Throughout his life he harked back to his idyllic rural childhood, and was ever aware of the continuity and values of rustic life.'[4] This upbringing within an agricultural community is a childhood experience he shares with Powell, although Powell's family were gentleman-farmer stock, not employees on a feudal estate. It is also an experience Pressburger shared with Korda, whose early life was startlingly similar to Pressburger's. Arriving in England after a history of insecurity (financial and political), Pressburger's rapid cultural assimilation was born out of necessity, was facilitated by his affiliation to Korda's Hungarian 'enclave' at London Films, and is inscribed into his work. Losing members of his close family to the concentration camps, there may seem to be an eloquent, topical silence in his screenplays, yet it is one which is spoken of through the idealisation of domesticity, Englishness and the pastoral, and through the romantic longing which figures so consistently in his films. The assimilation, then, was partial. Signs of exilic cinema litter his work. It is easy, too, to romanticise Pressburger's fondness for England, Arsenal football club and village life, and to see the dynamic of his life pulling him centripetally towards deep Englishness. As early as 1938, he wrote about his desire to emigrate to Hollywood. With the film industry in an unsatisfactory shape by the late 1940s he was seriously considering another emigration to Canada, only a few years after becoming a British citizen (he complained about the state of the Industry, the crippling levels of Entertainment Tax levied by the British Government, and the higher wages which had to be paid to technicians while cinema admissions were falling). By 1950, in a hiatus while *The Tales of Hoffmann* was in its extensive pre-production preparation stage, both Powell and Pressburger investigated the possibility of working in Canada, where there was no Entertainment Tax, and where ultra-modern new studios were planned in Toronto. At this time, they were under contract to Korda, were making *The Tales of Hoffmann*, and the move never took place.

Pressburger's response to exile seems to be typical. In her account of the assimilation of German Jews into English society as a result of the rise of Hitler, Marion Berghahn reports numerous interviews with second-generation settlers which suggested that 'certain characteristics of the English lifestyle are highly valued – as they are also by the older generation – and the relative lack of them in German society is criticised. The main one is "decency", but they also include fairness and the inclination towards moderation. The precision and clarity of the English language is especially valued in contrast to German, which so easily inclines towards obscurantism.'[5] An admiration of decency and of moderation; delight in the acquisition of a new language: the Prussian émigré Theo Kretschmar-Schuldorff in *Blimp* exhibits just these traits. He is the most obviously autobiographical of Pressburger's characterisations.

Native British film culture showed signs of anxiety about the foreign presence in its industry. Take, as a snapshot a few years before what is often seen as the high-water mark of 'British National Cinema', Graham Greene's review of *The Marriage of Corbal* (Karl Grune), written in 1936 for *The Spectator*. Greene notices the film's international credits and, finding his viewing experience to have been 'appalling', he strays beyond his specific remit to ask the question, 'What is an English film?'⁶ His comic yet bilious diatribe caricatures the English film industry of the 1930s. In a grotesque register, his profile is a pessimistic one:

> (Noting) the dark alien executive tipping his cigar behind the glass partition in Wardour Street, the Hungarian producer adapting Mr. Wells's ideas tactfully at Denham, the German director letting himself down into his canvas chair at Elstree, and the London film critics (I speak with humility: I am one of them) exchanging smutty stories over the hock and the iced pudding and the brandy at the Carlton, I cannot help wondering whether from this great moneyed industry anything of value in the human spirit can ever emerge.⁷

The superior tone is a mark of xenophobia. Greene regrets that Britons have 'saved (the industry) from American competition only to surrender it to a far more alien control', and he denounces 'a system of nepotism' in which émigrés find jobs for each other to the exclusion of English technicians. While he praises the English craftsmanship of films which are within the 'quality' documentary aesthetic, and which formed both the bedrock of British realism and a bulwark against American escapism, Greene has little time anyway for what he dismisses ironically as 'the art of the cinema'. For him, 'it remains almost as unrealized as in the days of *The Great Train Robbery*. The peepshow, the fun-fair, the historical waxworks are triumphant [and] in some moods appear to be a chamber of horrors.'⁸ The ideological links which Greene forges are familiar within the discourse around British cinema: qualitatively, the realism of a documentary filming practice which expresses a middle-class, liberal ethos is praised; popular entertainment, admitted to be part of cinema's pre-history, is disparaged; and a sensational, gothic terminology is used, paradoxically, to ridicule hated manifestations of gothic sensationalism and of the foreign. Greene draws on a tight and authoritarian definition of 'Nation' which sees hybridity as monstrous. His argument rests upon a policy of strict *containment*, in which a discretely signified England needs protection. That which falls within the confines of his definition is to be accepted, and he speaks pointedly of 'Englishness' throughout. But the sketched caricatures he claims to observe, and the 'darkness' of his Wardour Street executive, are indices of paranoia: there is a sense that borders have been transgressed. If Greene does not answer his own question ('What is an English film?'), his offended sensibilities suggest that his answer would draw upon the language of essentialism. The purity of the tribe has been defiled. Greene is having fun, and his own long involvement in cinema indicates a stronger hope for the medium *per se* than is suggested here. But the terms of his argument expose the problems of a 'national cinema': how far does the notion rely upon the politics of nationalism, and how far does the construction admit diversity and opposition? At a conceptual level, these are the crucial questions. What I wish to argue is that, following Homi K. Bhaba's recognition of an 'antinationalist, ambivalent nation-space [which] becomes the crossroads to a new transnational culture',[9] so too can a distinctively national cinema allow for difference, engage with international factors, and be enriched by hybrid and alternative voices, while remaining in some very real and cultural senses 'nationally specific', without necessarily peddling an authoritarian or conservative set of values.

The debate over how far 'British' cinema incorporated ideas from continental Europe, and how best to account for stark anti-realism in British films, is in part an argument about how open British culture was to the intellectual changes marked by European modernism. If for no other reason, the Archers' recruitment of German or Austrian émigrés suggests their own affinity with this foreign culture (most obviously, they team up with the designers Alfred Junge and Hein Heckroth, actors Conrad Veidt, Anton Walbrook and Albert Bassermann, and cinematographer Erwin Hillier).

In Sarah Street's judgement, the period from the 1920s to the 1930s marks the first phase of a period of Modernism within British cinema.[10] Street correctly regards the key cleavage in world cinema to have been that between Hollywood, marked early on by what would come to be termed its 'classical style' (and constructed as an overtly commercial cinema), and alternatives to it. Russian montage, German Expressionist styles, French Impressionism and Surrealism all present themselves as intellectual, 'artistic' alternatives to the American form, and they perpetuate a distinction between so-called 'high art' and 'mass entertainment' (favouring the former). Echoing Tom Ryall,[11] Street notes the significance of London's Film Society in developing ideas about film as artistic practice and as cultural protest, although at this stage notably less as an agent of tightly defined 'national' expression. Founded by Ivor Montagu and Hugh Miller for film enthusiasts, the Film Society existed from 1925 to 1939 and, in addition to showing new imports and old favourites, it arranged screenings of experimental European work often not exhibited elsewhere. The Film Society provided a platform in London to a minority elite for the intellectual consideration of an art-house cinema (the respectability of the Society can be gauged by a glance at its more eminent members: H.G. Wells and G.B. Shaw, Roger Fry and John Maynard Keynes, Ellen Terry, John Gielgud and Ivor Novello, together with names from the cinema such as Michael Balcon and Victor

Saville). It was nevertheless the catalyst for the development of a specialised, modernist film coterie, and its importance should not be overlooked. Bolstered by the publication of the periodicals *Close-Up* (which appeared from July 1927 until 1933) and *Film Art* (1933–37), the presence of the Film Society suggests an openness, during this period, to continental influences. The critical voice emanating from the Film Society gave forthright damnation to the Hollywood product, and promoted the European 'art' film. As an organisation it was both cosmopolitan and international.

Andrew Higson's writing on the 'Film Europe' project similarly reminds us that 1930s cinema could breach discretely constructed versions of 'national cinema'.[12] As a commercially motivated attempt to ward off Hollywood's hegemony, Film Europe established procedures of international co-operation during the silent era, pooling resources such as studio space and personnel, and setting up pan-national distribution to fend off US domination of the market. The significance of Film Europe is more than commercial: it is cultural, for it admits the permeability of borders and depends upon trans-national partnerships. The coming of 'talkies' did not utterly parochialise European cinema, because strategies such as multi-linguals (whereby different language versions of the same film would be filmed either back-to-back or simultaneously) sought to transcend national boundaries. This policy 'spoke the local vernacular', as Higson notes, 'but was bound by a stateless blueprint'.[13] Thus we find 'German' films such as Reinhold Schünzel's *Viktor und Viktoria* (1933) made multi-lingually – it was also produced in French as *Georges et Georgette* – before it was recast, rewritten and remade (in an adapted form) in Britain by Victor Saville as *First a Girl* (1935). Similarly *Michel Strogoff* (Jacques de Baroncelli and Richard Eichberg, 1935) was made in both German and French versions before it was subsequently remade by RKO in America as *The Soldier and the Lady* (George Nicholls Jnr., 1937). These works, with the exception of *First a Girl*, all starred Anton Walbrook, one of a group of actors who collaborated with Powell and Pressburger, and who can be seen to be genuinely international.

Film Europe and the Film Society's elitist critical voice point to a lively hybridity in European cinema, whether it is configured aesthetically, intellectually or commercially. By the mid-1930s, with the emigration of film technicians to Britain from Germany and central Europe, Film Europe itself either dissipated, or, in Higson's view, became absorbed into British cinema. This powerfully argues the case that British cinema (or at least cinema *in Britain*) in the 1930s had a cosmopolitan character. Certainly,

German technicians were important, and the presence of Alexander Korda and the émigrés around him suggests a strong international dimension. Michael Powell was irritated when the arrival of 'talkies' led to the foregrounding of the human voice over imagery. This was a debasement of his medium, erecting a language barrier across what was a pictorial and cross-cultural medium. 'And then,' he writes of this historic moment, 'when nation was talking to nation in the most direct and simple way, the blow fell. Synchronised speech had arrived.'[14] He praised Hitchcock's *Blackmail* (1929) for retaining the priorities of the silent era and is nostalgic for the primal perfection of the silent period. In *Black Narcissus, The Red Shoes* and *The Tales of Hoffmann* the Archers move towards what Powell terms the 'composed' film, using the soundtrack to construct 'an organic whole of dialogue, sound effects, and music'.[15] The pre-composed method of shooting these films, giving priority to a musical score and filming sequences with little or no speech, is a sign of Powell's ongoing commitment to the internationalism of the silent era and the subsequent multi-lingual phase.

TRAVELLERS' TALES

In *Blimp*, the central character Clive visits the theatre and sees a play about Ulysses, the epic wanderer exiled from his homeland. Ideas about mobility have long been central to Western culture, as John Peter Durham's survey of exile, nomadism and diaspora illustrates. Exile, he says, 'suggests a painful or punitive banishment from one's homeland, [and] generally implies a fact of trauma, an imminent danger, usually political, that makes the home no longer safely habitable'.[16] Exile therefore implies and defines its converse, homeland, and the sense of loss from it produces a process of idealisation: a nostalgia or a longing for utopia where, in Durham's words, 'Home becomes an impossible object'.[17] This is where exile differs from diaspora, another displacement from a centre but one which suggests a network of compatriots rather than a lonely pining, and from nomadism, a culture defined by its mobility, where there is no fixed centre at all. The senses of isolation and of a remote centre or homeland are exile's defining characteristics.

Exile is entwined with the condition of modernity, with its complex societal change, a loss of identity, the slow ache of alienation and a fractured relationship with the past. It is a facet of the twentieth-century Western condition, and some of its most significant writers have been émigrés, as Terry Eagleton has pointed out.[18] Arriving in an alien territory which lacks known cultural landmarks is disorientating and it produces a sense of anomie. It is natural, then, that the exile will try to take bearings from other co-ordinates, and that the self should become a new and central organising principle. Journeys therefore become journeys of self-discovery, where identity itself is discovered. This Robinson Crusoe-like arrival in a strange, new world is seen in *A Matter of Life and Death* (1946), where Peter Carter, washed ashore alone on an unplaced beach, becomes an existential hero. Pressburger's modernism, though, is reluctant, for he favours continuity rather than sudden breaks, and he shows an idealistic belief in transcendental absolutes rather than an ongoing sense of unresolved spiritual crisis. This relationship with the past puts him some distance from the rigorously critical, agnostic stance associated with more radical branches of modernism. The journey of self-discovery in Powell and Pressburger's films is often directed towards the past, in heritage, myth and memory. Joseph Brodsky has summed it up:

> A writer in exile is by and large a retrospective and retroactive being… Whether pleasant or dismal, the past is almost always a safe territory, if only because it is already experienced; and the species' capacity to revert, to run backward – especially in its thoughts or dreams…is extremely strong in all of us, quite irrespective of the reality we are facing.[19]

The cinema of exile is out of kilter. Where national, dominant cinemas are often defined in terms of their classicism, exilic cinema is 'accented', to use Hamid Naficy's term.[20] Naficy's important work has identified stylistic similarities among post-colonial, Third World and other displaced film-makers living in the West. He is careful to note that '[n]ot all transnational exiles, of course, savor fundamental doubt, strive toward hybridized and performative self-fashioning, or reach for utopian or virtual imaginings'.[21] That said, he identifies a set of 'generic' traits, such as border aesthetics, fragmented narratives, multiple subjects, self-reflexivity and hybridised forms. Naficy's focus is on non-mainstream, artisanal film-making, although his observations could be widened to embrace commercial cinemas and to look at differing experiences of immigration and displacement, such as that to Hollywood and across Europe in the 1930s. Signs of 'accented' cinema can be seen in Powell and Pressburger's work. They can be read as the imprint of Pressburger's authorial presence; they can be seen as instances of Powell's own brand of visual and dramatic romanticism. Either way, they are markers of the way authorial and contextual factors converge and of how Powell and Pressburger's cinema perturbs the apparent tidiness of 'national cinema'.

Boundaries between genres are often crossed. Few of the Archers' films pigeonhole themselves neatly into known popular genres. Spy thrillers masquerade as Expressionist horror films; documentaries become comic fantasies; an 'Imperial epic' becomes a mock-heroic satire and a wartime propaganda piece; a back-stage drama becomes a surreal exploration of female hysteria and a Trilby-like tale of mythic possession; a female-centred exotic drama becomes a full-blown horror film. It is difficult to categorise Powell and Pressburger's films in genre terms, because in part their films exhibit a greater structural similarity to each other than they do to other films. They are often idiosyncratic, and the creative freedom Powell and Pressburger won gave them latitude to experiment and to transgress generic boundaries.

Given the interest in the self, ethical questions about performative identities are often raised by the cinema of exile. The stable self is the product of modernity, and of the imagined community of nationhood. When this self is forced into alien territory it is jeopardised, which can cause an exaggerated sense of identity-in-performance. Among the geographical relocations dramatised in Powell and Pressburger's early collaborations, we find characters donning costumes unwillingly (Hardt in *The Spy in Black*), and others whose ability to masquerade their national identity is ingeniously subversive: it is crucial to the Dutch resistance in *'...one of our aircraft is missing'* and to press the theme of performativity one of the British airmen trapped in Holland is a professional actor. It is the basis of Powell and Pressburger's *The Elusive Pimpernel* (1950). Here, Sir Percy Blakeney (David Niven), a Regency fop, fussing over his elaborate toilette, is also 'The Pimpernel', a dashing undercover spy during 'The Terror'. Ethical questions about our ability to reinvent ourselves are central to debates about modernity and postmodernity, of course. The modern self is posited on an idea of depth and fixity, and belongs to a stable geographical territory; postmodernism celebrates performativity, denies depth, and is unrooted.

As well as giving us performances of identity, Powell and Pressburger's films also feature divided selves, and divided, embedded formal structures. This is a feature of belonging to borderlands, a product of the margins. Double agents exist on both sides, and a sense that human consciousness is disunified proliferates. Sister Ruth is a monstrous *doppelganger*, the unregulated flip-side of Sister Clodagh in *Black Narcissus*. Vicky and the character she dances in the *The Red Shoes* ballet mirror each other and are locked in a destructive relationship. This formally mirrors the embedded narrative of *The Red Shoes* film, where the diegesis struggles to 'contain' the mythic plot of the ballet, and the Lermontov ballet troupe self-reflexively mirrors the collaborative ideal of the Archers' team. The focus on theatricality pinpoints another variation of borderland aesthetics: self-conscious, staged performances which spotlight a sense of unnaturalness. Powell and Pressburger's use of artificial studio settings, trick shots and flagrant cinematic illusionism is an implicit critique of British 'quality realism', of course, but their idiosyncratic, anti-classical mise-en-scène is also a marker of their utopian yearnings, and a product of their dislocation from the mainstream. The framing narrative and contained tales in *The Tales of Hoffmann*, and the stark division between Heaven and Earth in *A Matter of Life and Death* are other, formal signs of split identity.

Another sign of Powell and Pressburger as 'auteurs', but also a sign of their accented relationship to the centre, and a marker of their wish to mark openly their acts of expression, is the appearance of alter egos on screen, or sometimes their own appearance in their films. Theo in *Blimp* is Pressburger's spokesman in the film, and Anton Walbrook's role in *49th Parallel* articulates sentiments which clearly spring from their author (although his anti-Nazi speech would, of course, find many sympathisers). There are other men in the films – charismatic, powerful men – and it is tempting to read them as expressions of Powell's persona (and Powell's interest in self-expression continues through to James Mason's role as the painter Bradley Morahan in *Age of Consent* [1969, Australia]). There are also brief glimpses of Powell himself on screen, in '*…one of our aircraft is missing*', in *The Volunteer* and then (as his real son's father) in *Peeping Tom* (1960). These cinematic inscriptions are signatures of authorship, yes, but the screen images are detached from their real, biographical originators. They are another instance of doubling, symbolically akin to the mechanical dolls in *The Tales of Hoffmann*.

What of the central characters Powell and Pressburger give us? There are 'special', individual men – Hardt, Anderson, Hirth, Colpeper, Lermontov, Hoffmann, Langsdorff – all in their own way outsiders who express a sense of alienation, and in the cases of Colpeper and Lermontov, they are also 'magicians', responsible for the magic spaces on screen. There are Peter Carter and Sammy Rice, anti-establishment figures who are reluctant to be incorporated. Many others are wanderers: Alison Smith, Bob Johnson, Peter Gibbs and Joan Webster. And there is an unnamed, shadowy figure in *A Canterbury Tale*. He appears in silhouette and speaks with difficulty. The area of the village he strolls around is clearly an artificial set. Alison, Bob and Peter happen upon him at night, and engage him in a brief dialogue. The dark stranger gives stammering, repeated, monosyllabic replies, his answers confirming the trio's suspicions about the answer to the film's own peculiar mystery. He is named 'the village idiot', and as he hobbles up-stage and waves farewell a cuckoo in the soundtrack mocks him. He is played by Archers' stalwart Esmond Knight, a character actor who has just played another comic role in the film's previous scene, and whose voice provides the film with its opening voiceover. The text therefore triplicates Knight, albeit covertly. The village idiot is a mannered stereotype. He is affectionately indulged, although the trio of protagonists do laugh *at* him. He is tolerated in the village, but is not apparently housed there – a vagrant in a film which venerates homes and buildings. He is a peripatetic outsider, inside the village, and his appearance is a jarring, sadistic moment, a stylistic discontinuity in the film. When the trio laughingly identify him as 'the village idiot' they admit that they exist within a self-conscious 'representation' of village England, and this is an alienating moment for an audience which has so far been lured by Edenic footage of the Kentish countryside. The wandering idiot's presence, awkwardly telling awkward truths, is emblematic of Powell and Pressburger's films.

HOME

I have said that exile and home are co-determinant. The sensibility of the Powell-Pressburger films, even if reduced to a set of signs of exile, is therefore intimately bound up with 'Home', and by extension with the sort of indigenous expressions which typify 'British National Cinema' in the 1940s. The longing for 'Home' is a form of idealism, and it explains many of the 'magic spaces' in Powell and Pressburger's films. 'Home', and other expressions of the familiar, are inevitably emphasised in times of upheaval. Nostalgic conservatism like this, engendered by violent socio-political convulsion, displacement and apparent breakdown, is not necessarily a reactionary commitment to the past, or a simple flight from the present. Often it signals social conflict brought about by a readjustment to the present. Ideologies of nationhood frequently draw on a sense of the domestic. National ideology can offer a safe haven to the alienated, and is all the more persuasive when historical turmoil exacerbates the sense of displacement. Anthony D. Smith suggests that it is through a sense of national identity that 'we are enabled to know "who we are" in the contemporary world. By rediscovering that culture we "rediscover" ourselves, the "authentic self", or so it has appeared to many divided and disoriented individuals who have had to contend with the vast changes and uncertainties in the modern world.'[22]

Entrance to the new world finds the immigrant stimulated by new signs. Sights and sounds can be riddled with an uncertainty which at times verges on the surreal. This is the experience of Bob Johnson on his arrival in Chillingbourne: he is as unfamiliar with the modern British telephone system as he is with the archaeology of the area and the significance of Canterbury Cathedral. His reactions are mirrored by those of Joan Webster, spellbound in the Hebrides, and even by Bob Trubshaw, a lost boy seeking a familiar face in an austerely monochrome Heaven. Each wants to belong. What is timely is that 'Home', and the 'Home Front', became intensely charged expressions in wartime culture. Paradoxically, therefore, the exilic, outsider perspective characterised by Pressburger's wartime screenplays actually articulates just the sort of utopian ideological commitment which the nation was calling for. For Pressburger, the new cultural identification is grafted at an apt historical moment, when his own search for an identity with a social dimension coincided with the necessary recalibration of national characteristics, brought about through the mobilisation of a 'total war' and the cultural retrenchment which this involved. However, the glorification of Britain which Pressburger often makes us face is characteristically qualified. It is at once homely, wonderful, outmoded, infuriating, parochial and neurotic. There is nevertheless a sympathy between the 'British National Cinema' of the Home Front, re-establishing a set of values coded as vigorously English and gearing the nation to victory, and the personal experience of Pressburger, the refugee seeking roots in a host nation. Pressburger came to Britain at the very time when the *incorporative* ideology of the nation was particularly powerful. The actual treatment of aliens notwithstanding, his arrival coincided with a broad and inclusively profiled national character, popularly peddled under the democratic banner of the 'People's War'. The culture of the Home Front expressed utopian idealism. It was ingrained with a principle of hope: hope of victory in the first instance, although that would translate into the rhetoric surrounding the establishment of the Welfare State and the 1945 Labour landslide.

As Chantal Mouffe's analysis of Antonio Gramsci spells out, the securing of hegemony involves 'a complete fusion of economic, political, intellectual and moral objectives' – a condition which results in what Gramsci himself termed 'intellectual and moral unity'.[23] The ideology of Britain at war, founded as it was upon terms such as unity, common direction, shared interest and the relegation of the private in favour of the public, achieved an astonishing centrality and strove to forge that sense of oneness. It was obviously not universal, as history records markers of dissent, yet the discourse nevertheless held together, and the *myth* of universality was kept aloft. And the themes which this ideology chose to valorise (explicitly or implicitly) were close to Powell and Pressburger: the pastoral; anti-materialism; groups; tolerating foreigners; the insignificance of class. In short, the State co-opted traditional, romantic values as part of mythologising propaganda.

The journeys undertaken in *A Canterbury Tale* and *I Know Where I'm Going!* are frustrated. The films themselves decelerate, and during their stoppages their protagonists are re-educated and taught to reprioritise their lives. Images of velocity – trains, boats and cars – are pitted against the static: secure beds, castles, crofts, farmhouses, cathedrals, a caravan symbolically bereft of its wheels. In *A Canterbury Tale* plodding cart horses contrast with the destructive speed of Bren-gun carriers. Exploring the values for which the film believes the war is being fought, *A Canterbury Tale* calls for meditation, studied reflection and revelation. The rush of modernity is a temporary deviation from the revered stasis of Canterbury Cathedral. This tension between the frozen, photographic spectacle of landscape and monument, and the urge to move the narrative on, recollects Laura Mulvey's distinction between static, fetishised imagery and the powerful need to resolve anxieties created by the narrative. Of course, in Mulvey's specific terms, these anxieties are created by threatening images of 'otherness' which women represent to the patriarchal spectator and to his on-screen (male) surrogate. These *topographical* tensions are animated by anxieties to do with claustrophobia, incorporation and statelessness which express Europe's geopolitical upheavals in the 1930s and 1940s, and which relate to Powell and Pressburger's respective experience of expatriation. *The Life and Death of Colonel Blimp* takes a figurative journey too, through forty years of one man's life, and it is initiated by a shock moment in which he too is *arrested* (he is literally taken hostage), forcibly giving him time/space to reassess his values.

The Archers' wartime work contains an idealism which is consistent with their output as a whole. In their later work the idealism is there, but is redirected towards ideal, heroic masculinity, or the absolutes of 'Art'. During the war, with its patriotic credentials clearly flagged, their idealism finds itself flowing *with* the dominant cultural current, however much that ideological sympathy was unnoticed when some contemporary critics paid attention to matters of style and idiosyncrasies of narrative. A heritage of European influences may well have gothicised Powell and Pressburger's work, and put it beyond the tastes of these critics. There is a tension between the iconoclastic or eccentric characteristics in their films and the conservative ideology which often informs them. Nevertheless, the hegemonic ideals of wartime are ultimately what govern this period of their careers. Theirs is not, however, a bland compliance. Forms of national culture are subjected to an insightful interrogation. From the mid-1940s their romanticism is increasingly at odds with the cultural mainstream, although this post-war 'mainstream' is itself less organised around a dominant cultural myth than it was in the war years.

INDEPENDENCE

As the brief declaration at the head of this introduction indicates, Powell (unlike Pressburger) was neither coy nor modest about his cinematic ambitions. In his autobiography, he claims that his 'craft is a mystery' and that he is 'a high priest of the mysteries'.[24] In what amounts to a manifesto for the Archers, Powell noted down their shared feelings about artistic freedom and collaboration in a letter to Wendy Hiller written early in 1942, before her pregnancy removed her from the anticipated cast of *Blimp*. Significantly, he makes the following statements:

> We owe our allegiance to nobody except the financial interests which provide our money; and to them the sole responsibility of ensuring them a profit not a loss.
>
> Every single foot in our film is our own responsibility and nobody else's...
>
> No artist believes in escapism – and we secretly believe no audience does. We have proved at any rate that they will pay to see truth, for other reasons than her nakedness.[25]

From these extracts, we can picture Powell's sense of what the Archers were about. There is a clear, *idealised* sense of the magical potential of moving pictures, together with a notion of Powell's own role as a director, dedicated to serving his mystical medium and at the same time promoting his own directorial prowess. The Archers' independence is valued above all else, and it is convenient to point out here that at times they successfully negotiated a high degree of artistic freedom, particularly via their arrangements with Independent Producers, the production consortium set up under J. Arthur Rank's umbrella. By 1943, Rank headed his own vertically integrated empire. Geoffrey Macnab's history of Rank shows that the contract which established 'the Archers' company under the umbrella organisation of Independent Producers was as obliging an arrangement as any film artist could have wished for. Alongside the Archers at Independent Producers were Cineguild formed by David Lean, Ronald Neame and Anthony Havelock-Allen as a splinter group from Filippo Del Giudice's Two Cities, the team of Launder & Gilliat, and Ian Dalrymple's Wessex Films. Rank also controlled Two Cities and Gainsborough, and financially supported Ealing Studios, while he dominated exhibition and distribution through his acquisition of Odeon and Gaumont-British. During their peak years the Archers were therefore a central component in one of the most solidly organised industrial machines in cinema. Rank was investing in the creative freedom of his writers and directors. As Macnab points out, '[Rank's] reluctance to "cap" his film-makers allowed Cineguild and the Archers in particular to follow a bourgeois/ romantic creed of the creative individual artist…They were cine-poets, making "art" films within the mainstream.'[26] So the Archers' romantic ethos was, for a while, allowed to flower, and the patronage they enjoyed from Rank gave them their desired freedom. However, even when signed to the notoriously interfering Alexander Korda, Powell relished his own creative space: 'I didn't regard myself as working for Alex; not even with Alex. I had this passion for independence.'[27]

The third item selected from their 'manifesto' warrants closer inspection, because it implicitly touches on some of the aesthetic ideas governing the sense at the time of what British cinema should be. Given that the critical attacks levied upon the Archers' films were often spurred by a suspicion that they lacked a proper seriousness, and that their failure to meet the criteria of realism was a wayward indulgence, Powell sounds defensive. The distinction Powell makes between escapism and truth is important. In the mid-period of the Second World War, he stakes his colours to the cause of 'truth' and by dismissing its mere 'nakedness' he nudges towards something deeper than the superficial reportage of topical events. That deeper quality may well be a sense of realism, an aesthetic strategy which, as understood within the British documentary tradition, is based on formal qualities and seeks to expose hidden meanings and connections. Location shooting is one of the markers of 'documentary realism'; Powell had by this stage already used landscape creatively in his own film, *The Edge of the World*, and with Pressburger he had further developed a realist style in *49th Parallel*. When Powell speaks of 'truth', though, he may have a more imaginative meaning in mind. Romantically inspired artists have always striven to capture an artistic 'truth', a subjective sense of reality culled from the imagination's response to external stimuli. What distinguishes the Archers' romanticism is the notion of a 'transfigurative' art born out of this interplay. On his boyhood enthusiasm for film-making, Powell reported that 'the end was art, the end was to tell a story; the end was to go out into the real world and *turn it into a romantic fantasy world where anything could happen*' (my italics).[28]

Powell's maxim that 'all art is one' – it is the opening motto to the second volume of his memoirs, and is repeated throughout – suggests a romantic idea of totality and controlled expression. The utopian ambition continues: 'Unity of purpose among all my collaborators towards an ideal film became a religion for me.'[29] Film gives him the opportunity to synthesise music, drama, design and dance, and he enthuses about this potential. Despite the Wagnerian overtones of the motto, it is taken from Rudyard Kipling's story 'The Wrong Thing' (originally published in 1911 in the collection *Rewards and Fairies*). In Kipling's tale, the motto endorses general craftsmanship and creative community. Its hero, Hal o' the Draft (a medieval artisan) is spirited across the centuries to meet Mr Springett, an old Sussex builder who is his twentieth-century counterpart. Hal waxes lyrical when describing the teamwork he enjoyed in building the old king's chapel: 'Twould have done your heart good, Mr. Springett, to see the two hundred of us – masons, jewellers, carvers, gilders, iron-workers and the rest – all toiling like cock-angels.' The catchphrase articulates an idealised work ethic and argues against restrictive practices, a sentimental yearning for a pre-capitalist era safeguarded from the brutal exigencies of the cash nexus and the market-driven economy. This fits with the spirit of Powell and Pressburger's most Kiplingesque work, *A Canterbury Tale*, which commences with a similarly spirited match-cut from the Middle Ages to the twentieth century, and where distinctions of gender, race and class are effaced in the interests of a shared wartime identity based around a common history of feudal practice (that film's aged blacksmith, Horton, is a counterpart to Kipling's Springett). Significantly, Kipling's Mr Springett, in his pastoral haven, has been unaffected by historical developments. His magical communion with Hal depends upon a shared value system remarkably unimpeded by the rigours of capitalism. The 'labour' they each speak of is not the alienating, dehumanising factory work associated with the industrialised or commercialised world. Rather, it is the life-affirming stuff of dignified craftsmanship. Just as Kipling's tale recounts the relationship between the various medieval craftsmen and the king who has commissioned their work, Powell's chosen motto is bound up with a longing for artistic freedom granted by a bountiful and yet detached patron (a gong sounds and enter J. Arthur Rank?). And just as Hal's recollection anticipates the collaborative ideal of the Archers' production team – an ideal which is represented in *The Red Shoes* as the Lermontov ballet troupe, where dancers, choreographer, designer, musicians, conductor and composer pool their talents in the name of the dance – so Powell's depiction of the director as a 'craftsman' and a 'jack of all trades', who marshals the expertise of his chosen craftsmen, echoes Hal's call for co-operative endeavour.[30]

Creative independence; utopian yearnings; mysteries: the Archers' aesthetic is highly romanticised, and as Raymond Williams reminds us, the celebrated notion of the special subjective space is strongly established in Romantic culture:

> The artist perceives and represents Essential Reality, and he does so by virtue of his master faculty Imagination. In fact, the doctrines of 'the genius' (the autonomous creative artist) and of the 'superior reality of art' (penetration to a sphere of universal truth) were in Romantic thinking two sides of the same claim.[31]

Furthermore, the very notion of 'Art', in the language of the Romantics, has magical properties itself. This is determined by the relationship of both art and artist to economic conditions: rather than engage with the alienating effects of the market, 'Art', or 'high culture', inhabits a sequestered, rarefied and superior plane. This is the approach to art in *The Red Shoes*, and is expressed in the anti-materialism of *A Canterbury Tale* and *I Know Where I'm Going!* It is the abstraction from reality which dictates the subjective-fantasy space in *Black Narcissus* and *The Tales of Hoffmann*. The artistic history Powell writes himself into, then, is given to thinking in terms of reified spaces removed from reality.

NATIONAL IDENTITY, 'NATIONAL CINEMA' AND THE ARCHERS

Part of the project of this book is to examine how national identity figures in Powell and Pressburger's films as part of their wider tendency to romanticise homely (and unhomely) places and situations. Concepts of travelling and tourism – and their inverse, stasis – can be used to think this through. There is also a need to reconsider where these films are placed in relation to Britain's national cinema, and how definitions of national cinema might take account of them. As I write, proposals for regional assemblies in the

United Kingdom are being formulated, the European Union is being widened, and the United Kingdom's possible adoption of a single European currency is the nation's most significant pending political issue. There is a supposed crisis about how to assess (or limit) incoming asylum seekers. In the wake of devolution to a Scottish Parliament and the establishment of a Welsh Assembly, there has been an awakening assessment of what it has meant, and will mean, to be English. Of course, this specific form of identification has long been used, vaguely, inaccurately and with imperious assumption, to represent the United Kingdom at large. Yet if the signifying function of 'Englishness' is indeed being resettled, this need not necessarily invoke the clarion call of a muscular or bullish nationalism. The debate has more to do with reconceptualised forms of identity. Although appeals to an assumed sense of Englishness often *are* bound up with a specifically *right*-ist agenda, there is nothing automatic in this association. The issue may rather be phrased to take into account what sorts of identity are imaginable, what badges of belonging are being tabled, and to whom these badges are offered. In short, Englishness need not connote a 'Little Englander' mentality. If Englishness suggests an awareness of tradition, it can also suggest an acceptance of the modern. Neither *need* it invoke a sense of racial purity, for 'England' can be a wide and pluralistic idea, celebrated for its 'incomingness', allowing claims to tolerance, generosity and diversity, admitting its post-imperial circumstances, its multi-ethnic communities and its broadening integration within Europe. Such aspirations can be part of the idea.

The shifting parameters of this debate expose how national identity is a process, ever in the making. It is not an 'essential' quality, however much it is wrapped (and thereby naturalised) in such a myth. The crucial dilemmas underpinning Britain's currently disputed sense of nationhood are these: how far can the psychic boundaries of what we mean by the nation be stretched; how far can restrictive definitions be overrun by an acceptance of difference; how far can the foreign be incorporated or the 'alien within' be granted a devolved self-determination, before the once-understood concept of the authentic nation state ceases to have any substantive meaning? At what stage does a national discourse, so 'diluted', lose its place within a culture determined by international or regional factors, and ultimately when does the idea of national discourse itself become redundant?

Settling such questions is part of the process of negotiation and consent by which civil society holds together. Antonio Gramsci, in his *Prison Notebooks*, makes an important distinction between the 'direct domination or command exercised through the State' and the 'function of hegemony which the dominant group exercises throughout society.'³² It is this hegemonic operation, defined by Gramsci as the 'intellectual and moral leadership' of a social group, which aims to secure stability by winning and actively maintaining consensus, bringing the masses to identify socially with the interests of the governing group. The form of ideology conceived by Gramsci is dynamic, marked by consolidation, resistance and incorporation. This is how power is won. The hegemonic, however much recourse it has to the use of force, engages in strategies of containment. Bolstered by its prestige, it ceaselessly monitors its borders, checking dissent and renegotiating its encounters with 'otherness'.

Because of these inclusive strategies, it can be argued that the hegemonic strength of a modern state (it is particularly so in liberal democracies) depends upon the degree to which it entertains diversity. Whether or not we care to see such containment as an 'entertainment' or as a 'suppression', what is constant within the Gramscian paradigm is that it at least acknowledges a continually articulated interaction between dominant/authoritarian voices and the margins. This is a less monolithic view of the 'national'. It is de-essentialised, and is made ambivalent, conditional and double-voiced. In his subtle account of the discourse of nation, Homi K. Bhaba homes in on the critical question: 'What kind of cultural space is the nation with its transgressive boundaries and its "interruptive" interior?' The intrusion of the marginal into what he terms the 'cultural organicism, the deep nation, the long past' quizzes the hegemonic assumptions of the centre, and as a result, the boundaries of the nation are 'containing thresholds of meaning that must be crossed, erased, and translated in the process of cultural production'.³³ The nation then is an always unfinished discourse, a cultural stage on which Gramscian dynamics can be witnessed.

A clear and articulate instance of the current debate is to be seen in a dialogue between Andrew Higson and John Hill, both of whom have done much to push forward the study of British national cinema. The function of British cinema, as Higson suspiciously views it, is 'to pull together diverse and contradictory discourses, to articulate a contradictory unity, to play a part in the hegemonic process of achieving consensus and containing difference and contradiction'.³⁴ While he chooses to emphasise differences at the point of *consumption* and endorses reception studies with their notion of the active audience, Higson remains mindful of film *production*, but what he calls for is the renewal of minority cinemas (such as black, feminist, gay/queer, green or socialist cinemas) rather than for a re-energised 'national' cinema *per se*. John Hill disputes Higson's premise of what a national cinema is:

for him, 'the idea of a national cinema in itself does not necessarily imply this sense of "fixity"'.[35] Consequently the idea of national cinema is worth preserving. Higson is accused of running together the issue of national specificity with the rather different categories of social coherence and stability. Second, Hill's suspicions are directed to the potentially legitimising and politically quietist directions taken by academic study into audience research. He warns that 'although motivated by "progressive" cultural impulses, the combination of critical suspicions of the "national" and populist celebrations of audience preferences may simply end up endorsing the operations of the market place…and hence the restricted range of cultural representations which the market provides'.[36] Higson's liberal voice rejects 'national cinema' because his own model of it suffers from an innate conservatism; Hill's leftist voice, more solidly within the politicised discourse of Cultural Studies, redefines national cinema broadly and plurally as a site of potential resistance to the marketplace and to multi-national capital.

Given his premise, Higson's shying away from national cinema is laudable. Yet what he downplays is that the Gramscian sense of the hegemonic is neither settled nor monological. This is merely its utopian goal. Hegemony may well be the attempted containment of diversity, but containment suggests acknowledgement, and it is the site of internal pressure. What is more, to be contained is not to be erased: incorporated deviancy may, after all, continue to harry the dominant. More importantly, the 'other cinemas' Higson calls for may well be configured differently (gay, black, feminist etc.) but, given the prowess of nationally determining factors, it is difficult to see how they could exist without reference to the social and historical conditions of national subjecthood, and thereby belong and contribute to the nation's culture. Neither can the texts of such cinemas be ideologically compartmentalised as tidily as Higson suggests. 'National cinema' is still a necessary term, as long as we remember that national culture is criss-crossed with alternative strands, differences and accented voices.

These differences are marked within concrete, specific texts, the structures of which contain the same eddying cross-currents and conflicts. These structures offer masquerades of spurious coherence: plausibilities of storyline and consistencies of subject position which it is the task of what Alan Sinfield terms 'dissident reading' to expose.[37] This charting of polysemy and observation of deviance worries away at dominant meanings and hegemonic structures. British wartime cinema, conforming more closely to Higson's unifying institution than any cinema in the country before or since, clearly offers up texts whose commitment to central, dominant ideals invites such investigation. Given the strength with which a mythic version of the English 'spirit' permeated accounts of wartime, and strove to mute any of the more mongrel instances of British culture which had arguably had freer rein in the pre-war years, the period stands as an exemplary instance of popular and official culture's collaborative establishment of what can only be termed a 'national ethos'. That national cinema – consensual, broadly appealing, offering leadership – is an exemplar of hegemonic activity. As such it is a site of negotiation.

The place of Michael Powell and Emeric Pressburger within this cinema (however defined or redefined) is also contentious. As guilty of foreign input as Graham Greene's witheringly reviewed *The Marriage of Corbal*, their collaborations challenge definitions of both the nation and the national cinema, particularly given the tone of British celebration which is in part to be found in their work. Given the wartime prestige ascribed to documentary realism and to the communal aesthetic, Powell and Pressburger's reputed 'Continentalism' and 'Romanticism' placed them at times beyond the strictly defined parameters of suitable 'British National Cinema'. In some of the wartime work, governed by propaganda needs, and in the male-centred films made in its wake, there is some confluence between their work and hegemonic ideals. The post-war Technicolor works seem to violate more rudely the 'restraint' with which 'British Cinema' was associated. They speak more of a failure to 'contain' or be contained, drawing more on a melo-dramatic genre which articulates, in whatever contorted fashion, both fracture and dissidence. They replace wartime narratives of hope with tales of dashed aspirations. Highly wrought they may be, yet despite their outright rejection of realism, what are *Black Narcissus* or *The Red Shoes* if not British?

'National cinema' as a critical construct remains problematic, suggesting an attempt to stabilise and to institutionalise a complex, shifting dynamic of economic, ideological and aesthetic parameters. Nevertheless, placing Powell and Pressburger within that paradigm throws their stance towards 'nation' into relief. They have no truck with xenophobia, they are clearly committed to nationhood, yet there is still a resistance to the dominant constructions by which Britishness was known. A kinship with foreigners – Theo in *Blimp*, Bob Johnson in *A Canterbury Tale*, June in *A Matter of Life and Death* – imply a trans-nationalism, or at least an acceptance of permeable borders. Clive's link to Theo, Horton's to Bob, Peter's to June: these are relationships which transcend boundaries of nation. In some ways they are reducible to class: the characters are knitted together more by their shared value systems and lifestyle than they are separated by geographical accidents of birth.

However, these international bonds do not suggest that borders should be jettisoned in favour of a globalised world community. Theo is metaphorically orphaned from his own fatherland and seeks a surrogate in England, but *Blimp* emphasises the need for local, homely roots and badges of belonging (as Candy asks, without 'home' what are they fighting for?). The most unredeemed character in these films is Kaunitz in *Blimp*, a German double agent, equally despised by the British and the Boers because he violates any sense of certainty, and as such he is an insult to good Germans. Not only does he defy the film's code of honour, but he ultimately lacks affiliation to any service other than his own. He travesties any real sense of belonging.

1

Alien Territories and Enemy Lines – *The Spy in Black, Contraband, 49th Parallel, '...one of our aircraft is missing'*

> Many stories have been told about the North-West Frontier, the territory dividing India from Pakistan. I have attempted here to show another aspect. What to India is the 'North-West Frontier' is, to Afghanistan, the 'South-East Frontier'.
>
> Emeric Pressburger, 'South East Frontier'

NOSFERATU IN BRITAIN

Shortly before meeting Michael Powell, Emeric Pressburger was developing scripts for Alexander Korda. One of his projects was provisionally entitled 'South East Frontier'. It was based on W. Somerset Maugham's play *Caesar's Wife* and is a conventional Korda-esque tale, similar to *The Drum* (Zoltan Korda, 1938). The script, which Pressburger soon worked up with Powell as 'The East and the West', was never filmed. It focuses on a 1920s aristocratic and military set, and tells how a group of Europeans escape a mullah's uprising in Kabul. Pressburger's own early draft version of the script, dated December 1938, opens with the characteristically skewed observation noted at the head of this chapter. He is drawn to a borderland theme, but inverts commonplace Western assumptions about it by imagining it from the other side.

Powell and Pressburger's first realised collaboration, *The Spy in Black*, was released in August 1939, just before the outbreak of war. Alexander Korda, who first brought the pair together for the project, was seeking a vehicle for his contract star, the German actor Conrad Veidt. Such was Veidt's success in *The Spy in Black* that he went on to appear in Powell and Pressburger's next film, *Contraband* (1940), released in May 1940. These films are companion pieces and they share not only their chief male star, but also their leading actress, Valerie Hobson (who had starred in *The Drum*). Both films are spy thrillers, a genre which allows Powell and Pressburger to initiate their career-long, collaborative exploration of some key motifs and themes: fascinating, fascinated aliens, cloaked in gothic mystique; border crossings, and a willingness to examine how place operates to shape or to threaten our identity. Echoing Pressburger's interest in those on the 'wrong' side of the border, the central character in *The Spy in Black* is an enemy alien, and the audience is asked to identify and sympathise with someone beyond their accustomed frame of reference. If there is a Germanic influence at work here, it is partly because Veidt himself, with roles such as Cesare the somnambulist in *The Cabinet of Doctor Caligari* (Robert Weine, 1919, Germany) and Ivan the Terrible in *Waxworks* (Paul Leni, 1924, Germany), embodies a history of German film-making. To Powell, 'he *was* the German cinema'.[1] It is also because the spy thriller's contours closely follow those of gothic fiction and because gothic structures also informed the Expressionist narratives associated with German cinema and with Veidt's early career. Both *The Spy in Black* and *Contraband* demonstrate a generic wedding, vamping up British territorial anxieties of the late 1930s into a gothic mode by intertwining the genealogies of the spy genre with some of Expressionism's uncanny motifs.

In both of Veidt's roles, he is sent undercover into a foreboding wartime Britain. *The Spy in Black* is a period piece, nominally set in the First World War with Veidt playing an enemy spy, Captain Ernst Hardt. Despite the quarter-century shift back in time, the film is clearly animated by some topical and urgent concerns, appearing at the commencement of the 1939–45 conflict and dealing with the themes of national security and military secrets. Hardt mistakenly trusts a double agent whom he is sent to meet in the Orkneys, and German plans to attack the British fleet are discovered in time for a counter-attack to be launched. In *Contraband*, Veidt plays Captain Anderson, a neutral Dane in the Second World War, although again he has to journey onto British soil without his identity papers. It is this very loss of identity which each film explores: forced to abandon the security of his old self, the Britain which Veidt has to negotiate is a dark, hostile place. The schoolroom in the Orkneys where much of *The Spy in Black* is set takes on the feel of a haunted house, claustrophobic and unsafe. The blacked-out London of *Contraband* is another uncertain regime: it has both safe havens and dangerous enclaves, and is plagued by Nazi infiltrators. These territorial displacements bring a sense of new discovery and even erotic possibility to Captains Hardt and Anderson, but at no time is there any easy or cosily secure sense of being at home, or much less any sense of joy at the possibilities which border crossings might bring: new spaces are alien territories, generally viewed with trepidation, and never with less than guarded caution.

While *The Spy in Black* has signs of what would later be trademark motifs for Powell and Pressburger, it is not the work of confident auteurs. It is fundamentally a genre piece based on popular fiction and stylistically it draws heavily from Hitchcock. Pressburger's remit was to rewrite an existing screenplay, which itself was an adaptation of a story by J. Storer Clouston, and to make the star's role more central. The film's broad parameters were therefore pre-set for him, yet in revising the original material he stamps his authorship on it. He elevates Veidt's role, and emphasises the acts of looking and of deception – activities which are central to the spy genre, of course, but which prefigure some of the characteristics of the Powell-Pressburger aesthetic.

The Spy in Black's allusions to Expressionist cinema within the conventions of the spy story are not so improbable. The spy thriller derives from popular entertainment fiction and deals with disguise, misinformation and paranoia. It therefore borrows from the same gothic writing whose horror elements were so influential on Expressionist film. Spy stories, horror stories and Expressionist film belong to the same family, even if the prestigious works of early German cinema raised the thrills of the 'penny dreadful' to 'high art'. The gothic, with its melodramatic plots, hidden secrets, malevolent forces and outbreaks of irrationality, forms part of the same sensational entertainment culture as the spy story. The spy story reframes those gothic motifs within narratives that foreground the ideologies of nationhood. Each of these forms feature dramatic encounters with demonised 'others' and *The Spy in Black* is readable, therefore, both in terms of the popular British taste for spy stories, and as an Anglicisation of German cinema styles which drew on fundamentally gothic motifs. Spy thrillers are clearly part of an indigenous culture of sensational escapism. As such, *The Spy in Black* is partly rooted in popular English writing harking back to nineteenth-century melodramatic fiction. These elements, though, are mediated through the 'horror' narratives of German cinema. Hence the film bears traces of F.W. Murnau's *Nosferatu, Eine Symphonie des Grauens* (1922, Germany), itself a trans-nationally hybrid work. *The Spy in Black*, as a vehicle for Veidt, is Powell and Pressburger's homage to the German film industry.

In British cinema, the spy thriller genre in the 1930s was dominated by Alfred Hitchcock, and *The Spy in Black* reworks the mixture of suspense, comedy and romance found in Hitchcock's work at Gaumont-British studios from 1934 to 1938: the sextet of films *The Man Who Knew Too Much* (1934), *The Thirty Nine Steps* (1935), *Secret Agent* (1936), *Sabotage* (1936), *Young and Innocent* (1937) and *The Lady Vanishes* (1938). Hitchcock's work represents the best of a spate of spy and crime thrillers in the 1930s. As James Chapman notes, with Europe stumbling into political instability, they work through topical anxieties regarding national identity and the menace of the foreign.[2] Just as Carol Reed's *Night Train to Munich* (1940) trades on its similarity to *The Lady Vanishes*, the plot and the dark mise-en-scène of *The Spy in Black* echoes the Langian feel of *Sabotage*, with its strange yet partly sympathetic villain, while the Conrad Veidt/Valerie Hobson relationship in both *The Spy in Black* and *Contraband* repeats the Robert Donat/Madeleine Carroll coupling in *The Thirty Nine Steps*.

Spy stories encode fears for the well-being of the nation. The genre deals, after all, with international politics – although in its modern manifestations it also deals with corporate espionage in a world of multi-nationals and global economies. Its 'thriller' elements descend from the violence and mystery of Poe, Conan Doyle and Wilkie Collins, where the lines between the detective story, the spy genre and the gothic tale of horror are deliberately blurred. In more bullish periods, such as high Victorian Britain, national ideology is more strident. Adventure tales of the British Empire fulfil this task, often covering similar territory to the spy story, but doing so with confidence. Rudyard Kipling's *Kim* (1901), with its boy hero recruited into a world of imperial espionage, Erskine Childers' *The Riddle of the Sands* (1903), with its discovery of an invasion plot, and the work of John Buchan, such as *The Thirty Nine Steps* (1915), illustrate the affinity between the adventure fiction of the day and the conventions of the spy genre. Epic stories of the nineteenth century often celebrated and affirmed the twin virtues of Englishness and masculinity, and tended to invest the fate of the nation in an emblematic hero. Powell and Pressburger will later alight on these imperial myths in their own, epic assessment of British military masculinity, *The Life and Death of Colonel Blimp* (1943). But where the adventure tale arrogantly shores up the ideology of Empire, the spy thriller, as Michael Denning has argued, indicates a crisis of faith in that mission.[3] Confident certainties give way to anxiety, and by unpacking the implications of this change, the noirish look of *The Spy in Black* can be accounted for. The tropes of noir – chiaroscuro lighting, unstable situations – are visual imprints or externalisations of fear, and in *The Spy in Black* and other espionage tales, that fear is immediately political: the literal threat of invasion or subversion by a foreign power. It is a fear, though, which may also be read more generally as an expression of existential insecurity, as an uncanny encounter with evil which threatens the stability of the subject. Broadly speaking, the hitherto assertive stance of the Kiplingesque imperial adventure tale is replaced by a more defensive posture in the spy genre. Any simple binarisms (Good/Evil, Us/Them, Dominant/Subservient) are complicated by confusions of identity, by ethical problems, and ultimately by a troubling realisation that even the Self may be corrupt.

The Spy in Black commences stably enough. On-screen graphics tell us that we are in Kiel, in 1917, and that this is the base of the German navy, while we hear a snatch of the German national anthem over the opening credits. Place, time and culture are known. The opening sequence shifts us to the Kielerhof Hotel, where a newspaper headline announcing the success of the German U-boat food blockade is welcomed. A pre-production treatment for the film opens with a note about 'how' war should be fought, anticipating the key theme of *The Life and Death of Colonel Blimp*: '17th February, 1917, marked the end of the war as gentlemen played it. On that date the German High Command decided to institute ruthless submarine warfare on all neutrals, sinking all ships without warning in an attempt to starve England out by submarine blockade.' Captain Hardt's return to the Kielerhof Hotel, exhausted and hungry after a completed mission at sea, marks him out as the hero of this maritime campaign. Hardt embodies a set of heroic principles, based on honesty, consistency and duty, as his name, Ernst Hardt – 'earnest heart' – signifies. His solitude and his leadership qualities are romantically etched, and Veidt's frame and mature bearing convey a sense of gravitas, combining the attractiveness and the austerity which would become a feature of many Powell and Pressburger authority figures. Hardt's throwaway comment that he '*never* smokes a pipe' clues us into his character more specifically, implying that he is proud to be a creature of habit, and an observer of permanent, solid parameters. Later, when he is back at sea, he is pedantic regarding time, correcting his subordinates to the minute and ensuring that their sealed orders are not opened until exactly '11:15'. He stands for the military virtues of clarity and precision and is committed to the rational.

Yet already in the opening sequence, and long before Hardt is sent onto enemy turf, there are hints of the unfamiliarity to come. The story's triumphal opening rhetoric regarding food shortages in Britain seems to be contradicted by the Kielerhof's apparently empty kitchens, while a close-up of the newspaper headline shows most of the story of the blockade blanked out by a large 'Censored' sign. Tensions between disclosure and non-disclosure are a characteristic of the uncanny, as Freud's reading of the semantic levels in the German words *heimlich* and *unheimlich* has shown. The newspaper's secrecy fits in with familiar paranoid gothic motifs relating to authority, hidden knowledge and conspiracy, while the evidence of the senses (the severely depleted menu at the Kielerhof Hotel) disagrees with the purported 'truth' of received wisdom about the 'success' of the German blockade. The film therefore imbues the misinformation and propaganda of the First World War with romantic-gothic ideas. The gothic's sense of unfamiliarity and of the unconscious is also put into play: Hardt's occupation as the captain of a submarine symbolically acknowledges the importance of what is psychologically submerged and, soon, Hardt will be ordered undercover, and will be forced to descend into the morally corrupt and potentially corrupting world of espionage. Tidy national demarcations, coded in the fragment of the German anthem we hear at the opening of the film, are set to blur, and clearly flagged national loyalties will grow foggy and confused.

Hardt's orders are to go ashore on Hoy in the Orkneys and to make contact with Fräulein Tiel, a German secret agent who is posing there as a schoolteacher. His unseen superiors provide him with his own tweed suit as a disguise, relabelling it with a Savile Row trademark and anglicising his name. With a passing allusion to a German literature of doubling, collapsed identity and the fantastic, we are told that the suit was originally bought from 'Hoffmann' in Berlin. Hardt himself cannot be relabelled so easily. 'Try to make a spy out of me!' he snorts, and later, while still in uniform, his response is that of the professional soldier: 'If I am to be shot, it will be as an officer.' He claims a moral high ground of honest soldiery by declaring his disgust at the world of espionage, a world in which the German agent Fräulein Tiel has seemingly prostituted herself to win the confidence of a disloyal British officer. Hardt's arrogance about Tiel's moral fibre is soon undone with the simple accusation which she makes in her defence: 'Have *you* ever fired a torpedo at an unarmed ship?' His own ethics are more muddied than he would care to admit, his 'heroism' is compromised. The key debate here, though, is more to do with the fixity of identity than with the nature of the heroic.

Hardt's identification with his uniform is an open declaration of his personal integrity and national identity. To don a disguise is to perform a masquerade, and in psychoanalytic terms to masquerade is to open up a space between our identity and our social roles, a space which then, by definition, puts into question the very nature and existence of fixed identities. Joan Riviere was the first to use the word in this sense, and to her, it is a creative, sophisticated mechanism used as a coping strategy. While Riviere talks about a defensive exaggeration of signs of femininity in women, rather than an adoption of 'alien' traits, she nevertheless opens up implications of performance.[4] Here, despite Hardt's resistance, he is dispatched into a spy genre in which subjectivity is mutable and *national* identity is masqueraded. To Hardt this is far from liberating. It is an invidious regime of faulty vision, sophistry and betrayal. The film thus addresses the condition of having to reinvent oneself because one is forced into the unknown, and, negatively, it can see that reinvention only in terms of loss. The roles Hardt is reluctantly forced to adopt exile him from his erstwhile existential security and launch him into a radical no-man's-land of expressionistic disturbance. He is a modern man launched prematurely into a postmodern condition of performativity: that is the trauma of his exile.

Hardt's experiences are characteristic of the spy genre. National fate determined by the actions of an emblematic individual (part of its romantic heritage); hero and/or villain positioned as outsider (likewise a trace of romanticism); secret operations to be identified; a world of conspiratorial menace: these are its traits, and they create suspense and excitement. Where *The Spy in Black* most obviously departs from this is in the identification it encourages with its alien protagonist, a sympathetic investment which has important ideological repercussions, given the confused and collapsing identities in the film. The cross-national identification promotes the sense of tension which the thriller demands, but it also undoes any easy distinctions between 'us' and 'them'. Perhaps the most important characteristic of the spy genre is the inevitable and highly cinematic interest it shows in the act of *looking per se*. As Tom Ryall has noted, in the spy film, '[a]ppearances, the focal point of cinematic attention, are deceptive for both hero and spectator', with this shared experience forming what for Ryall is 'the definitional heart of the genre'.[5] *The Spy in Black* is no exception. Mirrors, windows and doorways – all framing and bringing attention to the field of vision – feature strongly throughout the film. They underscore the process of spying itself, and they also mark the entrances to new dramatic spaces in which discoveries will be made.

The plotlines of the film are confusing, and they explore confusions of national identity. As its complicated lines of espionage, counter-espionage and subterfuge are initiated, appearances are shown to be deceptive. Anne Burnett (the original, 'real' schoolteacher on her way to start work in the Orkneys) is driven unwittingly to what seems to be her doom, to be replaced by Fräulein Tiel, the German agent whom Hardt is sent to meet. As Anne is duped into accepting a ride from disguised villains, a knowing point-of-view shot of what the car's chauffeuse sees in her rear-view mirror first alerts us to the sinister turn which the plot has taken. Anne is oblivious of this, and innocently provides her life story to the disguised German agents planning to impersonate her. The theme of vision returns when Hardt is later guided to the Orkney schoolhouse by a light which Fräulein Tiel displays from her window (a light which the security-conscious local constable, Bob Bratt, being mindful of wartime strictures, is quick to put out). As would become common during war narratives, the idea of 'showing a light' (or of merely being visible) is connoted with treachery. Once Hardt reaches the schoolhouse, his entire frame of reference is limited to the views offered from its windows and roof-light. He is shown imperiously gazing at his target, the British fleet in the harbour, and we also see him looking down at Fräulein Tiel in Anne's class-room. Each of these views proves deceptive: the British cruiser squadrons are not Hardt's target, as he takes them to be, but are a British trap to lure the German U-boats into the bay; and in a shock narrative twist, the woman whom Hardt takes to be Fräulein Tiel turns out to be a British agent (eventually named as Mrs Blacklock) who has taken Tiel's place before she reached the Orkneys.

Initially, though, our range of knowledge is limited to Hardt's, and we share his ignorance of the British counter-deception. We see the schoolteacher being abducted and assume her to have been substituted by Tiel. We do not see Tiel being substituted by Mrs Blacklock. For most of the film, we assume that the English actress Valerie Hobson is playing a German spy who masquerades Englishness, whereas in fact Hobson is playing an English spy pretending to be a German agent passing herself off as English. If nothing else, this multiple confusion flags up the need for vigilance during wartime, suggesting that appearances of national identity are not to be trusted. At the denouement of the film the British commander asks of Constable Bob Bratt 'Where were your eyes, man?' As *The Spy in Black* demonstrates, though, our senses are easily deceived.

When distinct binary categories such as good and evil are jeopardised we shift into a liminal space, where the self is threatened. John G. Cawelti and Bruce A. Rosenberg have suggested that the psychological tension brought on by a spy hero's clandestine life is like a state of schizophrenia. The spy must map out 'a boundary area in which the anxiety surrounding divergent worldviews can become so great that the secret agent passes beyond [any] stage of rational control over his divided self'.[6] What this hesitant, untrustworthy condition most resembles is the fantastical structure associated with the gothic. While *The Spy in Black* exhibits no explicitly supernatural economy, a subversive 'other' still threatens to invade. Gothic fiction throughout the nineteenth century moved away from a purely supernatural regime to a secular one in which the 'other' was allowed to be an externalisation of part of the self. The nature of good and evil which the gothic summons up is the marker of a culture realigning itself towards the post-sacred. With *The Spy in Black*, the presence of real, Germanic factors – Veidt's nationality and the Expressionist tone – pulls the genre's centre of gravity closer than usual to the gothic. Presenting a circulation of desire, and a string of substitutions which makes identities illegible, the film consciously draws on this tradition (one which Veidt personifies). The very 'blackness' of its title is a relic of the spy genre's gothic history of diabolic flirtation.

Crossing boundaries is a key motif of the gothic. As a transgressive gesture, this marks it out as progressive or radical. Bakhtin, for example, has established the connection between the fantasies of writers such as Hoffmann and Poe and the fragmentation and disorderliness of the carnivalesque, with all its anarchic potential. To cross into the territory of the fantastic is to abandon a rational knowledge founded in empiricism and anchored to the authority of the studied 'look'. It is to enter an alien and alienating other-place which is strange, where signs are confounded or inverted. In her detailed analysis of this fantastic regime, Rosemary Jackson offers the following conclusion, worth quoting at length:

> Fantasies of deconstructed, demolished or divided identities and of disintegrated bodies, oppose traditional categories of unitary selves. They attempt to give graphic depictions of subjects *in process*, suggesting possibilities of innumerable other selves, of different histories, different bodies. They denounce the theses and categories of the thetic, attempting to dissolve the symbolic order at its very base, where it is established in and through the subject, where the dominant signifying system is re-produced… [F]antasies image the possibility of radical cultural transformation through attempting to dissolve or shatter the boundary lines between the imaginary and the symbolic. They refuse the latter's categories of the 'real' and its unities.[7]

The Spy in Black offers us states of 'process' (transitional spaces, mutable appearances), multiple metamorphoses of character (which can be read as projected fantasies) and a dissolution of the symbolic (signs hidden or misread). If these realignments are clued from the start, they are amplified at key moments in the narrative, first with the abduction of Anne Burnett on the Scottish mainland, where evil first shows its hand, then with the sexualised atmosphere between Hardt and the woman he takes to be Fräulein Tiel, and finally with his discovery of the British counter-plot.

The events leading to the abduction of Anne Burnett contain superstitious portents of what is to follow. As Anne's nanny shouts that it is time for her to commence her journey north, her packed travel bag tumbles downstairs into an over-emphatic close-up. 'The handle broke,' she explains prosaically, although other than being an omen of bad fortune (Anne will, it seems, soon be thrown over cliffs to her death by her German abductors) the event has no other narrative motivation. We then learn that Anne is unmarried, and is engaged to Reverend John Harris. As her nanny fusses over her, her innocence becomes clear. Her family's lack of worldliness is later revealed – her deceased father was an unsuccessful architect and a teetotaller. As a fresh virgin, vulnerable on the eve of her wedding, with absent or deficient parents, Anne is an archetypal gothic female victim. That moment on the brink of marriage – with the fear of the unknown given a specifically sexual coding, and the lack of a (father) figure to offer guidance – is a gothic condition *par excellence*. As Anne and her nanny ponder the late arrival of her lift to the station, a dog barks to alert them to the arrival of a rich old lady in a car, a lady who will offer to take Anne herself. In the strange logic of the horror genre, animals instinctively detect the presence of danger, and Anne's good-natured nanny is blind to the irony of her words: 'It's certainly the hand of Providence that brought you here today,' she innocently tells the apparently harmless old lady.

Much like Hitchcock, Powell and Pressburger play with hierarchies of knowledge allowed to their audience, to create suspense and tension. We alone are shown that the old lady's chauffeuse has not taken the expected road to Dingwall. The old lady's false appearance is typical of the genre. Later, the script makes explicit this scenario's indebtedness to myths of endangered virginity. 'Do you know the story of Little Red Riding Hood?' the disguised Mrs Blacklock asks Captain Hardt, pointing out that for Anne, that story did not have a happy ending. The old lady is a conflation of grandmaternalism and wolfishness, her black furs ambiguously suggesting the menace she represents. Once Anne has been smothered, and malevolence has shown itself, the first of the film's substitutions can take place. A close-up shows Anne unconscious in the car. As readers of *Dracula* know too well, virgins are never more at risk than when asleep. Moreover, the association between sleep and dreaming suggests an obvious parallel between the endangerment brought on by the presence of evil, and the fantasies, desires and fears of the unconscious.

A sexual charge between Hardt and Mrs Blacklock (whom he still takes to be Fräulein Tiel) is set up when the two are cooped up in the remote schoolhouse. After their first meal, a post-prandial cigarette draws them together, and Hardt notices her stockings. She adjusts her dress to hide them. The sexual politicking between them places 'Fräulein Tiel' in charge, as she is Hardt's superior within the German secret service. Hardt attempts to reassert his compromised masculinity in the film's romance plot. The spy's world is traditionally one of male domination, yet here Hardt's heroically male credentials are jeopardised and a power play takes place between them. Hardt's troublesome journey to enemy territory has brought with it another less literal migration out of his homosocial enclave and into a world where gender difference causes insecurity. The tense intersecting of power and desire is intentional here, and was consciously part of Pressburger's use of his star actor. As early as the revised treatment for the film, an aside from the authors suggests, 'Certainly [Fräulein Tiel] must be feeling something, but she has herself under control, that is as much under control as it is possible for a young lady to be, who is alone with Conrad Veidt at midnight.' When 'Tiel' rejects Hardt's initial advances and locks him in his bedroom, a brief fade to black (denoting a temporal elision) is barely sufficient to separate this proof of *her* domination from the footage which follows: shots of phallic naval weaponry, with close-ups of machinery and of guns firing, indicate a fantasised displacement of – or an ironic compensation for – Hardt's impaired martial credentials. It is a nostalgic splicing back to the simple world of male warfare which Hardt knew and understood in the first reel of the film. In microcosm, this spectacular display of 'boys' toys' reasserts a safe male ethos, and it is a strategy Powell and Pressburger would revert to again in such films as *The Small Back Room* (1949).

To capitalise on Conrad Veidt's early career, and make fuller use of his exotic, erotic and yet threatening potential, *The Spy in Black* draws atmospherically on vampire myths. Repeated images of either Hardt or 'Tiel' gazing out of windows resemble similar images in Murnau's *Nosferatu*. Hardt's way to the schoolhouse is signalled, as I have said, by a light shown from an upstairs window, and numerous cutaway shots of moonlight associate him with subversive nocturnal behaviour. Features which are entirely (and realistically) appropriate to the spy/war genre are thus also readable from a gothic-romantic perspective. That beam of light from the schoolroom lures Hardt to 'Fräulein Tiel' just as surely as Dracula is drawn to his victims. The point to be made about Hardt is that while Dracula, as a gothic villain, is entirely 'other' and defies rationality, Hardt is ordered invidiously and unwillingly into this regime and becomes threateningly 'gothic' only because of the clandestine mode of existence he is forced into. Indeed, with his fixed characteristics, his efficient military outlook and his pedantic punctuality (established in the film's opening sequence) he is first marked out as Stoker's emblem of rationality and clerkly precision, Jonathan Harker. Harker is likewise dispatched into alien territory to be infected by the seductive approaches of the 'other'. During their spell in the schoolhouse, Hardt becomes increasingly menacing. Hence, while it is sufficient for Lieutenant Ashington, a disloyal English officer, to tap his fist rudely on the schoolhouse window to gain admittance to the German spies hiding inside, Hardt's similar signal to 'Tiel' is overloaded with gothic mise-en-scène: a silhouetted close-up of his long, skeletal fingers rapping on the window pane, bare dead branches in the background and great swathes of mist in the darkness gothicise his return to the schoolhouse. 'Tiel' is woken by his sinister rapping on a window, and the fact that a sexual desire has already been registered between them forces us to read the sequence psychologically. Just as *Dracula* plays with an oneiric interplay of fear and desire, so too is Hardt's arrival summoned by 'Tiel's' eroticised dream-state.

As the German plot to demolish the British fleet seems to have been safely concluded, Hardt again attempts to seduce 'Fräulein Tiel'. Although again she offers resistance, this time his seduction is rather more successful. She protests vocally ('*If* I am in command, I order you to let me go'), her simultaneous language of militarism and romance emphasising a mixture of masculine adventure narrative and love story. Her opening 'if' implies a possible shift in the power play between them, granting some authority to the man, and despite her protestations, it is she who half-unconsciously opens the hatchway which has been separating her from Hardt. While Veidt is rarely given much rein in this film to fully draw upon his wide acting range, he is allowed to touch upon a hypnotic quality which recalls earlier roles, most famously Cesare in *Dr Caligari* and Ivan the Terrible in *Waxworks*. Frequent beautifully lit close-ups of his face, handsome, strong and intelligent, but also suggestive of a concentrated menace, capitalise on this quality. Fascinated by the German, Anne lets him enter through a highly symbolic doorway. This recurring fascination with doorways – whether locked or open – is an architectural rendition of the film's exploration of crossed boundaries and transitional spaces, and it is given a very sexualised emphasis.

The kiss between Hardt and 'Tiel', from which she recoils, forms the next dramatic shift in the narrative, for it is at this belated stage that our assumptions regarding 'Fräulein Tiel's' loyalties are shown to have been misled. Hardt too learns that his trust in the 'schoolteacher' has been misplaced. 'Fräulein Tiel', assuming Hardt to be safely locked away, runs out to meet the man we have taken to be the disloyal Ashington, and the truth is revealed that she is Mrs Blacklock and is working for the British. In a crudely symbolic gesture, 'Ashington', whom we now discover to be David Blacklock (the husband of Mrs Blacklock) takes off his coat and gives it to her. His noble, knightly virtues are coded by the white jumper he is wearing. The contrast with the 'spy in black' could not be clearer.

The claustrophobically designed mise-en-scène of the schoolroom (by Vincent Korda) becomes far more meaningful as the style of the film grows more Expressionist. It is a recurring feature of gothic tales that landscape and buildings assume the characteristics of their protagonists. Secret rooms in old buildings, hidden entrances, labyrinthine passages, haunted places, Poe's 'House of Usher': they are all concrete metaphors for psychological conditions. The awkward staircase and low, forbidding beams in the schoolhouse depict the panic of entrapment, the destabilising effect of the narrative's reversal, and the rapid realisation of betrayal with which Hardt has to contend. He is no longer the hunter but the hunted, lurking in shadows which represent visually his sense of persecution. Yet, liberated from his room he still presents a threat. In the emblematic image of the film (a photographic still from this shot features emphatically during its opening title credits), he is seen silhouetted from behind in long shot blocking a closed doorway with his arms outstretched. He is leaning against the door frame, listening to the disclosure of the British counter-plot. It is an arresting image, a dramatically ambiguous pose expressing both defiance and submission. It recollects a heritage of threatening or foreboding gestures, drawn from the gothic and familiar to the horror genre. Indeed, while Powell and Pressburger seize the opportunity to overlay their spy story with elements of horror, the point can only be reiterated that the irruptions of malevolence and irrationality which structure the spy genre derive from this older form. In Jerry Palmer's words, 'Underneath the paraphernalia of medieval castles and persecuted virgins the core of the Gothic is terror through incomprehension. It is this that the thriller has borrowed, and incorporated.'[8] Hardt manages to flee the island by boarding the *St Magnus* steamer disguised as Reverend Harris, the fiancé of the real Anne Burnett. In this ministerial cloak he looks like a caped, melodramatic stage villain, and the danger he represents to the passengers on board the steamer is evoked by what seem like conscious allusions to the 'ship passage' sequence in Murnau's *Nosferatu*. Hardt moves about the ship silently, spying through port holes, masquerading as that most comfortably familiar and established of figures, an English parson. This is a prime instance of the *heimlich* becoming its opposite, the *unheimlich*, and the disguise also acknowledges the spiritual dimension with which the gothic genre was once associated. This, of course, is part of the significance of his disguise. Just as a grandmaternal old lady was earlier revealed to be a murderous secret agent, the uniform which Hardt wears hides a threat, and as Powell points out, in Storer Clouston's original story the 'spy in black' had been a Scottish minister who had likewise used the uniform as a respectable disguise.[9] Lotte Eisner found this structure of deceptive appearances littered throughout Expressionist German cinema. She suggests that in the process of doubling and mirroring which such narratives present:

> Caligari is both the eminent doctor and the fairground huckster. Nosferatu the vampire, also the master of a feudal castle, wishes to buy a house from an estate agent who is himself imbued with diabolism… It would seem from this that for the Germans the demoniac side to an individual always has a middle class counterpart. In the ambiguous world of the German cinema, people are unsure of their identity and can easily lose it on the way.[10]

While there are problems with Eisner's generalisations about the German race, it is true that the films she looks at are characterised by confusions between the familiar and the uncanny, and something of this echoes through to *The Spy in Black*.

The German prisoners-of-war taken on board the *St Magnus* at Stromness fortuitously furnish Hardt with a 'tribe' to assist him in taking over the steamer. Pressburger suggested early in the scripting process that the prisoners should speak German, to emphasise the menace they represent. There is an irony that these prisoners have been rescued after their own vessel was blown up by one of their own mines. It anticipates Hardt's imminent destruction by his own U-boat, and (like the hidden omens earlier which anticipated the abduction of Anne Burnett) it suggests that predestination may be at work. One of the passengers announces that they are 'all in the hands of Providence', while the *St Magnus*'s engineer is troubled by the Germans' presence on board: 'I am not a superstitious man but I don't like it. They're Jonahs, pure Jonahs!' The complicated and confusing chains of male and female substitutions in the film hardly map out a tidy circulation of desire, but there is some logic to Hardt's assumption of Reverend Harris's place. The real English schoolteacher, Anne Burnett, was to have wed the distinctly un-dashing Reverend Harris. Later, her substitute (Mrs Blacklock) is tempted away from her own husband by a genuine desire for the magnetically attractive Captain Hardt. There is a strange reasoning, therefore, in Hardt's eventual disguise as the original unsatisfactory partner, as he becomes an exciting alternative to the dull Reverend Harris. It is also in accordance with a perverse gothic order that Mrs Blacklock is herself aboard the *St Magnus*, fulfilling her position as maiden-in-peril as Hardt becomes the vampire, summoned by her expression of unregulated sexuality.

In the concluding moments of *The Spy in Black* the certainties of its opening reassert themselves and all the deceptions are exposed. The convoluted complications of identity and loyalty repolarise, and the narrative backs away from its Expressionistically inflected chaos to restabilise itself into the simple verities of the war film:

> Veidt: You are English. I am German. We are enemies.
> Hobson: I like that better.
> Veidt: And I. It simplifies everything.

Significantly, this re-ordering into the norms of a clearly recognised genre cues conventional footage of Royal Navy vessels and of the ensuing sea battle. In her assessment of Conrad Veidt's work in British cinema, Sue Harper focuses on the lines of dialogue quoted above as evidence that 'Powell had an over-simplified notion of the tendency of Veidt's work...Veidt by that time excelled in portraying men who were torn *apart* by their duty; he specialised in evisceration.'[11] With Veidt's huge experience of acting in Germany, Harper is surely right to note that he best represents 'a dystopian persona riven by contradiction'.[12] While it is true that Powell's direction of Veidt could have made more of this aspect of his star image, given the constraints of genre (at heart it remains an 'action'-based genre) and of storyline (inherited by Pressburger and rewritten to expand Hardt's role for Veidt), it is unfair to take these lines to represent the film as a whole. Clearly and emphatically, they mark a shift in the text back to a clearly demarcated conflict-based drama and away from a plot which has been so complicated that points of identification have begun to crumble. Until this moment, Veidt's Hardt has struggled with just the ambiguity which Harper finds to be lacking. The movement to a clear, concrete resolution where 'true identities' are unmasked is typical of melodrama, which is, as Christine Gledhill has pointed out, 'a drama of misrecognition and clarification, the climax of which is an act of "nomination" in which characters finally declaim their true identities, demanding a public recognition till then thwarted by deliberate deceptions, hidden secrets, binding vows and loyalties'.[13] Hardt's wish for a simple, polarised world of clear demarcations is a sign that at this early stage in their collaboration Powell and Pressburger's imaginations are fired by ambiguous states brought on by border crossings, but that their sympathies are anchored in more stable, modern identities born out of a sense of being rooted.

A final closing irony, the last vestige of Expressionistic homage in the film, is exhibited in Hardt's fate. Recognising that his own U-boat is about to torpedo him, he attempts to semaphore the message 'Hardt ist Hier' to his old crew. They fire nevertheless and he is destroyed by that with which he most identifies: the German navy. It is a self-destruction, as his own symbolic double, an uncontrollable extension of himself, turns on him at the moment when he reaffirms his identity and authenticity. But while his death is ironic, Hardt's cry reasserts his individual ego. Having shifted into a paraxial regime where selves were blurred, the narrative now finds and restores the centrality and value of the stable personality. Self-consciously, a close-up shows Hardt on the bridge of the steamer, cranking the controls to the 'Finished With Engine' position as the narrative itself grinds to its own halt. As he is left alone on the sinking steamer, he quietly expresses the rediscovery of his heroic self by repeating the personal motto of his opening scene: 'I never smoke a pipe.' The last shot of the film shows where its dramatic investment truly lies, resting not on the romantic reunion between the Blacklocks, but on debris littering the ocean, marking where Hardt has gone down with the *St Magnus*.

Mannered and abrupt – marionette-like – Hardt's flailing semaphore recalls the exaggerated movements of Veidt's early film career, which, of course, blossomed before the arrival of synchronised sound. Those movements are codified and concretised into Hardt's futile physical gestures. There is something here of the style of Expressionist acting we find later in, for example, Anton Walbrook's performance in *The Red Shoes* (1948). Edward Gordon Craig, the internationally famous theorist of drama, whose writings on acting at the turn of the century had been so influential on Max Reinhardt, wrote that to express moments of acute passion, the actor should utilise a technique of screaming which abandons constraints of realism. *Der Schrie*, the scream of horror and anger, should thus distinguish the impassioned will of the actor. Furthermore, Craig was alert to the tragically ironic potential when that emotional excess was trapped within a regulated clinical language.[14] This is what Hardt's semaphore signifies: vital crisis articulated physically – not with a raw flailing physicality, but struggling within a brutally mechanised sign system. It repeats the irony of Veidt's furiously articulated cry, 'Hardt ist Hier!' as his fists pound his chest: it is a call to his second-in-command, Schuster, aboard his old U-boat, and is also an existential assertion, made at the moment of his destruction.

This highly melodramatic register is clearly more full-blooded than the body of the film, most of which has been a more prosaically crafted genre piece, albeit one which is enriched by a redrafting of romantic motifs. *The Spy in Black*, then, can be conceptualised as a product of a popular, indigenously British, cultural tradition. This is its 'dominant' coding. But an alternative set of codes, dovetailing into that tradition, also claim our attention. They are presented through Vincent Korda's design (and the industrial practice which produced such tight studio designs), through Pressburger's narrative which takes the conventions of a genre and plays up the romantic traits embedded within them to Germanicise the film, and through the presence of Conrad Veidt, for whom the screenplay was rewritten. The film is most successful when this alternative set of codes is deployed in the name of gothic sensationalism. If it is only in its last brief moments that Veidt's potential is fully realised, his presence nevertheless complements a film which betrays the characteristic traits of a 1930s Anglo-German aesthetic.

CONTRABAND

Powell and Pressburger's next film, *Contraband*, reworks some of these themes, and in its very title there is a connotation of transgressed boundaries. Plainly, the repetition of both the Veidt/Hobson pairing and the theme of espionage links the film with *The Spy in Black*, and like its predecessor this second collaboration opens with a concretely signified place and time. Positioning itself at both the geographical frontier of the nation, and at the moment of transition into war, the graphics displayed over location footage establish where we are: 'In August 1939, Eastgate on Sea was just a holiday town on the South East coast of England. In November 1939 – '. The sequence proceeds to show subtitled Morse code scripted across the screen telling us about the interception of a Danish freighter, the *Helvig*. Like Captain Hardt's semaphore, this language is a mechanical, logical sign system, clearly decipherable. Again, the narrative takes its protagonists into a deceptive and confused paraxial space. Partisan loyalties, though, are complicated by the nationality of Captain Anderson (Conrad Veidt). He is Danish, and thus politically neutral. The plotline, about military intelligence relating to enemy ships sailing under neutral flags, is weakly thought out, but it perpetuates a motif from the previous film, namely the distinction between actual national identity and displayed or admitted badges of belonging. Again, the masquerade of national identity is foregrounded. Captain Anderson becomes a stateless being when he has cause to follow one of his passengers, Mrs Sorenson (Valerie Hobson) to London in pursuit of his identity papers. Here he enters the noir world of Mrs Sorenson's espionage, although, as with Hardt, Anderson stands for a commitment to rationality. The narrative's interest in clocks, schedules and deadlines (putatively a source of suspense) marks this commitment – Anderson's treasured watch, inscribed with his name and playing a Danish sailors' tune, neatly equates rationality with his sense of being Danish and with the navigational skills of his maritime career.

1. Gender boundaries: Conrad Veidt hesitates as Valerie Hobson draws the line in *Contraband*. (BFI Stills)

Here again, we then find that the abandonment of national identity, and the journey away from 'home', are the occasion for anxiety.

There is, however, a clear development in the sense of space associated with the émigré's experience. In *The Spy in Black*, the Orkneys are a marginal and exotic other-space for the German exile Hardt, for the British officers and agents, and also for the bulk of the British audience. In *Contraband*, the presentation of the 'Three Vikings' restaurant in London marks out a type of area not overtly dealt with elsewhere in Powell and Pressburger's work. They tended at this stage in their careers to use concrete locations or buildings as spatial metaphors, giving visible rendition to social relations, forms of society and to states of mind. The 'Three Vikings' is an enclave, a safe haven for Danish immigrants, and it marks out a process of distinctly sub-cultural, minority affiliation, here of Danish 'foreigners' within Britain. Clearly, the friendly and helpful Danes working in the restaurant are sympathetic, and there is a sense of home created within its walls. It is a little bit of Denmark. Their restaurant represents an ambiguously separatist strategy: perhaps it is a transitional stage, preceding a deferred incorporation into the main culture. It is also a defensive policy resulting in an exaggerated sense of belonging to the old country. The condition and status of the alien begins to change in the new host nation, as new associations develop. Conservative tendencies are brought out in nostalgic performances of identity. Here, one of the Danes is even costumed as a Viking, clinging to (and revelling in) a Scandinavian stereotype. Emeric Pressburger himself sought out and enjoyed the company of fellow expatriates when he arrived in London, and here we find that sort of clubbishness celebrated. If the 'Three Vikings' restaurant is little more than a sketched-out space, it at least indicates that migration does not necessarily bring with it alienation and personal isolation.

The secret base from which the Nazis co-ordinate their clandestine activity in London forms another of the film's set-pieces. It is no arbitrary accident that they are hidden in a cinema. Hitchcock had used a London film-house, showing popular thrillers and cartoons, to mask Verloc's evil activity in *Sabotage*, acutely suggesting a demonic dark side to the cinematic medium. In *Contraband* we see a cinema audience standing to acknowledge the playing of the British national anthem, and thus the public image of the building squarely signifies popular patriotism. But the audience is oblivious to the truth hidden behind the screen. Tempting as it might be to see this as a metaphor for a British cinema permeated by foreign personnel (something which had been a cause of anxiety in some quarters), it is also part of the film's play with appearances and essences. The other secret hiding place of the German infiltrators is the warehouse of 'Patriotic Plaster Products', with its store of Neville Chamberlain busts, for which, presumably and understandably, there is no longer a market. A satirical joke about the futility of 1930s appeasement, with the then Prime Minister relegated to history, Chamberlain is at least redeemed when one of the plaster busts of him is used to fell Van Dyne, the film's German villain ('They always said he was tough,' jokes Anderson). *Contraband* had its trade screening on 20 March 1940, and was released in the UK in mid-May. In the intervening period, Germany had occupied Denmark (on 9 April) and the ensuing revolt against Chamberlain led to his resignation as Prime Minister on 10 May, on which day Hitler invaded the Netherlands and Belgium. The Danish community in the film, and the Chamberlain joke, could not have been more topical. Michael Powell would later recall that Chamberlain 'was already the laughing stock of the Nazis and of his own people' when the film was released.[15]

There is a marked Expressionist moment in *Contraband*, used for exaggerated effect. Unlike the sustained atmosphere of *The Spy in Black*, this hallucinatory moment, when Anderson is knocked unconscious by Nazi spies, is injected artificially into the film. The images superimposed over a close-up of Veidt's face when he is insensible are very much a stylistic eccentricity, set to a percussive soundtrack. In an acknowledgement of one of Germany's most celebrated directors, the instigator of this extreme moment is a female German agent whose name is 'Lang'. Names are further played with in this sequence, as Anderson reveals his 'Christian' name to be Hans, and Lang's German thugs joke that they must therefore be 'the Brothers Grimm'. Like *The Spy in Black*'s nod to E.T.A. Hoffmann, this signpost to a culture of nineteenth-century fantasy and fable looks forward to *The Red Shoes* and *The Tales of Hoffmann* (1951). Similar to Sammy Rice's gigantic whisky bottle in *The Small Back Room* (a film which claims its place within any canon of British noir), Anderson's hallucinations mark a crisis of identity, as he tries to persuade his captors that he is 'not Mr. Pidgeon', the man they have mistaken him for. Taken alone, however, such technical displays of virtuoso film-making are little more than curiosities. Tim Bergfelder dismisses the importance of such expressively psychological effects in British cinema, writing that 'most Continental art directors adhered in their British period to a "classical" organisation of space,…and most of the rare aberrations from these principles can be explained as "highlighting" markers for isolated dramatic effect. But this does not amount to a

German aesthetic.'[16] It is a valid point. With these twinned early collaborations, however, it is possible to argue that the over-riding stylistic tendency in Powell and Pressburger's work leans heavily towards Germany but is related closely to the structures and appearance of the Hitchcockian thriller. The similar narratives in these two films each treat British soil as alien. Only with the onset of the Second World War, with an increasing dialogue between their developing personal style and an over-riding, patriotic, national discourse, do we find Powell and Pressburger addressing England as 'Home'.

PLAYING AWAY: THE TEAM ABROAD

Powell and Pressburger's next two films together, *49th Parallel* (November, 1941) and '*…one of our aircraft is missing*' (June, 1942) are as closely related as their first two, and together they develop the directors' ideas about alien space. However, for *49th Parallel* a very different look is created. Gone is the Hitchcockian tone, the spy theme and any sense of homage to Expressionism. Both of these films were conceived primarily as anti-Nazi propaganda, and they contain traits which Powell and Pressburger elaborate in their later war films: the treatment of territory; the sense of teamwork (a defining feature of 'classic' wartime British cinema); and eloquent rhetoric given to a key character in a 'big speech'. *49th Parallel* is filmed extensively in Canada and is dedicated to encouraging America to enter the war. It was part state-funded, the result of a briefly held Ministry of Information policy to produce feature films. Just over half of the budget was met by J. Arthur Rank, indicating, as James Chapman has noted, that a friendly relationship had been fostered between the government and commercial film-makers.[17] Chapman's sharp history of wartime film-making in Britain details Whitehall's attitude to cinema, and points out that Powell and Pressburger's film fulfilled the official desire that good propaganda should also have an entertainment value. *49th Parallel*'s picaresque narrative follows a German U-boat landing party which has been stranded in Canada. Led by Lieutenant Hirth (Eric Portman), the group travels from Hudson Bay via Winnipeg to the American border. In distinct stages of their journey they meet different communities, with each encounter illuminating themes of warfare, racial brotherhood, pacifism, Hitlerism, leadership or 'home'. Its episodic structure marries deliberately with the casting: each stage on Hirth's journey introduces one of the film's stars making an important cameo appearance. The film's ideological project could not be clearer: Nazism is repeatedly contrasted with democracy. As Hirth and his men venture on, they meet a French Canadian trapper, Johnnie (Laurence Olivier), a group of Inuits, a mainly German Hutterite religious settlement (led by Peter, who is played by Anton Walbrook), crowds of Anglo-Saxons and native Americans, and an English aesthete and anthropologist (Leslie Howard). With the rest of his group either dead or captured, Hirth hides on a train and makes it over the border into the United States, where lies either internment or escape back to Germany. His escape is frustrated, though, by Andy Brock, a Canadian soldier (Raymond Massey). In the film's final episode, Andy connives with US Customs men to reverse the train back to Canada, where Hirth will be captured. As if to emphasise the importance of these stages in the journey, the actor playing the chief protagonist of the film, Eric Portman (Lieutenant Hirth), is billed fifth, after its 'stars' Howard, Olivier, Massey and Walbrook, each of them sketching out a very specific ideological position. Together they constitute a chorus of disapproval of Hirth's ideals. Wartime British cinema would create and perpetuate a myth of Britain (and its allies) as a team, with each individual sharing a common purpose. In contrast to the Canadian individuals and communities, Hirth's landing party is deficient as a group, bickering and self-destructing.

Separated by spectacular location footage of the Canadian landscape (including panoramic aerial shots), there is space enough here to entertain culturally diverse groups which together constitute a racially plural population, united in a recognition of its shared Canadian identity, yet also loyal to more local and ethnic forms of organisation. Canada's structures of national identity therefore deliberately mirror the constitution of the film's target audience, the USA. *49th Parallel*'s aim is to advertise a shared purpose between the Allies and the as yet neutral United States. Olivier's trapper is therefore adamant that he is neither French nor Canadian, but French-Canadian, and he respects both British dominion and the native Eskimos. The most successful episode in the film is centred on the Hutterite community which unwittingly provides the U-boat crew with food and shelter. They are farmers, living and working co-operatively and peacefully. One of the Germans, Vogel (Niall MacGinnis), is so seduced by their lifestyle that he decides to stay with them. It is a highly idealistic community, and its treatment is just as highly idealised. A short montage sequence shows the settlers reaping and gathering their crops, with their leader Peter surveying the harvest as a wistful and genial orchestral accompaniment (composed for the film by Vaughan Williams) plays comfortably in the background. Vogel had been a baker before the war, and is understandably drawn back to his old lifestyle. Agrarian imagery such as this has a powerful ideological charge, and here the making of bread takes on well-nigh Biblical connotations. The 'garden of England' is similarly celebrated in much of *A Canterbury Tale*, and the abundance of the Hutterite harvest anticipates the representation of a 'homeland' in that later film. Indeed, Peter tells Vogel that their community is his 'home' and, in a passionate response to Hirth's openly declared Nazism, he gives thanks for the 'security, peace, and tolerance and understanding' which the many settlers in Canada have discovered. The 'new horizons' of the New World are bitterly contrasted with the 'filthy disease' of Hitlerism. The film presses the point by having Hirth find Vogel guilty of desertion and ordering his immediate and brutal execution.

There is another appeal here to the film's target audience. Peter's speech, the biblical undertones and the democratic ethic of the Hutterite community deliberately echo the original Adamic ideals of the American Dream. The 'long straight line athwart a continent' which expressly gives the film its title is, in contrast, an *artificial* border. The snowy mountain scenery of the film's establishing sequence clearly pays no heed to the man-made division separating the Commonwealth from the USA. It is, thus, only 'natural' that, in what is strictly speaking an illegal act of collaboration with Canada, the American customs officials at the close of the film return Hirth to Canada and to justice. It is also natural that the film's final episode should impinge geographically on America's territory just as its propagandising agenda is designed to weigh upon its conscience.

The purpose of *49th Parallel* was to illustrate the proximity of the war to America by transporting a Nazi ideologue across the Atlantic. Much of it seems as exotic to a British audience as it does to Hirth and, as James Chapman notes, some resentment was expressed during its production about the provision of state funding to a project which ventured overseas rather than to genuinely domestic film-making.[18] The Canadian location footage has a travelogue feel to it, and the shots of Inuit fishermen, hunters and native Americans resemble anthropological documentaries (Robert Flaherty's *Nanook of the North* (1922) had been shot in the Hudson Bay area where *49th Parallel* opens). This gives a sense of objective distance to the film, however much its more melodramatic sequences appeal to the emotions. As a narrative device the encounter with the foreign was very much what had structured Powell and Pressburger's Conrad Veidt films.

In *49th Parallel*, a stereotypical sketch of Britishness is offered through the character of Philip Armstrong Scott, played by Leslie Howard. He is aristocratic, effete and non-bellicose, yet he shows backbone and grit when eventually roused. His surnames betray him as a compound of eminent Victorian industrial endeavour and heroic polar exploration, and so we are not surprised that his mettle is eventually proved when he physically fights back against Nazism. Powell and Pressburger's next film, '... *one of our aircraft is missing*', is one of a group of films, like Charles Frend's *The Foreman went to France* (1941), which attempt to imagine what is happening in occupied Europe. The focus here shifts to an entire British aircraft crew caught behind enemy lines in occupied Holland. This variation on a theme allows for a more sustained exploration of the British character, and in their study of group dynamics (a familiar wartime theme) Powell and Pressburger abide by propaganda expectations by ensuring that the six British airmen stay committed to their shared purpose. This contrasts starkly with the divisions in Hirth's team. As soon as the British crew reunite after bailing from their aircraft, they discuss whether to stay together or to separate, and agree that their survival depends upon selecting a leader they can follow. Democratic, egalitarian order clearly contrasts with Hirth's autocratic domination. The theme of teamwork is explicitly foregrounded again when one of the airmen, Bob Ashley (Emrys Jones) – a professional footballer before the war, and therefore unused to working alone – is temporarily separated from the group after bailing out. The team's integrity is paramount. At the end of the film, the eldest team member, George Corbett (Geoffrey Tearle) is shot and badly wounded. By this late stage in their narrative, to leave George behind is simply unthinkable: 'We can't do that,' one says. 'We're all the one crew, you see.' The emphasis on teamwork articulates the sense of community which was a cornerstone of British wartime ideology, and the documentary approach Powell and Pressburger take to the film further emphasises the confluence of their own developing style with the central, hegemonic discourse of wartime. There is no soundtrack music – even over the film's opening, and its 'lower case' title with the important preceding three dots reminds us that this is not just a film title but the familiar understated and formalised way in which the dramatic and often fatal loss of aircraft and crew was announced by the press. The first shot of the film is a close-up of a note of remembrance from the Netherlands Government Information Bureau to five Dutchmen executed for assisting the escape of a British air crew (we hear the sound of the execution on the soundtrack but the event is not re-enacted). After a brief fade we see a plane returning to an English airbase, and the first person to speak is Michael Powell himself, playing a dispatching officer. One plane,

Alien Territories and Enemy Lines   51

'B for Bertie', has failed to return. Ghostly shots of an empty plane then follow (these shots anticipate the opening footage of Peter's stricken aircraft in *A Matter of Life and Death* (1946). Its crew have bailed out, and we see the plane crash. Only then do we hear a radio voice announcing the film's title, as we see a series of graphics announcing that 'British National Films Presents / "...*one of our aircraft is missing*" / With the crew of B for Bertie'. A camera in the plane moves from airman to airman, as they introduce themselves into their radios and the actors' names are displayed as sub-titles on the screen. The performances of the key players are therefore advertised, although the diegetic images tend to have authority over the sub-titles, and the admission of artifice is downplayed. Other technical credits follow before a flashback to 15 hours before the air crash initiates the film story 'proper'. What is interesting about this series of shots is the way they demonstrate Powell and Pressburger's 'qualified' commitment to the documentary form. They take the familiar grammar of fictional film and deconstruct it playfully (as they would do later with *The Volunteer* (1943), their 24-minute recruitment drama-documentary for the Fleet Air Arm). The fictional status of the narrative is thus downplayed. At the end of the film there is another curious directorial intervention. As the drama concludes, graphics read, 'That was going to be the end of our story, but...' Then the cast and credits are listed ('First the Actors' / 'and then the Technicians') before another title tells us ' – All of them wanted to know what happened to B crew'. An inspiring coda then flashes forward three months to show a new plane, and George fully recovered from his injury. The target is now Berlin, and the final graphics promise that 'The Netherlands Will Rise Again'. We are given a closing montage of propaganda images, and at the same time they quiz the meaning and syntax of the closing credits, drawing attention to the actors' and technicians' names and underscoring the fiction. Paradoxically, they divorce the actors from their roles, give a 'truth' status to the 'real' 'B' crew, and align the film 'crew' with its audience in shared curiosity about the fate of its protagonists. Rather than showing an impatience with the rigidity of the documentary style, this attention to the cinematic 'form' of what is normally a standardised formality is characteristic of the Archers, and anticipates the directors' more sustained, meta-cinematic investigations in their feature films. It is a sign of their developing auteur status within the strictly governed parameters of the wartime fiction-documentary genre.

The theme of nationhood naturalised, mystified or masqueraded is emphasised again (another mark of Pressburger's exile status?). The English crew are not long in Holland before they are discovered by some Dutch children, with whom they are soon able to establish a basic dialogue. The children take them to their schoolteacher Els Meertens (a luminous performance from Pamela Brown). With her own safety at stake she is suspicious at first about the airmen's identity, despite Frank's (Bernard Miles') simple insistence, 'But we're English, Miss!' National identity is something which cannot be taken for granted. A hidden photograph of the Queen of Holland confirms Meertens' affiliation with the Dutch resistance. National identity is something which may be tactically veiled. The talk is of Quislings. National identity is also something which may be betrayed. With an episodic structure very like *49th Parallel*'s, the crew make their way towards the coast, where they are appointed to meet with another strong woman, Jo de Vries (Googie Withers). She too has masqueraded loyalties: she pretends to be anti-British following her husband's supposed death following British air raids over Haarlem, whereas in reality she is a key figure in the Dutch resistance. As they travel to the sea, the crew have to disguise themselves. In *The Spy in Black* Captain Hardt's enforced disguise was an assault on his straightforwardness, and everyone else's disguise was the cause of narrative confusion. The tone here is more playful, and the ingenuity of the crew's undercover survival is celebrated. Shoes dissolve into clogs (a trope of stereotyped Dutch national identity) and forged Dutch papers for the crew dissolve, for the British film audience's benefit, into their English translations. Gramophone records of the Dutch national anthem are given different labels and delivered, as a politically charged joke, to German soldiers. These instances of role-playing and re-branding inch towards a postmodern sensibility with one of the crew, Frank (Hugh Williams), being a professional actor, at one point disguised ridiculously as a Dutch farm girl. Frank's admission to Jo that 'the way you handled those Germans taught me something about acting' is a reminder that for Jo, dramatic realism is a matter of life and death, and that the masquerade is a tactically deployed and crucial survival mechanism. The 'performances' in the film do more than celebrate the crew's ingenuity, though. They imply that British men have corresponding equivalents among Dutch men (and women) and that the international dimension is as important as the national. Parallels between nations are sought: a characteristic of Powell and Pressburger's later work. 'You know, that's funny,' Tom observes during an air raid, 'Them blacking out because of us.' Jo in Holland tunes into her husband's broadcasts from London on 'Radio Orange', while Frank is able to hear his wife (a singer) performing on the

BBC. When the crew observe the bravery of some Dutch girls, they reflect that British girls would do as much if needed. Tom Earnshaw looks forward to trading wool in the Low Countries after the war – a sign that his experiences in Holland are going to produce a healthy internationalism in this gruff Yorkshireman. This ability to envisage and interact with the foreign becomes a motif in Powell and Pressburger's work.

With the cover of night being so crucial to the airmen's survival, and the subterranean work of the resistance being so vital to their escape, '*...one of our aircraft is missing*' at times veers towards the noirish feel of the Veidt films. There are hidden subterranean passages, disguised buildings, secret codes, and a need for constant vigilance. Point-of-view shots into a distorting convex mirror reflecting Jo de Vries' hideaway for the airmen inscribes the spy theme into the film's visuals. What one carries away from the film is the sense that the beleaguered courage of Els Meertens and Jo de Vries signifies a special and reserved area, a genuine light in the darkness. The Dutch resistance forms a circumscribed pocket of heroic national identity, not unlike the London-based Danes in *Contraband* (although that unlikely haven is in relative safety and receives a far more comic treatment). As Jo de Vries remarks, although the Germans have occupied the physical space of Holland, she and her compatriots can still 'Think and hope and fight'. George, as the eldest of the air crew, offers their love, gratitude and admiration to Jo and the Dutch resistance, and his rich voice is just beginning to warm to its theme of the forces amassing in opposition to Germany (the film's 'big' propaganda speech) when the drone of a British air raid signifies it is time for them to make their final bid for freedom. Hirth's rhetoric in *49th Parallel* is hubris in comparison. It was after '*...one of our aircraft is missing*' that Powell and Pressburger formed their own production company, the Archers, and what one publicist referred to as their 'true marriage' commenced.

2

Satire, Epic and Memory – *The Life and Death of Colonel Blimp*

When, amid the blasts of hell, the towel is torn aside, the secret places of the heart are revealed.

David Low, 1936

THE ANATOMY OF A HERO

'Englishmen are by nature conservative, insular, unsuspicious, believers in good sportsmanship and anxious to believe the best of other people.' This is how Michael Powell, in a letter to the War Office in 1942, begins to defend the Archers' forthcoming production, *The Life and Death of Colonel Blimp* (1943), the first film they directed for J. Arthur Rank. 'These attractive virtues,' he continues, 'which are, we hope, unchanging, can become absolute vices unless allied to a realistic acceptance of things as they are, in modern Europe, and in Total war.'[1] Notably, Powell considers English conservatism and insularity to be *virtues*, and longs for them to remain fixed in the nation's character, alongside a rosy (and possibly naïve) commitment to fair play. He implicitly admits, though, that such virtues can become dangerous if they are divorced from *realpolitik*. Powell's catalogue of qualities draws on well-recognised if mythical tropes of Englishness. Imaginary elements play an important part in the formation of national identities, but Powell recognises that sentimental imaginings of a 'Little England' and cosseted notions of sporting, gentlemanly fairness would have to be jettisoned if Nazism was to be squarely faced down. Simply put, this is what *Blimp* sets out to demonstrate, by tracing – wittily and sentimentally – the personal history of a representative army officer, Clive Candy (Roger Livesey), from his youthful bravado to the reactionary authoritarianism of his old age. This life is seen sympathetically. Clive's disappointments are marked, and his gentle innocence, bred out of that English sense of fair play and 'good manners', is treated with gentle irony. Yet from the film's opening sequence, in which a herd of aged military types, including Candy himself (as an old man), is caught off-guard and is taken hostage during a military training exercise between Candy's Home Guard and a troop of eager, insubordinate soldiers led by Spud Wilson (James McKechnie), the high ranks of the British army are held up for ridicule. Spud sneers at Candy, and this provokes the old man to justify himself by recalling his military life, initiating an extended personal flashback to 1902, where a magically rejuvenated Clive has just returned from the Boer War.

Blimp is a satire, directly attacking a very particular attitude within the military elite, and it naturally caused disquiet among those whom it set out to ridicule and those to whom the expression 'military intelligence' contains no hint of the oxymoronic. The film became, and remains, a *cause célèbre* – a myth – because of Churchill's efforts to stop it being made, and the War Office's refusal to release Laurence Olivier (originally pencilled in to play the lead role of Clive) from the Fleet Air Arm. Its export was for a while hampered by officialdom, and the publication of the Sidneyan Society pamphlet *The Shame and Disgrace of Colonel Blimp* (1943), which declared the film to be the product of rampant pro-Nazism, helped to fuel its mythical status, and to bolster its reputation as a rogue film. The Sidneyan Society – run by, and possibly consisting solely of, E.W. and M.M. Robson – set out to expose pro-German tendencies in British cinema, and in no way should their pamphlet be read as a typical response, as its claims are for the main part ludicrously out of kilter with most contemporary reviews. With hindsight, it looks as if the film's rogue reputation was overstated and undeserved. Despite its boldness in presenting a sympathetic German in 1943, it looks now like a film in which the dominant myths of the Home Front are expressed, and in many ways it conforms to some of the ideals of its time. Indeed, while it is shot through with spells of anti-realism, Powell's recorded 'realistic acceptance of things as they are' is readable as a rejection of romantic fantasy, and as a manifesto to produce something which would fall in line with the governing realism of 'British National Cinema'. It would be difficult to argue that a truly 'documentary spirit' enters the film, but its contemporary sequences record the 'look' of the 1940s and, importantly, they contain some of the key motifs of classic wartime British cinema, such as the London blackout and the mobilised woman. The film also undertakes an 'incorporative' mission, drawing together a new army to fight Nazism. It is sympathetic, therefore, to the over-riding ideology of its time. Yet, as a satire, it injects tones of romantic sentiment and quirky jokiness to stake its critical distance from any realistic, documentary aesthetic.

As if to emphasise this anti-realism, the central character, Clive Candy, is identified with a popular newspaper cartoon figure, David Low's 'Colonel Blimp'. Yet Clive Candy's character never merges with Low's caricature. 'Blimpery', the outmoded reactionary force which the film sets out to dispel, is a frozen mindset. The film rejects the fixity of the caricature to chart the 'life and death' of the Blimp type. It maps this transition onto the figure of Clive, marking not only an ideological shift in the history of the nation, but doing so by dramatising the life-long development of its central, iconic character. In this respect, the film is about memory, nostalgia, loss and recompense as much as it is about military endeavour, and herein lies its status as a genuinely national epic, albeit one which crucially leans on the mock-heroic rather than the heroic. It draws out links between personal individuated characteristics, national types and processes of identification by offering to Clive a gallery of role models – epic, historical, fictional – on whom to fashion himself. In part, this is a normal process of his class-bound socialisation, but as he internalises these heroic types, so too does he project idealised values onto the women in his life – each of them played by a single actress, Deborah Kerr. Either way, the process is sentimentally blinkered from the truth. With British imperialism forming a subtext to the film, *Blimp* rewrites tales of Empire, and by extension (for the two are inextricable) it quizzes idealised versions of British masculinity. Scripted almost entirely as Clive's personal (unreliable?) memoir, his idealisations and the false consciousness in which his view of the world is encrusted become the magic space the film explores – magic because his life's theatre is imaginary, extracted from history and deeply imbued with a sentimentality with which it is hard not to sympathise.

Blimp successfully pensions off an antiquated, reactionary officer class, and to fill the vacuum it simultaneously recruits new (and renewed) cultural types as agents in the war against Fascism. Elitism is replaced with populism, as the dominant myth of the 'People's War' comes into play, and the film gestures towards representing a united nation, chronicling a shift from a once dominant form of leadership to a more broadly hegemonic sense of collaboration. Because this complex negotiation is presented with the Archers' customary idiosyncrasies, it is not surprising the film has always been seen as an ambiguous or contradictory work. The *Observer* critic C.A. Lejeune (13 June 1943), in a typical review, praised the film as 'a work of quality', but asked the question 'what is it about?' Subsequent writers have nodded to undefined ambivalences in the text. Kevin Macdonald deems it to be 'a hot-house of contradictions'.[2] There *are* real contradictions, for this is an untidy, broad-ranging (and highly ambitious) text, but its cross-currents can be charted thus:

1. A dominant military Old Guard ('Blimpery') is satirised and dispensed with.
2. The way in which 'Blimpery' is inculcated is examined.
3. Modes of masculine behaviour associated with this imperial mindset are critiqued.
4. A more broadly based, hegemonic form of community is developed, incorporating disparate groups united against Hitler.
5. The experience of loss and nostalgia which this change enforces is romanticised, and Candy (as distinct from 'Blimp') is treated emotionally.

The film's title, with its explicit reference to David Low's newspaper cartoon of 'Colonel Blimp', emphasises the satirical credentials. Low wrote of his Colonel that he typified 'the current disposition to mixed-up thinking, to having it both ways, to dogmatic doubleness, to paradox and plain self-contradiction'.[3] Insofar as the Archers' film uses Low's caricature, its purpose is also to expose such flaws within the British officer class system. Pressburger had set about researching this mindset. Powell, in a note to his 'Angel Imre', advised his partner not to neglect *Punch* magazine, 'a mine of banality, an artesian well of Blimpish sources'. Others were also noting the spread of 'Blimpishness'. In *The Lion and the Unicorn*, written in 1941, George Orwell charted recent shifts in the country's power structure and pointed out that the decay of the old ruling class in the inter-war years had been accompanied by a wilful blindness to reality among that class: 'They (the ruling class) could keep society in its existing shape only by being *unable* to grasp that any improvement was possible. Difficult though this was, they achieved it, largely by fixing their eyes on the past and refusing to notice the changes that were going on around them.'[4] Myopia like this is the stuff of Powell and Pressburger's film, and Orwell's indictment is closely echoed in Powell's letter to the War Office setting out the thesis behind the film. Orwell's judgement is that the Blimps (he too uses the name) 'are not wicked, or not altogether wicked (but) they are merely unteachable'.⁵ Here, Clive parts company with Blimp, for Candy is not merely a three-dimensional rendering of the cartoon figure: he also exists in time, and is mutable. In short, he can be taught. He changes belatedly, and after some humiliation, as his gentlemanly Home Guard exercise is hijacked by a younger generation of pragmatists, but he does at least reach a personal epiphany in the last reel. His transformation indicates that ultimately the Archers have some faith in the ruling order: it is certainly part of their rosily affirmative conclusion that Clive is regenerated, although in this the Archers merely echo the generally positive tone of wartime national discourse. Clive is reincarnated into a new world order with his old carapace cast off. Orwell, too, with characteristic nuance, expressed some hope for the body politic: 'Patriotism and intelligence will have to come together again,' he concludes. 'It is the very fact that we are fighting a war, and a very peculiar kind of war, that may make this possible.'⁶

Caricatures are, by definition, fixed, two-dimensional exaggerations. 'The aim of the caricaturist,' in David Low's own words, 'is to discover, analyse and select essentials of personality, and by the exercise of wit to reduce them to appropriate form.'⁷ Low ironically concedes, however, that 'the caricaturist for the Press is urged to think of the sentimental disposition to hero-worship on the part of the "Constant Reader" and "Regular Subscriber". He compromises with kindness.'⁸ David Low's suggestion of self-censorship suggests that he had a less agreeable relationship with his employer than was actually the case. The left-wing New Zealander Low (like Pressburger, another outsider) arrived in Britain in 1919 and worked for the right-wing Express Newspapers, but its maverick proprietor Max Aitken, the 1st Lord Beaverbrook, prided himself on his iconoclasm and gave his star cartoonist as much latitude as he could have wanted. Thus Low found himself working alongside other such radical writers on London's *Evening Standard* as Aneurin Bevan, Michael Foot and A.J.P. Taylor. In their film, Powell and Pressburger soften the satire further to mollify Low's caricature. Thus, while the cartoon Blimp's catch-phrase 'By gad, Sir, Lord Prendergast was right!' is given to Candy in the film's shooting script, it is not present in the finished film. Other changes make the film more popularly palatable. During the First World War sequence, the intimidation and murder of German prisoners, explicit in the script, is lessened to an uncomfortable implication. The militarism of Clive's German friend Theo Kretschmar-Schuldorff is downplayed (and, as Theo, Anton Walbrook's performance is generally a sympathetic one). In the script, he clicks his heels as he arrives to plead to the British authorities against his internment as an alien; in the film he is dishevelled, tired, vulnerable. Pressburger's early manuscript outline of this sequence suggests that Theo would tell us, with a bitter poignancy, that his wife Edith committed suicide in Germany five years earlier: however much it serves as a sign that there was something rotten in the state of Germany in the inter-war period, Pressburger's early bleak suggestion does not even make it as far as the shooting script (Ian Christie, 1994) has carefully edited the shooting script and final film to show where additions and deletions were made).

Would the reference to the cartoon of Colonel Blimp have been lost on most of the film's provincial audience? Compared with the *Daily Express*, the best-selling daily paper in the United Kingdom at the time with a circulation of around 2 million, the *Evening Standard* sold only around 400,000, but with syndication to the regions (including local papers in Glasgow, Birmingham, Manchester and Newcastle) Low's cartoons had a circulation of another million or more daily.[9] World-wide, Low was syndicated to more than two hundred other newspapers and magazines, making him one of the most influential cartoonists and caricaturists of the twentieth century. Low had introduced the Blimp figure in 1934, although the caricature was admittedly a less frequent sight by 1942. By this time, Low's cartoons predominantly featured caricatures of real people – notably the Nazi High Command. Yet Blimp remained a national type, with his knee-jerk outbursts of reactionary, war-mongering and jingoistic stupidity. He was fixed in the national psyche, and is securely identified with the film, most forcibly during the opening and closing credits, the only place where Low's cartoon figure is directly acknowledged (although Low's *Evening Standard* cartoon was regularly set in a Turkish bath, and Alfred Junge's design for this sequence of the film closely resembles Low's drawings).

Behind the film's opening credits we see a tapestry, a woven establishing shot which gives an appropriately stylised impression of the film's cultural topography. It presents its landscape symbolically, a tableau-pastiche clustering together an anthology of familiar signs. Its antiquated style of outdated craftsmanship mirrors the survey offered by *Blimp* of a military caste ossified in tradition. In the background, to the right of the screen, there are scenes of horsemanship: foxhunting, a lady sitting side-saddle, a game being played (rugby or cricket?) – Old Tory values, gender divisions, the gentry, the unwavering certainties of village life. Like a sampler inspired by Siegfried Sassoon's *Memoirs of a Foxhunting Man*, this is just the sort of rustic Englishness which Powell and Pressburger's *A Canterbury Tale* (1944) will interrogate, and precisely the *olde worlde* of good sportsmanship, *noblesse oblige* and disastrous military acumen which *Blimp* exposes. In the centre of the tapestry is Blimp himself, in medieval costume, and behind him in the distance, aeroplanes fly past. This jarring temporal collision anticipates the famous shots in the opening prologue of *A Canterbury Tale*, where five hundred years are elided in a match-cut from a Chaucerian falconer's hawk to documentary-style footage of a soaring Spitfire. *Blimp*'s tapestry is a spatial rendition of the same creative dialogue between the historical, the mythical and the topical, a stitched-together collocation of heterogeneous signs, jostling with and against each other. Significantly, the tapestry's scenes of modernity are placed in the more dominant position, to the left of the picture, the village life to the right remembering that lifestyle which was swept away with the First World War (or an archaic rural ideal, still held in the minds of the modern fighters to the left).

In the centre, Blimp mediates between the two. The displayed crest of his family emphasises the class bias of the film, although it is not a class which the film necessarily endorses. The tree on which this piece of heraldry is resting – it seems to be an old oak – symbolically conflates longevity and Englishness as twin virtues. This metaphor of permanence figured through timber is, again, echoed in *A Canterbury Tale*. The presence of the Archers' own production company trademark on the trunk of the tree reinforces the theme. The famous archer's target is itself a piece of medieval iconography, and alludes at the same time to the concentric circles which form the insignia of the RAF. Nailing their logo to an oak, the Archers' patriotic colours are clearly posted. To reinforce this mark of authorship, an enigmatically codified sign of Powell himself is stitched into the scene, for Blimp's spoof family crest includes the director's two cocker spaniels, Eric and Spangler, beasts which regularly make appearances in Powell and Pressburger's films – they are also in *Contraband* (1940), Powell's own *An Airman's Letter to his Mother* (1941), *I Know Where I'm Going!* (1945) and *A Matter of Life and Death* (1946).

As a knight errant on his white charger, the Blimp on the tapestry is part Don Quixote, part Sir Lancelot, part hero of classical Greece, and part indulgent, bloated satyr. Immediately, then, the stability of the sign is undone. With its multiple connotations it begins to cut loose from any single anchorage. Blimp is the satirical distillation of a type of Englishman. Low occasionally portrayed him as Britannia, and he clearly owes something to John Bull. As Peter Mellini records, C.S. Lewis found Blimp 'the most characteristic expression of the English temper in the period between the two wars',[10] while Robert Graves offers a mock genealogy, noting that 'the oxheaded Saxon strain has always been dominant in the Blimp family', and also joking that 'the Elizabethan de Blympe was satirized by Shakespeare as Sir John Falstaff'.[11] The meaning of the cartoon sketch, which seems superficially to be so clear, begins to dissolve, as the discreet and autonomous meaning of Blimp as a national 'type' disperses into a range of inter-textual sites. This interwoven set of identification points indicates one of the key arguments of the film. The model of national character it offers (embodied by Candy) is made out of a collage of historical elements, where identity is a matter of selection, something acquired from a store of available discourses. Social identity derives from a sense of shared cultural depictions, and is a matter of representation and recognition. *Blimp* intertwines the fictional, the fantastical and the factual, such as the references to Conan Doyle and J.B. Priestley, and to actual events – the film is fastidiously accurate in this regard. The national profile, according to the strategy of the film, is a composite of disparate parts, and national identity is a matter of imaginative investment. Clive, identifying with his culture and background, is offered to us as a coherent centre, a protagonist with whom we might identify, and his lifespan forms the narrative and embodies the stable continuity he stands for. The film manifestly worries some of this sense of stability, however, by exposing Clive's 'cohesiveness' and reliability to be myths. National identity, therefore, is shown to be provisional and contingent.

Nominally the epic hero, Clive's own subjectivity is, itself, primarily based upon his identification with stereotypes and idealisations. Candy's own Christian name, of course, echoes the renowned imperialist, Clive of India. Early on, Candy decides to disobey the Foreign Office by going to confront the spy and anti-British propagandist Kaunitz. He dashes to Berlin, telling his friend Hoppy to make his excuses to Lady Gilpin: 'Say I've gone on some secret mission – make me out the most serious romantic figure' (and he promptly sends a postcard back to Hoppy from Berlin signed 'Sherlock'). In his first dialogue with Edith Hunter (Deborah Kerr), the governess who has alerted him to Kaunitz's propaganda, she refers to him as Livingstone. He is an accretion of popular heroic types, the product of an investment in adventure, and his heroic function is donned as if it were a costume. The meticulous pageant of external details in the film, particularly the clothes and uniforms forming the cluttered mise-en-scène of the 1902 sequence, is an expression of this 'performative' quality. The film presents the viewer with a spectacle of colour and some dazzling moments of cinematography – all clearly an artificial construct – and it lets this display masquerade as history. It is no mere chronicle of the past. It causes the viewer to question how historical narrative is made. Clive is a player strutting through his life's gaudy drama, invested in the authority of his uniform, and of course, when he is caught napping and naked in the Turkish baths he seems bereft of that authority. His sense of self is pegged to a pantheon of great names littering the film, either explicitly or implicitly.

In the 1940s 'framing' sequence, Spud collects his troops to capture Clive, and his hijack of the artificially staged military exercise is a timely imitation of the Japanese attack on Pearl Harbour. Spud's regiment of 'Taffy', 'Geordie' and others recalls the Captains Fluellen, MacMorris and Jamy from Shakespeare's *Henry V*. His ironic interpretation of his orders that 'to make it like the real thing' means to report 'our losses divided by ten and the enemy's multiplied by twenty' echoes the implausibly accounted report of the English casualties at the Battle of Agincourt towards the end of the play (and his insistence that they should 'make it like the real thing' also echoes Powell's own statement about the need for the film to endorse 'a realistic acceptance of things as they are'). These nods to Shakespeare's history plays implicitly associate Clive with Sir John Falstaff, a figure who connoted a rejected past by the time of Henry V's reign. The utter rejection of the aged Clive's Blimpery at the end of the film is comparable to Prince Hal's repudiation of his own erstwhile companion: 'How ill white hairs become a fool and jester!' in *Henry IV (II)* (V.v. 47–8).

The influence of contemporary American popular culture on the younger generation of the 1940s is also admitted (one of Spud's soldiers is nicknamed 'Popeye'). Spud soon discovers that his girlfriend Angela (Deborah Kerr) has 'gone to warn the Wizard' and chases after her. *Blimp*'s indebtedness to Victor Fleming's film version of *The Wizard of Oz* (1939, US) anticipates *A Canterbury Tale*'s use of it as a semi-conscious influence. Clive, like *A Canterbury Tale*'s Colpeper, is simultaneously magus-like and foolish, and both films' ultimate quest, like Dorothy's, is for a sense of 'home'. The identification between Clive and the 'Wizard of Oz' can be taken further for, although they are both shown to be foolish and relatively powerless, they are warmly genial and avuncular. Ironically, as soon as Spud refers to Candy as the 'Wizard', he grabs his tin hat, unconsciously casting himself as Dorothy's 'heartless' friend, the 'Tin Man'.

The contrast between the military dragoons of Clive's youth (resplendent turn-of-the-century cavaliers in scarlet) and the modern, utilitarian troops in 1940s khaki echoes the history of the English Civil War. In the final minutes of the film Spud's 'New Model Army' is heard marching across the 'Cromwell Road'. *Blimp* also points to the classical world: at the opening of the Café Hohenzollern sequence the band finishes playing Offenbach's can-can, a popular piece from a satirical theatrical comedy, of course, but one which nevertheless initiates a series of gestures in the film towards relinquished loves. Orpheus, bereft of Eurydice, anticipates Clive's romantic losses. Later, the foolish Clive finds himself cast as Odysseus. Returning to London without Edith Hunter (his 'Diana' perhaps – she too was a 'hunter'), he takes Edith's sister to Her Majesty's Theatre to see a new musical play by Stephen Phillips entitled *Ulysses*, a happily topical coincidence, for the play was being performed there at the time the narrative is set. There, he sees his old friend Hoppy now married to his old acquaintance Sibyl (another classically unobtainable woman). Clive sits in the audience watching the performance and identifies with the play's heroic wanderer, 'the most unhappy of mankind', in Athene's words, longing to 'view the smoke of his own fire curling blue'. This classical world is further alluded to, of course, in the architectural mise-en-scène of the Bathers Club sequence, while the sense of exile (whether Dorothy's or Ulysses') picks up and reflects Clive's sense of loss.

What *Blimp* shows, then, is the importance of cultural representations in forming identity. Cinema audiences, too, locate their desires and establish their sense of selfhood in mobile and fluid forms of identification, with the protagonist of the film providing a focal point for such identifications. Here, Clive, the film's supposedly integrated hero, serves as a conduit. Through him, the viewer is likewise bonded into a seemingly endless imaginary cultural matrix. Much of the film, of course, is a flashback, the hermeneutic pretext for which is deeply personal. 'You laugh at my big belly, but you don't know how I got it! You laugh at my moustache, but you don't know why I grew it! How do you know what sort of man I was,' Clive bellows at Spud, 'when I was as young as you are – 40 years ago – 40 years ago…?' Flashbacks are often initiated subjectively, at character level. What we see here is private memory rather than public history, directly connected to the current, and to the living, 'narrating' individual.

Past and present, therefore, are rendered concurrently. The very continuity of Clive – he is the one thread tracing through the entire film – seductively causes us to identify with him yet, of course, if we look at the memory he gives us, it is one frustrated by elliptical punctuations, galloping accelerations and frozen moments. Time pirouettes and leaps. There is a constant tension between this fragmented view of the historical and the appearance of constancy offered by a protagonist whose sentimental and insulated foolishness is repeatedly shown to us.

HISTORY AND GENRES

No culture can successfully be placed into discrete, hermetically sealed and internally coherent epochs. While a part of the culture will always be in some ways dominant at any one time, fresh ideas and positions are always surfacing. Likewise, retrograde aspects sink into relative obscurity, even though they may continue to exert influence. Raymond Williams uses the terms 'residual' and 'emergent' to account for such intra-cultural transitions. The residual, as opposed to the 'archaic' (which is wholly recognised as an element of the past) is that part of the culture which was formed in the past, but which still has some active part in the cultural present.[12] Residual elements may be either alternative or oppositional to the dominant culture, or may have been incorporated partially or fully into it. Here, Williams touches on the notion of tradition, for what is tradition if not the selective incorporation of either the actively residual or the truly archaic within our culture? Blimpery, as a dogmatic, rigid belief system, is just such an example of a residual culture. It fails to recognise its out-datedness, and it continues to hold sway, but new ideas about warfare move forward by the 1940s. When Clive's Home Guard exercise is hijacked by Spud, he belatedly learns his lesson about the aims and means of modern warfare. *Blimp* traces transitions within a culture over a period of half a century and marks Candy's increasing obliviousness to these changes.

New meanings and new relationships may often crystallise. Some develop within the dominant culture; others are genuine alternatives or oppositions to it. The more oppositional they are, the more the dominant culture is triggered into activity to recuperate and disarm them, a process which seems like recognition or acceptance, but which in reality works to nullify rebellious sections of society. By containing dissidence like this, the dominant group maintains its position. The all-inclusiveness we associate with the ideological myth-making of wartime Britain is a sign of just this form of incorporation. As we see in *Blimp*, women are mobilised, as are lower classes and regional types, and, as if to test the strength of the social alliance against Hitler, a German army officer, Theo, is finally accorded a privileged place within the generously reconstituted national 'family'. The 'broad church' of the 'People's War' uses the vocabulary of leadership, direction and commonality, and this sustained presentation of hegemony was a structuring ideology of the war effort. *Blimp*, for all its attacks on a once dominant military elite, for all the opprobrium it excited from some official circles, throws its weight behind this new ideology.

From the fixed position of the Blimps to the new populism which replaces it, there is a shift in power. What the film therefore diagnoses is gear change in the leadership of the nation, a 'crisis of authority'. It reflects the situation sketched by Antonio Gramsci (in his *Prison Notebooks*) to finesse his concept of hegemony or political leadership:

> If the ruling class has lost its consensus, i.e. is no longer 'leading' but only 'dominant' … this means precisely that the great masses have become detached from their traditional ideologies, and no longer believe what they used to believe previously, etc. This crisis exists precisely in the fact that the old is dying and the new cannot be born; in this interregnum a great variety of morbid symptoms appear.[13]

Blimp negotiates this interregnum, charting the 'life' and 'death' of the now dogmatic old order, and exposing its wilful blindness to the symptoms of change. Blimpery is constructed as an outmoded, residual force which, through the apparent permanence of social relations, has retained an active position within the power structure. Candy, in absenting himself from the historical process of development and redefinition, increasingly becomes a dinosaur and, while behind Roger Livesey's good visage he seems harmless, the very *appearance* of harmlessness among the military elite is figured as something paradoxically more dangerous when facing the candid might of Fascism. It is part of the film's propagandising agenda to denounce as derelict this aspect of the dominant order. While rendering it archaic, the film also seeks the active incorporation of that which is supportive of the establishment. Sue Harper argues that Powell and Pressburger's works defend elite groups, and that *Blimp* is also a defence of the past *per se*, with the 'Blimp class' being 'the cement of society's disparate values'.[14] Harper's reading suggests that the film portrays a world where *society* is marching out of step, not Clive. Surely, though, it is the 'elite group' (by which Harper is speaking of the 'old order') which is shown to be fatally detached from the mass of society. It is the imagined community of pragmatists which the film endorses, the hegemonic and utopian social matrix of classic wartime British cinema allied in opposition to the enemy.

This debate between reactionary and progressive forces is figured musically within the soundtrack. Allan Gray's score is constructed from a handful of motifs. Later in their career, Powell and Pressburger would explore the adventurous possibilities of 'composed films' more thoroughly, collaborating with the composer Brian Easdale on both *Black Narcissus* and *The Red Shoes*. With *Blimp*, the patchwork of cinematic styles benefits from Gray's musical pastiche style. Two military marches, one a jazz tune reminiscent of the American big band sound, the other a more conventional piece of brassy triumphalism, each signify linearity, purpose and dynamism. The former suggests modernity; the latter is more traditional. The jazz tune features prominently in the introductory sequence set in 1942, and is heard a second time as the extended flashback returns us to the contemporary frame narrative. Towards the end of the film, it is played on a jukebox, specifying it as a recent popular hit, one fittingly associated with the young Spud's 'New Model Army'. The other march tune sympathises with the aged Clive's re-engagement with the mainstream culture of the modern world, and their shared beat signifies that a reciprocity between old and new is to be achieved. These tunes each accompany sequences of energetic progress – the race to London, Candy's career within the Home Guard depicted with a montage of *Picture Post* photo shoots, and the triumphant shift into the major key which brings the film to a close. Contrasting with these dynamic marches, there is a German waltz motif, identified by Edith in Berlin as 'The Mill Went Round and Round' during the 1902 Café Hohenzollern sequence. This dance tune nostalgically evokes an easy time of pleasure (the strange potency of cheap music?), but its circularity also connotes a fatal, endless repetition. It is first heard being played by the Café orchestra, as Clive disappoints the radical suffragette Edith by abandoning his adventure to expose the anti-British propagandist Kaunitz. Clive's rebellious trip to Berlin has been stifled by the operations of the diplomatic service, and he begins his excuse to Edith, 'I know a chap in our Embassy here. We were at school together...', and goes on to explain how he has been brought to realise the danger of 'a possible scandal'. Symbolising a world of old school ties, reactionary fixity and the purposeless vacuity of social rounds, this tune is a death-waltz. It stands for all the archaic principles the film rejects. We later hear it over the montage of snapshots and Embassy invitation cards which constitute almost all we see of Clive's married life travelling the world, a montage which culminates, of course, with a shot of his wife's death notice in *The Times* and then with blank album pages. Like the *Picture Post* montage of his Home Guard career, this brief pictorial sequence marks a temporal elision, but what distinguishes this 'married life' sequence is the direct implication, coded through the waltz on the soundtrack, that these years of society high-life represent Clive's failure to develop, and his abstraction from *realpolitik*. Of course, this is also psychologically justified, as Clive's entire relationship with Barbara is shown to be a re-enactment of his unconsummated first love for Edith. The other significant tune on the soundtrack is a graceful Elgarian slow piece, poignantly connected to Edith.

Just as the opening credit sequence of *Blimp* is a hotchpotch of images, matched to a disparate musical score, so too does the film resist the constraints of any one genre. Part of its pastiche-like feel derives from the way it brings together a range of cinematic topographies. In its closing frames it finds repose squarely within the style of classic wartime British cinema, but the quizzical critical attitude towards the work's 'ambiguity' may reflect the film's reluctance to align itself along any obvious or guiding generic co-ordinates, and its consequent refusal to clue the viewer into recognising a known environment in which s/he feels 'at home'. In her survey of British genres, Marcia Landy catalogues *Blimp* as a 'War Film', although her study also includes assessments of other forms, most notably the 'Film of Empire', the 'Heritage' and the 'Historical' film, and *Blimp* salutes each of them meaningfully.[15] While Landy is right to connect *Blimp* with the war film, it is a problematic conclusion: it foregrounds the film's topicality, addressing the conditions of the Home Front, for example, but the work is a hybrid. With its leap back in time from 1942 to 1902 it partially adopts the stance of Korda's 'Imperial epics', such as *The Four Feathers* (Zoltan Korda, 1939), but then this nod towards these Kiplingesque works is also soon questioned, as the earlier genre is interrogated, and its elasticity is tested. *Blimp* exposes the fixity of mind associated with the Imperial epic by attempting to bridge the gap between it and the contemporary war film. It signals towards many of the features which exemplify the 'Empire' genre – such as location shooting, the exotic, scenes of armed conflict and conspicuously muscular bouts of heroism – yet it denies the viewer any of the expected spectacle. Such spectacle may be non-seen, but it is clearly articulated in an off-screen space, and the very act of displacement significantly undermines the bravado of the

British military hero. Clive becomes a disorientated wanderer, outcast unwittingly from a world of nineteenth-century, 'Fringe of Empire' adventure to renegotiate a relationship with the present. He is part of a residuum of meanings, a cultural inheritance whose validity and worth are entirely implicated with Britain's military and imperialist past, and whose relevance to the 1940s, the film suggests, is in need of urgent revision. By the 1930s, the 'Empire' genre itself was arguably already outdated, harking back to the heyday of colonisation just before the sun began to set on that period. Korda's 'Empire' films endorse his adopted homeland somewhat jingoistically, affirming the verities of the 'white man's burden' and harking back to what would soon become a largely redundant imperial ideology. They use popular myths and popular history, just as Candy is seen to do in *Blimp*. *Blimp*, however, reformulates the crude construction of 'otherness' associated with the British Empire adventure yarn, and in this respect it is distinctly a more modern work.

The 'Empire' films produced by Alexander Korda's London Films draw largely on popular literature. *Sanders of the River* (Zoltan Korda, 1935), *Elephant Boy* (Robert Flaherty and Zoltan Korda, 1937), *The Drum* (Zoltan Korda, 1938), *The Four Feathers* (Zoltan Korda, 1939) and perhaps Korda's 1942 American production of *Jungle Book* (Zoltan Korda) form a coherent group, with the Arabian fantasy *The Thief of Bagdad* (1940), directed in part by Michael Powell, vying for inclusion. *King Solomon's Mines* (Robert Stevenson, 1937), produced by Gaumont-British under Michael Balcon, also belongs to the genre. These films are united in their treatment of the exotic, their apparently simplistic constructions of national, racial and gendered identity, and their imaginative investment in the virtues of adventure, wherein lay their international marketability. Adventure is bound up with the affirmation of the British imperial ethos, with the sound physical health and good mental state of the British elite abroad, and with the equation of a certain type of masculinity with various heroisms done in the service of the Empress. Raymond Durgnat once observed that 'the war film is the European Western'.[16] It is an interesting point, given the genre's focus on male same-sex relationships, action and heroism, and the fact, of course, that the Western was one of the means by which the formation of the USA as a nation was mythologised. Differences may be noted: the hero of the Imperial epic is likely to be an agent of the Crown, rather than a lone individual, expressing existential virtues, but the civilising mission is common to both. The war film itself, which first developed during and after the World Wars of the twentieth century, is descended from the imperial adventure tales which had their heyday in the late nineteenth century and which provided the cinematic 'epic' genre with its material. It is a genre so well-defined as to have been met with close parodic treatment: in *Carry on up the Khyber* (Gerald Thomas, 1968); and earlier in Robert Hamer's *Kind Hearts and Coronets* (1949), whose General Rufus D'Ascoigne tediously restages his African campaigns at the dinner table enlisting as props whatever food, crockery or cutlery is available, in close parody of General Burroughs' identical (and, to be fair, similarly comic) re-creation of Balaclava in the 1939 version of *The Four Feathers*.

Epics celebrate the achievements of heroic people in history or tradition. The Oxford English Dictionary goes on to state that 'the typical epics…have often been regarded as embodying a nation's conception of its own past history'. It concludes, though, with the tellingly nuanced afterthought, 'or of the events in that history *which it finds most worthy of remembrance*' (my emphasis). The epic protagonist is of course the ideal heroic type on whose actions the fate of the nation depends. Alexander Korda had always been drawn towards the biopic form, mythologising the lives of such iconic figures as Helen of Troy, Samson and Delilah, Catherine the Great, Henry VIII, Elizabeth I and Lord Nelson. His investment in tales of British imperial adventure was part of the same international marketing strategy, a projection of national myths relying on action sequences, formulaic constructions and sketched 'types' of English temperament to entrance the foreign market, both in America and the colonies.[17]

The late Victorian and Edwardian works of popular fiction upon which the Korda films are drawn are soldiers' stories, selling heroism. They are bound up with Britain's sense of self, the soldier (he is almost always an officer, and the aristocratic is almost always celebrated) returning to Britain a mirrored image of its ideally constructed masculine type, one whose gendered identity is at the same time an exemplary model of *national* virtue. Real manhood is mapped onto the political terrain of the 'Empire' and, as Graham Dawson observes, the one endorses the other.[18] Their emergence in the British cinema of the 1930s serves as a popular re-investment in manhood in the wake of the losses of the First World War, for these tales record the potency of British masculine energy marshalled in the vigorous assertion of the imperial assumption. They form part of a culture industry which for the expanding popular readership of the late nineteenth century had offered a *Boy's Own* national story. They are fantasies in the sense that they are metaphors or displacements, part of the cultural machinery by which images of subjectivity are made available, gendered social identities are internalised and built upon, and the social order is reproduced.

Georges Perinal, who was responsible for photographing *Blimp*, had been the cinematographer on *The Drum*, *The Four Feathers* and *The Thief of Bagdad* (all in Technicolor), and *Sanders of the River* (in black and white). The bright colour code of Powell and Pressburger's film clearly reproduces Perinal's earlier style. Michael Powell viewed *Blimp* as something of a throwback: 'I looked on it as an old-fashioned film, a relic of the pre-war days of which the key was the exquisite photography of George Perinal.'[19] Later in his film-making career, he famously strives for the symbolic use of colour, and for a synthesis of all aspects of film language towards a single expressive whole. With *Blimp* the impetus is emulation and pastiche, rather than any heady synaesthetic experience in a high romantic register. '*Blimp* was, after all,' says Powell, 'a conventional film, a black and white film coloured', with Allan Gray's imitative music 'applied on, as it were ... like the rich glazing on a ham'.[20] In *The Drum*, Captain Carruthers is played by Roger Livesey, and this reinforces the connection with *Blimp*. The film also stars Valerie Hobson, Raymond Massey and Sabu, familiar faces in Powell and Pressburger's films. Carruthers, posted to the remote base of Tokot, faces down and defeats the rebellious usurper Prince Ghul, played with relish by Massey as an uncomplicatedly evil madman. With its location shooting (albeit with the hills outside Harlech substituting for India), its military music, its action sequences and its dancing (both Highland and Indian), *The Drum* offers an unproblematically polarised and *spectacular* justification of the British imperial adventure. Typically this genre supposes a strict gendered division of space allotting the private world of domesticity to women and the public active outdoor life to men. While *The Drum* ships Valerie Hobson to the front line, and permits her to save Sabu by shooting his pursuer, her subservience to her husband is stressed and her presence is marked as a token embodiment of bourgeois 'Home Life'. India is here less a geographical reality than a psychic arena, where men and nation may be tested, where the alien or the exotic are either disarmed by rendering it childlike, or demonised in order that it may suffer a decisive exorcism. The purity and good health of Britishness is sustained by a paranoid projection of otherness.

The Four Feathers operates on a more epic scale, extensively shot on location in the Sudan and containing some very effective Technicolor photography, with a large cast of extras, and grand spectacles of battles shot as dynamic action sequences with a highly mobile use of cameras, echoing the ambitious scope of D.W. Griffith and anticipating Olivier's *Henry V*. It repeats many of the tropes of *The Drum*. Harry Faversham's apparent cowardice in resigning his commission on the eve of the campaign to retake the Sudan and to avenge the 'murder' of General Gordon is marked as an illness, denoted by the sympathetic attendance of a friendly doctor, but his bravery is proved, as he works disguised as a mute Arab to rescue his erstwhile companions. This donning of a disguise, a masquerade of identity, betrays the imperial adventure story's affiliation to the spy thriller genre and does suggest a lack of confidence in simplistic and overt 'displays' of uniformed Britishness. However, with the retaking of Khartoum, the myths of the British imperial mission and of the efficacy of the military aristocracy are restored. Despite Harry's disguise as an Arab outcast (clearly a tactical incorporation of the 'other'), the natives really are little more than an undifferentiated mass of 'Dervishes' and 'Fuzzy-Wuzzies'.

In *Blimp*, Clive's biography is a chronicle of denials, repression and displacements, evasions which under-cut the settled image of the 'soldier hero'. His retreats and silences are issues of critical importance, for not only does his relationship to women and 'Home' cast the Empire hero in a new light, but his faith in the stainlessness of British public history is left open to question. At his most youthful, Clive is dynamic and vigorous, a man of his times, progressive enough to admire the 'lovely lines' of a new motor car which speeds past outside the Bathers Club. The motor vehicle as token of modernity is very much a feature of the film's opening sequence too: here, back in 1902 among the horse-drawn cabs, it marks a transition, anticipating the red car trundling through the opening tracking shot of turn-of-the-century America in Minnelli's *Meet Me In St Louis* (1944), although in spirit recalling Orson Welles' *The Magnificent Ambersons* (1942), another elegy to a fast receding world, released a year before *Blimp*. We quickly learn in the exchange between Clive, Hoppy and the so-called 'period Blimp' in 1902 that Clive has just returned from South Africa, where he has won the Victoria Cross. The strongest affirmation of his masculine credentials thus relates to an incident prior to the start of the narrative. It aims to establish his pedigree as soldier-hero, although, in a departure from the 'Empire' genre, it denies us any exhibition of actual military valour. The 'adventure' lies adjacent to the represented world of the film. Genuine heroic activity is displaced onto its signs and tokens: the medal and the uniform.

Almost immediately, however, the reputation of the British in the Boer War (and with it, Clive's VC) is tarnished. Clive is outraged to learn that the spy Kaunitz is spreading anti-British propaganda in Germany, alleging that women and children were killed in South Africa, and that they were starved in British concentration camps. He dashes to Berlin to silence the scoundrel, but the suggestion of British ill treatment is never satisfactorily erased. Scandals such as the shootings of prisoners were well reported during the Boer War. The court-martialling and subsequent execution of the Australian Bush Veldt Carbineers Lieutenants 'Breaker' Morant and Peter Handcock in 1902 had caused outrage, and Emily Hobhouse's campaign to publicise the conditions in the camps had successfully enlisted Lloyd George's support. At no point does Clive demonstrate any awareness of this.

Clive's Berlin showdown with Kaunitz in the Café Hohenzollern is not a noble affair but a squabble, and it descends into a dishonourable brawl, a slapstick parody of disastrous international relations, resulting in Clive having to fight a duel with a representative of the Imperial German Army. It is an early instance of the film's mock-heroics. Military spectacle is later displayed, but is more explicitly ridiculed. After Clive's duel with Theo, visitors to their nursing home are astonished by a diplomatically awkward collision in the vestibule between British dragoons and members of the German Uhlan Guards, all in full regimental dress. A hastily agreed protocol determines that the opposing armies should file through the doorway in parallel. This 'Vestibule Incident' is presented with full mock-heroic honours. The film thus deals with honest soldiery in two main ways. It either banishes it to an off-screen space, or it treats it comically (a third tactic, of course, is to suggest the full horror of war, and *Blimp* will broach this later).

This brings us to Clive's duel with Theo in Berlin, 1902, where an unreal attention to the artifices of honourable action is a sublimation of the real, the visceral, and potentially the homoerotic. The excessive observance of detail before and during the duel marks both the period and the officer class as one fatally disassociated from reality and fixated on form. This very addiction to high ceremony in a situation promising butchery undermines the full-bloodedness which the duel is meant to prove. Despite the assurance of heterosexuality in the ruse concocted by the Embassy that the duel is an affair of the heart (the men will seem to be fighting over Edith), this scene, like so many others of robust male conflict, is flushed with a blush of sado-masochistic homoeroticism which worries away at its presentation of heroic valour.

Writing about the spectacle of masculinity in screen, Steve Neale suggests that 'the anxious "aspects" of the look at the male...are...both embodied and allayed not just by playing out the sadism inherent in voyeurism through scenes of violence and combat, but also by drawing upon the structures and processes of fetishistic looking by stopping the narrative in order to recognize the pleasure of display, but displacing it from the male body as such and locating it more generally in the overall components of a highly ritualized scene.'[21] With its attention to formality and symmetry, these are just the displacements we see in the duel sequence. Glimpses of naked flesh – seen when the Swedish attaché Colonel Borg asks Clive to undo his shirt – and the cutting away of Clive's sleeve to free his movement, hint at the real damage about to be done to the body. With the arrival of Clive's hitherto unseen combatant, the curious and handsome Theo, a sense of mutual recognition between the men is shown in a conventional shot/reverse shot of close-ups. Soon to be 'blood-brothers', they mirror each other, and are spliced together. All that separates them is nationality. As this quasi-balletic bout of fastidiously staged male bonding is about to commence, however, the camera audaciously retreats. It does not simply pan back, but famously cranes overhead, up and out of the massive gymnasium, dissolving through the roof, into the snowstorm, and then descending again to meet Edith's waiting carriage in the street outside. The thrill of the kill is denied to us.

The crane shot is an act of vertiginous disavowal. While again the actual spectacle of combat is left off-screen, the motivation here is that this is an event governed entirely according to form and manners. It matters not that recoiling from the scene frustrates the narrative, for the outcome is, according to the values being satirised, immaterial: Candy's cohorts articulate a mindset concerned more with the rules of the game than with ends. As a piece of literal sabre-rattling it is another expression of the film's concern with circularity and teleology. While the extravagant preparations for this diplomatically necessary duel receive sharp satirical treatment, the exposure of ridiculous Prussian codes of conduct necessarily brings Clive's unwritten but equally rigid standards into question. Such a reading supports the text's quizzical attitude to military masculinity. Moreover, this is a critically anti-epic moment, another 'screening-off' of male bravado. It is also, of course, the most significant ellipsis in a film structured around the tension between the continuity of a biographical narrative (in which the personality marks a site of coherence), and a presentation of history marked by fragmentation and selectivity. The combatants each receive minor injuries and, with honour satisfied, they come to befriend each other while convalescing. When he is fully recuperated, Clive returns to London, leaving Edith to marry Theo. At this stage Clive is unconscious of his own love for Edith. He jokingly dresses up in Edith's extravagant hat and celebrates Theo's and Edith's engagement with a cordial toast, but the hat clues us to the drastic un-manning which this failure to accomplish union with Edith represents. Back in London briefly, he seems lost. He soon seeks compensation in the hunting life.

Memorable shooting-trophy montages follow, and these work to fast-forward the timescale of the film. Hunting of game was an integral ingredient in the imperial myth. The Boy Scout Movement, inaugurated by Robert Baden-Powell during the siege at Mafeking, contributed to this peddling of a popular image to aspiring British and colonial boyhood. It channelled together the necessary pioneer spirit and the need to dominate nature with rules of good conduct, patriotism and ideal manliness. While the British Empire remained a testing ground for young men, the pragmatic need to understand and respect the wild was something any domestic boy-child could similarly rehearse. However, the reality of game hunting was that it remained an exclusively elite activity. Born out of a public school mentality, it disguised as good sportsmanship a worryingly Darwinist supremacism, and offered a brutal apprenticeship into the skills and disciplines of soldiery. As John MacKenzie has argued, hunting was also an almost entirely male activity, one of the vigilantly guarded demarcation lines by which the gendered division of the imperial culture was maintained.[22] It follows, therefore, that hunting and chastity were necessarily seen to be concomitant, and the collection of hunting trophies was thus a substitution for sexual activity. With Clive, it is a clear displacement activity, a divorce from something more fulfilling.

Powell and Pressburger rely upon knowledge of this culture, but their deeply cynical allusion to it goes further to diminish its credentials. The first montage of trophies is initiated by Clive's realisation on his return from Berlin that he had loved Edith, now forfeited to Theo, and by his subsequent recognition that his effort to fill this loss by romancing Edith's sister is futile. Returning to Cadogan Place, Clive looks wearily around his 'den', and as he walks onto and then off the screen to the Elgarian tune once marked as Edith's motif but now connoting nostalgia and lack, his shadow is drawn out on the blank wall. The 'den' literally becomes his 'retreat', the site of his evasion from a full and fulfilling life, and Clive's cast shadow is appropriately and ominously ghost-like. To staccato gunfire and to exotically crude 'pastiche' music denoting parts of the British Empire, animal heads begin to clutter the blank space. The unwitnessed episodes of hunting suggest the traditional, familiar rhetoric of popular adventure and, seen as a succession of point-of-view shots, the trophies become tokens of a triumphant identification between Clive's ego and its imagined rugged ideal. Yet, of course, this is to ignore the deep irony of the sequence, for Clive's expeditions are clearly coded as a displacement. Hunting is a sign of the transmutation of sexual energy, and this reassignment of feelings suggests that adventure is nothing but a substitution. The evasion of reality is marked by Clive's two-dimensionalisation, as his substantial form is replaced on the screen by an ephemera, a walking shadow, an apposite nod to Macbeth, perhaps, for consequent upon the loss of his love, Clive's hunting life is a sound and a fury, a rampaging safari, signifying nothing. A similar montage immediately after the death of Clive's wife Barbara reinforces the point. Its status as a denial of historical progress is made clear as this second speeded journey through the inter-war period culminates in 1938 with a map of Munich and strains of the German national anthem. Clive later hangs Barbara's portrait in the 'den' along with his other trophies, emphasising what is now clear. It replaces, rather than proves, virility, and undoes Clive's self-appointed status as masculine epic hero. Of course, Clive's adoption of Barbara's family name 'Wynn' – after his marriage it is fixed with a hyphen to his own surname – is a nominal feminisation, further marking the actual distance between Clive and the archetypal gods of Empire with whom he wrongly identifies.

This connotation of hunting with sexual and emotional inadequacy directly critiques the popular justification of imperialism. Not only does it imply that the imperial adventure is a flight from domesticity, but the focus upon the collection of trophies rather than upon the supposedly skilful hunt forces us to read that imperialism as a grotesque acquisitiveness. The popularly imagined character-building attention to sportsmanship is invalidated by the relegation of hunting itself to another off-screen area, for all we are left with is the stuffed end-product of an already critically impaired masculine rite. Like Charles Foster Kane's Xanadu, Clive's Cadogan Place hideaway (with its 18 empty rooms) represents a desperate longing for plenitude, a need to fill a void. Paradoxically, the faster its walls are filled with trophies, the emptier the property seems to be. That each of the montages culminates in an image of armed conflict (the earlier sequence goes so far as to pan to a German helmet, appropriately labelled 'Hun, 1918, Flanders') links the ugly spectacle of hunting to the poetics of warfare, and serves as a denunciation of any glorious rendition of battle. The First World War sequence which follows the first montage is infiltrated by similar images of dead animals: Murdoch (James Laurie), Clive's batman, finds 'Dead Cow Cross-roads', and orientates himself by getting a scent of the two horses lying unburied by the road. This, incidentally, is another piece of cosmetic self-censorship, as in the shooting script it is the smell of dead 'Jerries' which marks Murdoch's way.[23]

The nineteenth-century rhetoric of heroic valour proved incompatible with the conditions of trench warfare by 1918. As the First World War sequence of *Blimp* makes clear, Clive begs to differ. During the Armistice Day sequence, he postures and 'speechifies' vaingloriously. He tells Murdoch that victory means not only that they can go home (and 'home' is a highly charged word in this film) but, in an emphatic close-up shot, that 'Clean fighting, honest soldiery have won', that 'Right is Might'. The mise-en-scène of this sequence is plainly artificial, with the war obviously played out on Alfred Junge's studio sets. These supposedly external scenes very strongly recollect the war paintings of the Official War Artist Paul Nash, particularly those works of his which date from after his return to near the Front Line of Flanders in late 1917. With pictures such as *The Front Line, St Eliot* (1917), *Void* (1918) and his massive canvas *The Menin Road* (1918) Nash gives a stylised rendition of a natural landscape raped and ruined. The skeletonised tree trunks splintering up from mud-brown earth to black-blue sky in the bleak, caricatured landscape of *The Menin Road* are three-dimensionalised on Junge's set. Nash's images have come to form part of the popular shared memory of the war. On this apocalyptic stage, though, Clive continues to wax lyrical, and is ironically counter-pointed by a skylark mocking the devastation beneath it. This is a forced and bitter pastiche, colliding two irreconcilable visual discourses, for Clive's blinkered ideals mock the traumatised environment. The visual code here, drawing as it does upon recognisable, iconic, 'imagined' memories of the battle scene filtered through art, reinforces the idea that the film is no documentary re-creation, but is Clive's (unreliably) remembered reconstruction of his own experience.

The irony in this sequence is so bitter because of what Clive *knows* (and yet denies) about allied activity during the war. Looting and the shooting of prisoners are witnessed, and while it is done by the South African Van Zijl (Reginald Tate), the geographical displacement cannot absolve the British. Van Zijl's looting is, we are told, something 'learnt from the English in the Boer War' (the ghost of that unhappy episode, disturbed by Kaunitz earlier in the film, is still not settled). After Clive's

2. The Great War: Paul Nash, *The Menin Road* (1918). (Courtesy of The Imperial War Museum, London)

3. The Great War remembered: Roger Livesey on Alfred Junge's set in *The Life and Death of Colonel Blimp*. (BFI Stills, © Carlton International Media Ltd)

failure to extract information from captured Germans by gentle means, Van Zijl is left to interrogate them in his own brutal way. Clive's unconscious denial of this is marked by the highly artificial pose of nobility he adopts as the camera pans back from his Armistice oration. This panning back merely refocuses and accentuates the dead landscape around him, making a heavy visual critique of Clive's head-in-the-clouds ideals.

INCORPORATION AND RESISTANCE

There is a two-way process at work in *Blimp*: one of rejection (of old world redundancies), and one of incorporation. Leaving old-style military manhood more or less undone, *Blimp* also tempers the (paranoid) projection of 'otherness' which characterised that pensioned-off ideology. It secures itself squarely within the outlook of contemporary 'Home Front cinema', the axiomatic premise of which was the denial of all partisan interests, other than those drawn along lines of battle. This 'democratic "everyone pulling together" ethos', as Robert Murphy notes, is the stuff of films like Reed's *The Way Ahead* (1945) and Launder and Gilliat's *Millions Like Us* (1943).[24] At a structural level, *Blimp* dramatises the same mythical community spirit. Operating as a fantasy of incorporation, it strives to construct a united Allied front. In doing so it leaves Nazism as the only significant 'other'. To incorporate is to unite into one blended whole, to break down foreign bodies into an undifferentiated compound, to absorb into the flesh. This was articulated by the so-called 'national cinema' of the war, committed to the effacement of difference and the propagation of consensus. In *Blimp*'s acceptance of the uniformed Angela within Candy's masculine army world, we see evidence of the process of hegemony: alert, flexible and ultimately pragmatic in securing its own perpetuity, tolerating the extension of women's labour into what were previously male arenas. Taking care to ensure that the meaning of this shift in social practice is clearly cued as temporary ('for the duration') such recruitment is encouraged through popular appeals to the national war effort.

Elsewhere, some of the film's inclusive strategy is cursorily achieved. The United Kingdom itself is geographically bound together in the opening sequence. As mentioned earlier, *Henry V* is echoed in Spud's selection of his team for the assault on the Bathers Club, calling on Taffy, Geordie and Dai Evans ('Oh we must have him, *look you*'), just as Shakespeare's Fluellen, MacMorris and Jamy exemplify a nation joined together. Regional stereotypes suffice to link together the nation. Similarly, a black American soldier in the First World War sequence goes totally unmentioned as a naturalistic detail. The fact that his presence is not underscored suggests an acceptance of the USA as allies in that conflict, and an indifference to matters of skin colour. In this small respect, *Blimp*'s distance from the 'Empire' film is clearly flagged. With the promised meal between young Spud and ancient Candy at the end of the film, a reconciliation is made between youth and old age, an harmonious conclusion which grants forgiveness to Spud for the bitter pill he has forced Clive to swallow. Conversely, the double agent Kaunitz, reported to have spied for both the British and the Boers during the South African War, violates any sense of stable political identity and is left unredeemed.

Where *Blimp* struggles more is in its representation of class, in part because Clive is himself so class-bound, and because the film focuses almost exclusively upon the Harrovian officer class (and its Prussian Junker equivalent), marginalising its attention to society as a whole. It is in this crucial aspect that any attempt to place *Blimp* squarely within a tightly defined notion of 'British Wartime Cinema' struggles, for so much of that cinema drew strength from its representation of the 'popular' – focusing as much on the image of the group (the 'masses', broadly conceived as the proletariat) as on the middle classes, and stressing a harmonious relationship between them. Yet when Clive makes damning reference to the 'army of loafers at Hyde Park', or when he rails bombastically against Murdoch, his batman during the First World War and subsequently his butler, it is his own prejudice, his own distance from the popular which is being exposed. Clive's dismissal of social groups such as these exposes his own intolerance: it is an attitude of superiority which marks his out-datedness by the 1940s. While Murdoch's inability to pronounce the name Theo Kretschmar-Schuldorff becomes a tedious joke at the expense of the quaintly small-minded commoner (like all those Shakespearean comic characters whose weak grasp of language is mocked), the representation of this token working man is otherwise largely positive. His active role as an air raid warden and his service in the Home Guard integrate him, and by extension his class, into the war effort. Spud himself belongs to no obvious class: an Everyman with an everyday nickname, his own code-name 'Beer Mug' contrasts with 'Veuve Cliquot 1911', the antiquated, elitist password selected by Clive for the Home Guard exercise.

The triple casting of Deborah Kerr as Candy's 'ideal' suggests a more engaged attitude to the shifting role of women. It is a radical casting decision, and its meanings are ambivalent. Primarily, it is an indictment of Clive's faulty vision: he is drawn, with a deathly repetition, towards identical women and, while he eventually admits that Edith came to constitute an 'ideal', the true significance of his inability to differentiate between these women is not really admitted. The presence of the same actress in three very different periods encourages us to see these characters less as individuals and more as representatives of their gender. As Edith, the articulate and politicised governess in Berlin, resenting the limits of her education but pragmatically capitalising upon what she has been taught (good manners and the English language), she is someone who at first alienates the young Clive with her intelligence, although he later grows more curious ('You know, it's a bit staggering to see a girl take such an interest in politics'). Deborah Kerr's performance here is sharp, pithy, feisty and intelligent. As the mill owner's daughter Barbara, she is a conventional support to her husband. With the role of Angela, Kerr plays the fully mobilised woman, so fully mobilised as to articulate her own nominal defeminisation: she rejects the range of meanings conferred upon her by her given name (an idealised Victorian 'angel'), and instead identifies herself as 'Johnny'. This name change echoes her altered career: before the war she was a photographic model and now she is an army driver. Discarding the passivity of her earlier willing objectification, she is now literally at the wheel. Her role in the film at this point is a clear comment upon the way women are viewed. Following hard upon Clive's revelation to Theo of the portrait of his dead wife, which clearly comments upon Clive's idealisation of the passive female form, there is a dramatic contrast in the next sequence where Angela is shown driving Theo back home through the London blackout. When a significantly *illicit* headlight illuminates her face, he recognises Angela's similarity to Edith and Barbara. This despectacularisation of womanhood is a rendition, through the lighting code of the film, of a definite shift in divided gender roles. As Pam Cook points out, this 'masculinization effect' marked a profound cultural change: 'Utility clothing (such as Johnny's uniform) was not just utilitarian, it was a form of cross-dressing which allowed women to try on masculine drag – sanctioned, moreover, by official sumptuary regulations.'[25] Angela's nominal and potentially destabilising masquerade of masculinity, or abandonment of femininity, is something which the film presents plainly: any implicit problems with Johnny's mobile gender are left unresolved. The message to be gleaned is that in the implicitly temporary conditions of 'total war', gender difference is an irrelevance and women are brought into what was hitherto a male public arena. A certain lack of reciprocity is suggested by the fact that men do not healthily come to inhabit the *domestic* space, but the military males who people *Blimp* are distinctly un-domestic, and the emphasis of the 'People's War' ethos is on public space. Ultimately, *Blimp* presents the metaphorical and literal eradication of 'Home' as a concept altogether. Even Clive's 'den' at Cadogan Place, a spatial rendition of his *Boy's Own*, juvenile, non-sexual life – a shrine/museum to his arrested development – is levelled by a German bomb. The explosive removal of his hideaway forces us to redefine our sense of what 'Home' might signify: the connotation of the physical property itself with permanence is shown to be a delusion. Until war is over, the home, figured psychologically as private space, will not exist. In a bold act of incorporative arrogance, hegemonic cultural energies attempt the universal conscription of the personal, the sentimental and the individualistic.

The most radical incorporation is clearly that of Theo, the exiled German, and it was the representation of this character, a 'good German', which raised most hackles when the film was released. The attack on *Blimp* from E.W. and M.M. Robson in their pamphlet *The Shame and Disgrace of Colonel Blimp* (1943) is lampoonable in parts. They find the film to be 'one of the most wicked productions that has ever disgraced the British film industry'.[26] There is, though, some merit in their analysis of Theo's role. Focusing on the immediate post First World War sequence, where Theo is a prisoner of war in Derbyshire, traumatised by defeat, unable at first to speak to his old friend Clive, then nonplussed at his genial reception by the British Establishment at Clive's house, and bitterly resenting the devastation wrought upon his homeland, the Robsons point to Theo's 'childish, petulant resentment and desire for revenge' and note in his attitude of contempt for Clive's class 'the very roots, the very ingredients of Nazidom'.[27] Theo does admit to Clive twenty years later, with some regret, that as he had left England for Germany in 1918 he regarded the British with disdain, and for a moment in the 1918 sequence Anton Walbrook's eyes narrow and a sinister tone creeps over him.

It is because of the pathos of Theo's situation in 1939 that this earlier bitterness towards the British tends to be forgotten. Theo's official admission into England as an alien is an important moment in the film, and is a critical exploration of the Archers' understanding of national identity and border crossings. Theo's tribunal, as he pleads his case, obviously reflects Pressburger's own exile to Britain. Theo admits that he fled Germany in 1935 after the death of his wife Edith and the loss of his two sons to the Nazi party. His explanation is that he was 'homesick', pining for a country he knew only as a prisoner of war, but one which feels familiar, through association with his wife, and the memory of a friendship struck with Clive almost forty years previously. 'Home' is redefined as an emotional state; the ideology of nationhood, paradoxically something one might expect to be dominant at this of all times, is subordinated to a form of identity born out of personal affiliations and a shared block of values all anti-pathetic to Fascism. Hence, the strength of the international friendship between Clive and Theo. *Blimp*'s integration of a 'good' German into its conscripted community daringly complicates any militant polarisation of nationhood, and that the intellectual weight of the film in its closing reels is allotted to this 'alien' voice marks the degree to which Powell and Pressburger advocate a strategy of incorporation.

At the end of the film, Clive learns his lesson. The plunge into the pool at the Royal Bathers Club which initiates his autobiographical narrative is part of a baptismal experience. After his defeat at the hands of Spud's army, he begins to see that his sense of fair play is bound up with inarticulable, romantic longings. He turns to face reality. What is most important about this moment, though, is that it is a *private* epiphany. Humiliated after his imprisonment in the Bathers Club overnight, Clive gazes into the space which was his Cadogan Place house, once his museum to escapism, and now flattened by a bomb. His old 'den', where his marriage to Barbara was anchored, has been commandeered. The basement of the property, open to daylight, is now an emergency water reservoir, ironically fulfilling Barbara's prophecy when Clive first brought her to his home. Recognising the house as a 'solid-looking property', Barbara had long ago asked Clive not to change 'till the floods come' and they have what Clive calls 'a *private* lake' in the basement. Remembering Barbara's words, Clive realises he still hasn't changed, and with the last word of the film, turns to face the present and the future. He also renounces the private in favour of the public.

This is the 'death of Colonel Blimp' promised by the film's title. However, *Blimp* has yet one more incorporative act to achieve. As Clive turns his back on the remains of Cadogan Place, Spud's modern army approaches unseen, and military band music grows louder. A parallel tracking shot, the last shot in the film, passes Theo, 'Johnny/Angela' and Clive in close-up, as they stand in the public space of the London street. As the camera reaches the reinvigorated Clive he salutes, in a gesture of respect to Spud's march-past, but the look to camera also acknowledges the cinema auditorium. It is an open recognition of the theatre audience, a piece of enunciation binding us into the film's integrated totality. Through this strenuous and consistent strategy of introjection, the film enlists us into its coherently marshalled new community. This is all very idealistic. Candy's salute to camera requires that we return it, and to do so we have to recognise that it is Candy we are acknowledging (not the now-dead 'Blimp'), and we have to be stirred by the triumphalism of the military fanfare which concludes the film. The sense of 'community' here is crucial, for the direct address to the cinema-goers is both intimate and 'local' and in a sense *always current*. A broadcast (diasporic?) audience for a mass cultural artefact is for a moment fantastically turned into a narrowcast network of compatriots, a band of Candy's kinfolk. This fits entirely with the film's ethos to put old fixed notions of home and homeland to one side and to find strength through new commitments and new relationships.

Insofar as the film is a satire and a propaganda piece, it engages in a public discourse. The audience is manipulated to agree with the exposure of military myopia, and to identify with the tenets of the war effort. All of this suggests that *Blimp* simply endorses the communal sphere and that notions of private space and subjective individualism are disowned. Part of the over-riding philosophy of the British at war was just this self-sacrifice, promoting social and public activity over private indulgence. It is not altogether clear from this reading where the film can be placed within Powell and Pressburger's output, because so often elsewhere they make ambitious forays *into* the subjective regimes of the imagination, romanticising it even in its destructive guises, as in the post-war melodramas. In part, *Blimp* shows the Archers idealising the Allied war effort and (through Theo) England is constructed as a sanctuary from Nazism. The literal and metaphorical destruction of Clive's inner sanctum demonstrates that the film wants to dispense with subjective flights of fancy ('for the duration'), and this is consistent with its endorsement of a 'People's War' mentality. Yet these overtly political goals do not explain the *affection* in which this film is held by many.

The ideology of popular culture often contains a utopian element. Social and political messages may well be communicated by popular texts, as the Ministry of Information recognised when it endorsed films which combined propaganda with entertainment and which appealed to the emotions. Such texts trade off their political message for something else, and in *Blimp* we can see the exchange in action. A spoonful of Sugar Candy helps the satirical medicine go down. In his essay 'Reification and Utopia in Mass Culture', Fredric Jameson has theorised how many such works of mass culture play this very significant double game. 'The drawing power of a mass cultural artefact,' he suggests, 'may be measured by its twin capacity to perform an urgent ideological function at the same time that it provides the vehicle for the investment of a desperate Utopian fantasy.'[28] It is thus that Jameson, after Gramsci, theorises the subject's apparently paradoxical acquiescence into a system which mystifies, falsifies and perpetuates a set of invidiously dominant class structures. For Jameson, ideology must have an appeal. It is a rhetoric of persuasion. Hegemony's wish to lead, of course, relies upon disciples willing to follow. As such, the 'ideology' he speaks of is not a bound set of parameters setting out a limited, repressive and utilitarian manifesto. At its core there is something excessive, a promised surplus of meaning. The emancipation to which the subject aspires is the reward for his/her recruitment (and for Jameson, the utopianism of the text waits to be identified and can be used to critique present social conditions). Because of this sense of boundless resource, the ideology he writes of is inherently idealistic.

The utopian sensibility at play in *Blimp* goes beyond the idealisation of the war effort itself. It is to be found in the elegiac tone of 'Edith's theme' on the musical soundtrack. It is there in the dignity of Theo's explanation of why he is in England in 1939. It is woven into ideas of 'Home' and loss and friendship. It is even there in Roger Livesey's burnished, honeyed voice. If it is hard to write about, this is because it is a realm of feelings, rather than thought. This is the magic territory in *Blimp*. However hard a dominant culture strives to recruit areas of social life (and the ideology of the 'People's War' is zealous in this regard), something remains outside the boundary of this public sphere. Incorporation is never total. Raymond Williams was shrewdly alert to this, concluding that, 'No mode of production and therefore no dominant social order and therefore no dominant culture ever in reality includes or exhausts all human practice, human energy, and human intention.'[29] Here, with his fond repetition of the 'human', Williams displays his credentials as a voice of the liberal left. While the dominant seizes the social, there are areas which it leaves alone, magic spaces kept out of the public cultural sphere, untouched by hegemony. For Williams, such areas include 'the personal or the private,...the natural or even the metaphysical'.[30] As Candy is recruited into Spud's 'New Model Army', finding a new social model to salute, areas of his private world are removed from him. But a part of Candy's 'human practice' is kept special. This is his sentimental, romantic mental space, his memory of his wife, and of his first love, and his old values, and his sense of friendship. It is one of the ways in which this film configures its own 'magic space'. Powell and Pressburger's recurring motif is not a physical location here, but an imagined one: a blurred mingling of memory, history and desire.

3

Two Pastorals – *A Canterbury Tale, I Know Where I'm Going!*

> England is a wonderful land. It is the most marvellous of all foreign countries that I have ever been in. It is made up of trees and green fields and mud and the gentry, and at last I'm one of the gentry.
>
> Rudyard Kipling

IMAGES OF ENGLAND

To begin to place *A Canterbury Tale* (1944), some words about 'classic' wartime cinema. Basil Dearden's prisoner-of-war drama *The Captive Heart* (1946) characterises much 'British National Cinema' of its time, advocating the stoicism and the group mentality associated with Ealing Studios and with the documentary movement, while also incorporating a romance plot which promotes audience identification and is the basis of its narrative suspense. This marriage between public, consensual virtues and distinctly private desires (frequently renounced, sometimes indulged, but generally the stuff of melodrama) is a characteristic of the 'quality' British film. In Dearden's film, we follow the experiences of a group of British prisoners-of-war during their time in a German camp. As such the film harks back to the period of the war, like Asquith's *Way to the Stars* (1945), Powell and Pressburger's *A Matter of Life and Death* (1946) and *The Small Back Room* (1949). One of *The Captive Heart*'s inmates, Captain Geoffrey Mitchell (Michael Redgrave) writes to his wife Celia, with an echo of Rupert Brooke's 'corner of a foreign field', that their prison has been gradually transformed into 'a little piece of England'. By creating their own tiny garden plots, the prisoners restage in miniature the 'pastoral version' of England which features so strongly in Captain and Mrs Mitchell's correspondence. In her replies, Celia (Rachel Kempson) describes a home life in England centred on the village green and on the Sunday game of cricket, so that her husband 'may picture it in [his] imagination', and as she writes her voice is heard on the soundtrack accompanying a montage of images of daily life in her village. This sequence recollects Dr Frank Reeves' casual remarks about his own village as it is reflected through his camera obscura in *A Matter of Life and Death*. The POWs' sense of 'Englishness' is central, although, in a familiar gesture of tokenism, the film embraces a Scot, Lieutenant David Lennox (Gordon Jackson), and a stock Welshman, Private Dai Evans (Mervyn Johns), both played by actors well used to representing their nation.

Captain Mitchell is not the only inmate imagining home, and neither is he the only one to echo Rupert Brooke. Major Ossy Dalrymple (Basil Radford) scrutinises a squadron of Flying Fortresses droning overhead and remarks that 'They'll be home in time for tea' (vaguely resonating Brooke's poem 'The Old Vicarage, Grantchester'). Quaint images like these, shared with poetry from Rupert Brooke to the Georgian poets of the post First World War period, are a common feature in 1940s wartime British cinema and are a key feature of *A Canterbury Tale*. Meanwhile, another prisoner, jaded by camp food, dreams of eggs, bacon and tomatoes with ketchup – his class betrayed by his diet. Yet another wonders what is happening in 'Jane', the *Daily Mirror* cartoon strip. This focus on a group mentality born out of a stoical sense of duty typifies the philosophy of Ealing Studios (who were responsible for the film), while the specific manifestations of nostalgia among the group depicts the class inflections of its individual members. The irony of the film's title, *The Captive Heart,* becomes clear: incarcerated though the prisoners are, their hearts are far from 'captive'. By imagining England, their sense of identity is affirmed, their right to liberty asserted. Specifically, as Jeffrey Richards has noted, '[t]he prisoners are sustained by a vision of England…a rural England: the village'.[1] This vision is shared by all, regardless of class. What Richards does not go on to explore is the way in which this identification is based upon a process of fantastic investment by the POWs. It directly expresses the critically psychological dimension of national identity. Benedict Anderson's notion of national identity as an 'imagined community' is effectively dramatised here.[2] The notion of 'community' seems clear enough, but the way in which that sense might be 'imagined' is more debatable. *The Captive Heart* fictionalises just how national identity is rooted in internalised representations of iconic and stereotypical images, a sense which is amplified by the inmates' exile from that homeland.

'Captain Mitchell's' emotional identification with the England depicted in Celia's letters and his tender feelings for their authoress are doubly and paradoxically significant because (as is quickly revealed in the first reel) the 'Mitchell' we are seeing is an impostor. Celia's real husband, Geoffrey, is dead: the character played by Redgrave is a Czech officer, Captain Karel Hasek, who has avoided detection after his escape from Dachau concentration camp by stealing the dead Mitchell's uniform. Masquerading as Mitchell by corresponding with the unknowing Celia, he is better able to sustain his disguise in the POW camp. From Celia we learn that the Mitchells' marriage had in fact broken down before the outbreak of war. The letters unwittingly exchanged between her and Hasek thus forge a new bond between the two: Celia imagines a reawakened affection for an apparently transformed husband; Hasek imagines a fantasy life to replace his own family killed by the Nazis. Their relationship develops within a textual rendition of English home life, the idyllic nature of which encourages their shared emotional investment (a similar attachment to an imagined England is to be found in *Blimp,* where Theo, made homeless by the Nazis, speaks of the love he has acquired for an English countryside he barely knows and which is for him inseparable from the memory of his deceased English wife). Hasek's very act of fraud, of course, foregrounds the constructed nature of national identity. As *The Captive Heart* concludes on VE Day, we finally see a happy resolution. Celia, recovering from the shock of learning that Geoffrey has been dead for four years, blissfully shares the moment with Hasek, who has telephoned her from London. Their conversation is drowned out by the triumphant soundtrack music and the explosion of fireworks in the garden of Celia's country house, signifying the end of war. Not yet physically united, their future happiness is nevertheless promised in smiling close-up shots and in the celebration of victorious nationhood which links them. Throughout the film, 'hope' and 'home' are inseparable.

In British national cinema of the time we find renditions of the Home Front (as it is either experienced or imagined) working along the lines established in this sketch of Dearden's film. In *A Canterbury Tale* a group of soldiers – Sgt Peter Gibbs (Dennis Price), Sgt Bob Johnson (an American GI played by Sgt John Sweet) and a land army girl, Alison Smith (Sheila Sim) – arrives in the Kentish village of Chillingbourne, which is effectively governed by local magistrate Thomas Colpeper (Eric Portman). Each of the young travellers has suffered from a form of loss. Alison's fiancé is missing in action, Bob's girl has stopped writing to him, and Peter has cynically abandoned his youthful musical ambitions. Alison becomes the latest victim of an attack by 'the Glueman', a miscreant who attacks girls by pouring glue in their hair. It becomes apparent that Colpeper and the Glueman are the same man, and we learn that his motivation has been to prevent casual relationships between the girls and the soldiers stationed nearby. Colpeper has a mission to teach the soldiers about English history, culture and landscape, and does not want them distracted. He gives public lectures about the meaning of the English countryside and is committed to traditional values. The trio of young protagonists attend his lecture (Alison, in particular, is mesmerised by it), and in their own ways they begin to commune with the spirit of the place. The film is structured around the idea of pilgrimage, and its four main characters journey to Canterbury to receive miracles or, in Colpeper's case, to do penance for his misguided campaign of terror.

It is typical that the nation should be pictured here as an Edenic countryside, with villages which ask to be described as 'quintessentially' English. This is a very specific image of England, and it achieves an iconic status. Essentially rural and southern, this particular version works as a trope which represents the central qualities of the nation at large. Other Britains (working class, municipal, suburban, northern, Midlands, Scottish or Welsh) may be in evidence, but the Home Counties arable rhetoric predominates, a partial rendition of the nation, ignoring its largely industrial profile and assuming a spurious completeness. No less than three British feature films, made in as many years in the early 1940s and exploring the nation's character, derive their titles from John of Gaunt's glowingly patriotic speech in *Richard II*. *This England* (David Macdonald, 1941) re-enacts historic moments in a country village for the benefit of a visiting journalist. *The Demi-Paradise* (Anthony Asquith, 1943) has Russian engineer Ivan Kouznetsoff (Laurence Olivier) shedding his misconceptions about the British through his encounters with a host of eccentrics (including Margaret Rutherford and Joyce Grenfell). Once more, village life, coupled to a sense of historical awareness, is emblematic of the nation, with a local fête presenting a set of victorious tableaux from England's past. David Lean's *This Happy Breed* (1944) admittedly differs in that it is London-based (it is also significant in that it is a chronicle of a specifically lower-middle-class family). Nevertheless it celebrates the 'British Commoner' as it charts the way its protagonists interact with moments in British history, and as such it articulates a clearly patriotic message. Elsewhere, from Ealing, *Went the Day Well?* (Alberto Cavalcanti, 1942), scripted by Angus Macphail (who also worked on the script for *The Captive Heart*), John Dighton and Diana Morgan from a story by Graham Greene, warns against complacency by showing the dramatic and brutal retaliation of another small village invaded by Germans: again the cosy and predominantly middle-class village exemplifies the nation at war. And yet again, *Tawny Pipit* (Bernard Miles and Charles Saunders, 1944) allegorically tells of a rare bird's nest jeopardised by the army and defended by local villagers, with a group of urban 'invaders' finding spiritual amelioration through contact with the values of the English countryside. These films rely upon a safe set of representational codes. Advancing the centrality of both the rural community and the middle classes they are resolutely unchallenging to the values and aspirations of the dominant social group.

Although these representations of the nation are directed primarily at the domestic market, in part at least they are geared to appeal to an international box office. Either way, they rely on the shorthand of stereotyping to maximise audience understanding and recognition. Conversely, the hugely popular American release, *Mrs Miniver* (William Wyler, 1942, US) deploys a set of images of Englishness which are remarkably consistent with many indigenous productions. Wyler offers another highly feudal, Home Counties, village view, with Lady Beldon (Dame May Whitty) at the pinnacle of its rigid class system. The Minivers (Walter Pidgeon and Greer Garson) enjoy a comfortable, in fact extravagant, lifestyle (perhaps more conspicuously consumerist than might be found in any English film of the time – this, as much as the casting, marks the film as an American product). Their family is a model for bourgeois aspiration.

Tradition is stressed again: the film focuses on a rose competition at the annual village flower show, which for years has been won by Lady Beldon because the other villagers deferentially refrain from entering any competing blooms. Lady Beldon acquiesces and gives the coveted prize to Mr Ballard the Station Master for his rose, which significantly has been named after Mrs Miniver, and so symbolises all of her maternal, patriotic, diplomatic and stoical virtues. Nevertheless, Lady Beldon's act of acquiescence merely confirms her popularity in the village. As an act of 'noblesse oblige' it perpetuates the feudal community. But 'international appeal' alone cannot and does not explain the persistence of these village-centred myths of Englishness. As Martin Wiener notes, the sociological survey Mass Observation asked the question in 1941 to respondents throughout the country: 'What does Britain mean to you?' Wiener's speculated response seems reasonable: 'One would expect expressions of affection for the threatened towns. Instead, the picture that "Britain" called to mind was for the great majority one of generalized rural scenery, or of particular, familiar country places.'³ The reaction might have been predicted, for the national myth of 'Deep England', an imaginary heartland to offset the devastation of the war, was a powerful and highly resonant emblem in 1940s British culture.

National discourses resonate with metaphors of centrality and marginality, depth and surface – oppositions which are often implicitly connoted with essential truth and distrusted superficiality. Homi K. Bhaba's aptly titled *Nation and Narration* is quick to identify a cultural rhetoric of 'homogeneity, cultural organicism, the deep nation, the long past (which rationalizes) the authoritarian, "normalizing" tendencies within cultures in the name of national interest or the ethnic prerogative'.⁴ *A Canterbury Tale* succumbs to this centripetal dynamic – it certainly explores the English 'heart' – yet at the same time it remains critical: it is a quizzical intervention into Bhaba's dominant discourse. Why, though, did such a highly illusory and pastoral version of the nation gather and retain its currency? From 1801 to 1911 the proportion of the population living in urban areas rose from 20 to 80 per cent, and the rise of industry was the dominant national characteristic. A strong current within the national mentality was clearly in denial about this irrefutable social shift, and the notion of power vested in the country estate proved hard to dislodge. In part, this valorisation of the countryside is a residuum of Romanticism, which as an artistic movement was forged from a reaction against the soulless alienation associated with industry and urbanisation. By the end of the nineteenth century, the land no longer formed England's economic base. But why, in a century marked by modernisation and technological progress, did a sense of national consciousness emotionally rooted in old, romantic myths achieve such a status, and how did seemingly retrograde cultural practices such as the excessive and indecorous 'gothic revival' become so dominant, particularly within High Tory culture (although medievalism like this was also found among dissenters such as Ruskin and Morris)? There was evidently something within that Tory mindset which rejected the advances of Capital. The opulent 'excess' of the gothic revival was less an expression of the nation's capitalist prowess, but rather an anti-utilitarian, non-materialistic insurgency against it. Like the emotional attachment to the land, it is evidence of an older frame of thought within hegemonic Toryism. In Wiener's neatly encapsulated history:

> The reconstruction of Conservatism in the Victorian and Edwardian periods was a two-way process. The Tory party shifted its base from the land to property in all its forms, making room for the new middle classes…[yet]

many of the attitudes of Toryism lived on within the reconstituted party, alongside industrial and capitalistic values. The party continued to invoke the rustic spirit of the nation. Conservatism was enamoured of rural England, as much an England of the mind as of reality. Conservatives imbued with the Southern Metaphor of the nation tended to look askance at a number of central characteristics of industrial capitalism – its ugliness (or at least untidiness), its 'materialism', and its instability.[5]

Never entirely modernised, the dominant patrician ideology accommodated itself to progress, but never concurred with the more aggressively entrepreneurial spirit of industrialisation. The attachment to the English countryside survived as a spectre of Romanticism and as a fondly embraced relic of feudalism, as a redundant although still active ingredient within the ruling bourgeois classes. Wiener's argument recapitulates that made by Eric Hobsbawm in 1968. Noting the 'assimilation of the British business classes to the social pattern of the gentry' from the mid-nineteenth century, Hobsbawm diagnoses that it was from this development that a particular 'mythical Britain' emerged. Thus, 'the heavy incrustation of British public life with pseudo-medieval and other ritual, like the cult of royalty, date back to the late Victorian period, as does the pretence that the Englishman is a thatched-cottager or country squire at heart'.[6]

British culture at times fixates on rusticity, not least in traditions of landscape painting, where organic countryside imagery and rural life became allegories of a society in harmony with itself and its environment. In the early twentieth century, Georgian poetry was likewise imbued with patriotic pastoralism. Popular writers such as Rupert Brooke, Edmund Blunden, Ivor Gurney, W.H. Davies, Walter de la Mare and Edward Thomas celebrated a very particular England, taking Hardy and Housman as their mentors to establish a genre of 'countryside literature'. Housman's poem 'In valleys green and still' and de la Mare's 'Dry August Burned' are unconsciously echoed in the early parts of Michael Powell's autobiography, where he remembers the excitement of seeing the 1st Sussex Yeomanry billeted around his Kentish farmland home as a child.[7] Expressions of Hardy-esque rusticity also saturate the novels of Mary Webb, whose *Gone to Earth* was later filmed by Powell and Pressburger. The popular patriotic and nostalgic mise-en-scène of Georgian poetry, with its hedgerows, country pubs, apple trees and village cricket, is informed indirectly by the events and sentiments of the First World War, and by the city's encroachment onto rural space. Tapping into similar cultural currents, English orchestral music of the late nineteenth and early twentieth centuries was associated with a pastoral aesthetic overlaid with a nationalist rhetoric, most notably in the cases of Vaughan Williams and Edward Elgar. An overidentification between Vaughan Williams and 'Englishness' has been constructed, often to promote the case of Benjamin Britten as a more modernist, less insular British composer, although this argument ignores the influence of Ravel and Debussy on Vaughan Williams.[8] Nevertheless, much of Vaughan Williams's work has been seen as deeply rural, with his interest in English folk-songs, and with works such as 'Lark Ascending' (1914) and the Pastoral Symphony (first performed 1922) echoing Shelley's 'Ode to a Skylark' and Wordsworth's 'Solitary Reaper'. The tradition therefore survives intact, surfacing again in works like Dearden's *The Captive Heart*.

Repeated and reformulated, a generally sentimentalised and universalised rendition of a fantasised nation became fixed in the cultural psyche. With the development of rail travel and, by the 1930s, the spread of bus services and private car ownership, popular tourism was easier for city dwellers. *A Canterbury Tale* acknowledges this developing leisure activity, as Colpeper prophesies that after the war the soldiers will want to holiday in his beloved Kent (a message which is also clearly directed at the film's predominantly urban audience). Such secular pilgrimages in search of 'Old England' are descended from the romantic retreats of the Lake Poets, which initiated the Victorian tourist boom to those parts of Cumberland and Westmorland made famous in their writing. The rise in tourism was mediated and promoted through widely sold 'travelogue' literature: the late Victorian Poet Laureate, Alfred Austin, made such a trip through England and published the popular *Haunts of Ancient Peace*. Later, publications such as the best-selling 'Shell Guides' promoted the burgeoning trade. W.H. Auden recognised the trend towards village-worship, and sounded his cynicism about the commodification of the countryside. Attacking the popular idealisation of the rustic, his poem 'It's So Dull Here' commences wryly: 'To settle in this village of the heart, / My darling, can you bear it?' He goes on to criticise the debasing effects of tourism and 'townee smartness' on the once welcome village home. While Auden remains ambiguous (would his dissidence have ever embraced this village, even in its unsullied, pre-commodified state?), in the main he recoils. One man's cosiness is another's claustrophobia.

The 'Shell Guides' and posters successfully created a popular iconography in the public mind. The pre-war head of publicity at Shell-Mex and BP was Jack Beddington (who was later in charge of film production at the Ministry of Information). Beddington commissioned paintings for these guides from artists such as John Piper, Paul Nash and

Graham Sutherland (and texts from John Betjeman). Along with Henry Moore, Ceri Richards and David Jones these artists belonged to what became a school of 'neo-Romanticism' in British art. This group expressed a mystical, often surreal view of the British countryside, drawing from Blake, and further back from Arthurian legend (I would place Humphrey Jennings with these artists – his own brand of surrealist painting, and of course, his film work, owes much to Blake). As Jane Alison and John Hoole have noted, 'Emblematic of the artists' vision and the neo-Romantic sensibility is "the quest",…a search whose object is the shrine, an Eden or Arcadia; a quest made by artists sensitive to the spiritual loss of their day, a society which was to be broken by a tidal wave of war carnage and subsequent consumerism.'[9] *A Canterbury Tale*'s agenda is almost identical. Pressburger described it as a 'crusade against materialism'.[10] In part it is an advertisement for the English countryside, an homage to Powell's own childhood stamping grounds and a celebration of the aspects of Pressburger's adopted homeland which seemed best to embody the alien's sense of Englishness. Erwin Hillier's cinematography presents the Kentish scenery as a glorious spectacle, and through the eager eyes of the Americans Bob and his buddy Mickey, Canterbury's 'sights' and 'things to see' are fetishised acquisitions, captured on Mickey's movie-camera. A shot of the cathedral turned upside down as it is seen through the lens of his camera visually underscores this process of commodification. The film has a general distaste for consumerism and commodity, and it satirises the souvenir mentality of its naïve Americans. The relegation of the landscape to an inventory of 'must-sees' is an inauthenticating act of reification. It turns heritage into 'Heritage'. The film, though, is *itself* an advertisement for the beauties of Kent, so in a sense this meta-cinematic moment self-consciously admits its guilt in packaging and selling its own landscape. The defence is this: Colpeper praises English heritage, wants post-war tourism and advocates environmental curiosity. In scoffing at Bob's love of the movies, Colpeper reviles what he sees as the blank passivity of mass cinema spectatorship and the un-situated, inauthentic nature of distributed, duplicated images. Colpeper tutors Bob, who then appreciates what the Old Road and the cathedral represent. He passes this understanding on to Mickey. 'Active', enquiring engagement is required. Hence, Colpeper's lecture is also addressed to us, the cinema audience, and we are urged to see the 'real thing'.

NOSTALGIA AND THE PASTORAL

In practice, any tradition which allows a major version of the nation's sense of itself to be invested in an emotional reservoir fatally dislocated from reality is one marked by decline, and the 'idea of England' harboured in these rustic evocations contains an element of almost desperate wish-fulfilment. The nation is paraphrased and a platonic 'essence' of England is concocted. 'This hinterland between fact and possibility', in David Gervais's words, 'has been the traditional territory of pastoral.'[11] In this territory, the countryside is used symbolically – and as a fantasy world. Delayed in Chillingbourne and then journeying to the 'magical' city of Canterbury, the healing process experienced by Alison, Bob and Peter is given mystical dimensions and the film culminates in a surge of optimistic idealism. But at the opening, its protagonists are less than whole. A vital set of values is deemed to have been obscured by modern civilisation but, like the Pilgrims' Road which runs near the village of Chillingbourne, they have managed to survive, and wait to be unearthed so that the urgencies of the war might be faced. Faith in these values will redeem both the three travellers and the film's wider constituency, the nation at large. As Alison remarks to the barman in the village pub, the 'Bend' in the Road was 'there all the same' even before its excavation, and now it can serve as a visual reminder of these values. The Road depicts the sense of mission (the answer to 'Why We Fight') which the film is aiming to instil: long shots of the cathedral from the Bend in the Old Road are an indication of the goal – the Bend gave the ancient pilgrims their first sight of Canterbury. 'Pilgrimage' metaphorically stands for the pursuit of the war effort itself, while the tightly knit feudal organisation of Chaucer's pilgrims is emblematic of the film's ideal community – a mythic model for the nation, bound by common purpose. As Colpeper points out, just like the modern recruits to the 'People's Army', the medieval pilgrims were ordinary tradesmen and craftsmen, making an unusual journey.

Esmond Knight's voiceover during the 'Prologue' sequence of the film explicitly directs us to the dangers of the current anomie: 'Alas! When on our pilgrimage we wend, / We modern pilgrims see no journey's end.' *A Canterbury Tale* gives us a representative group of people groping for orientation in the upheaval of wartime – which Colpeper refers to as an 'earthquake' (and at the opening of the film the group is literally lost in the dark). Paradoxically, however, the rigours and the devastations of war can also be seen to clarify things: as a passer-by points out to Alison as she rummages around the graveyard-like wreckage of Canterbury, the compensatory reward for the bombed-out streets is that 'you get a very good view of the cathedral now'. The cathedral stands for antiquity, permanence and resilience, and embodies pre-capitalist principles: it is a medieval variant of the value St Paul's Cathedral had for London during the Blitz, and it is used to denote the ideological commitment of the film – a hardy stoicism borne out of longevity. Discussing the links between Humphrey Jennings and Powell, Jeffrey Richards and Anthony Aldgate note that Canterbury Cathedral is for Powell what St Paul's is for Jennings, but they point out that Powell's symbol is an older, rural variant.[12] Yet, crucially, the image of Canterbury Cathedral is the object of a double investment, for it also suggests a romantic or sacred utopianism, manifested through the 'blessings' which are apparently granted there. The central symbol of the film thus has meanings which are at once immanent and transcendent, borrowing from a tradition of English pastoralism to find strength in the past through the invocation and reinforcement of a mythical old England.

Raymond Williams traces the perseverance of a set of cultural ideas and feelings about the countryside, reformulated by each generation to account for changes in material conditions, but nonetheless maintaining a broadly consistent structure. He concludes that 'the persistence indicates some permanent or effectively permanent need, to which the changing interpretations speak'.[13] The ideas we find in *A Canterbury Tale* are characteristic of the twentieth-century post-industrial response to the metropolitan and the rural experience: the city is associated with isolation and mobility; the countryside is a haven, and a place of honest cultivation. Although Powell and Pressburger belong within a romantic tradition, this is not the grand, sublime landscape of early nineteenth-century Romanticism, but the harmonious, rustic compromise of Constable – a painter whose work did not achieve iconic status until the early twentieth century. The film champions one myth – the organically cohesive community – to resist one which urbanisation has made prevalent: namely the myth of a society consisting of isolated, alienated individuals.

The urban/rural duality has an artistic and literary lineage in the 'pastoral', a form which is escapist and frequently nostalgic. Whether it represents an idealised time (the Golden Age) or an idealised place (Arcadia), this other space permits the exploration of attitudes and values which find no room in the here and now. The structure of *A Canterbury Tale* imitates that of classic Shakespearean comedy, placing a group of protagonists into a strange or exotic world to dramatise their preconceptions, their limitations and their encounters with the new or the strange. This key structuring motif of many Shakespearean pastorals is taken by Powell and Pressburger to express their own recurring fascination with opposed worlds, dream states, alien territories and magical spaces. At a literal level, *A Matter of Life and Death* incorporates a production of *A Midsummer Night's Dream* into its narrative (while Clive Candy taunts his opponent Kaunitz in *Blimp* (1942) with 'I am Titania', an aria from the opera *Mignon*). Antonia Lant has written of wartime British cinema that 'The blackout and the mobile woman were the basis of the new dramatic forms precisely because they were unstable, and embodied the perceptual and ideological reinventions of wartime'.[14] In her examination of fractured, decentred representations of womanhood, and the male anxieties excited by the conscription of active women, she finds a rich metaphor of disruption in the visual destabilisation of the blackout, which is often inscribed realistically into film narratives, as it is here. Alison's arrival in Chillingbourne causes the patriarchy which Colpeper embodies to reassess its presumptions regarding the role of women in society. Yet the pastoral form of *A Canterbury Tale* illustrates that these modes of representation are not as novel as Lant suggests. Although she gives them a nuanced topicality, Lant's 'new dramatic forms' bear comparison with the renegotiations of the gender system found in Shakespearean pastoral comedy. The prevalence of uniformed women brought with it a reassessment of femininity, just as Rosalind's cross-dressing allows for a contemplation of the construction of gender within the playful space of Arden. In *A Canterbury Tale*, both Chillingbourne and the anarchic, absolute and ludic potential of the blackout recall that forest, the enchanted woods outside Athens, and even Prospero's island. Powell and Pressburger explicitly call for a magical quality in the village's atmosphere in their shooting script: 'We would like to emphasize here, particularly to Alfred Junge and Erwin Hillier, that the Railway Station and Chillingbourne village at night are only described this prosaically because, in daylight, that is what they really are. But at night they loom, awful and mysterious, full of strange shapes, stranger sounds, menacing shadows and hard corners.' Their note to the film's designer and cinematographer indicates that the 'magical' quality of the film is to be registered visually, primarily through the lighting code, while comparisons which are to be made between Colpeper and Puck (both Shakespeare's and, more specifically, Rudyard Kipling's) confirm the cultural tradition to which the film belongs. Of course, the terms with which they describe this awful mysterious magic are far from delightful. The name of the village, 'Chilling-bourne', illustrates the qualified nature of this magic space: despite the welcome it grants its visitors, it is a 'cold domain'. It is no Paradise Regained.

Arcadia has often been imagined as a place of licence, contrasting with the moral hypocrisy of the court. Here, Colpeper strives to keep Chillingbourne a cradle of decency. Moral degeneracy is associated with the chaos of the modern city, and this licence is logically something the influx of unattached soldiers to Chillingbourne threatens to bring, and which Colpeper's puritanical campaign has tried to prevent. Here, Colpeper differs from previously wanton incarnations of the Puck/Pan character. Ludic spaces have often signified uncontrolled sexual desire. The alternative worlds which Gainsborough Studios throw together for their costume melodrama series turn the past into a fundamentally sexual fantasy. What motivates Gainsborough's displacement into pasteboard history is the licence it allows. In fantasies masquerading as history, the past is exoticised, eroticised and allegorised. *A Canterbury Tale* clearly differs, because, being more governed by the prevailing rhetoric of wartime, erotic energies are re-directed towards the war effort, where public achievement is incompatible with private (sexual) satisfaction. In *A Canterbury Tale*, sexual expression is displaced or perverted. Alison's holiday with her fiancé is an implicit sexual memory (did she lose her virginity in that caravan in the woods, within sight of that image of fulfilment, Canterbury Cathedral?) but the memory is of a time before the war, and her longings for her fiancé are now transformed into a heady sense of oneness with Chillingbourne's natural landscapes and with the past it represents. We are left, then, with the behaviour of the Glueman and a few risqué recollections of casual encounters from soldiers and land army girls. Governed by the war ethic, chance sexual liaisons seized in the upheavals of the conflict are denounced. So while Colpeper's Glueman campaign is a lunatic extreme, one which certainly undermines the legitimacy of his apparently feudal power base, the film holds back from censuring the ideals he struggles to impart. The *carpe diem* indulgences of Gainsborough find no place in frigid Chillingbourne.

This Arcadia is staunchly patriarchal and, in this sense, the film is deeply reactionary: its support of continuity and tradition manifests itself through an obsession with patrilinearity. In the character of Colpeper, the film seems to admit that a deep misogyny is implanted within the national male psyche (paradoxically, Colpeper, the local embodiment of the Law, is also – if we allow a perverted sexual motivation to his glue-throwing fixation – a libidinal figure, a warped eruption of unconscious drives normally kept repressed). His opinion of women is certainly striking. His approval of the ducking-stool, his curiously rationalised Glueman campaign and his refusal to accept Alison on his farm all point to a paranoid horror of women. Patriarchy is strengthened by the film's commitment to repeating the assumptions of male succession: Horton is proud that his father and his father's father were blacksmiths; Bob is a 'Johnson of Johnson County', and he eagerly anticipates a future son; a plaque outside the village lecture hall states: 'Colpeper Institute 1886. Ceded to the Borough of Chillingbourne by the former owner James Colpeper, J.P.' Colpeper, too, perpetuates a tradition of masculine inheritance. In his lecture, he talks only of a fascination with the 'father's house', and the tower of Canterbury Cathedral can be read as an architectural expression of phallic supremacy. History is on Colpeper's side.

Yet Alison's has a strong-willed nature. She forms a strong platonic friendship with Bob, and shows her readiness to understand the importance of the past. The warm force of these characteristics brings Colpeper to apologise for his misplaced attitude. When Alison tells him it is a pity he had not simply invited the local girls to his lectures, he implicitly admits his error. Ambiguously, it is unclear whether Colpeper is redeemed: his crimes go unpunished but he receives no 'blessing' himself (although he is last seen entering the cathedral to do penance and seek forgiveness). In part, he exists outside the 'natural' world of the film, a supernatural incarnation of Puck. As such he transcends the mortal sphere of Alison, Bob and Peter. Yet, as a final endorsement of the restorative power of the film, its penultimate shot, played over the final credits, shows hordes of couples – men and women – entering the village lecture hall together. Colpeper has learned some of the value of equality.

What remains constant in the tradition of the pastoral, though, is the imagining of another place of possibility, a heavenly playground, where damaged individuals may be healed (apparently miraculously), in which the deficiencies of the present may be overcome, in which desire may be staged. Hence the individual pilgrims have their own sense of disappointment and damage, while at a national level, a social fracture is mapped out in the division the film draws between Chillingbourne and London. The crisis is summarised by Alison: 'Why should people who love the country have to live in big cities? Something is wrong.' It is a simplistic dilemma, but is one on which the film depends. As long ago as 1887, the sociologist Ferdinand Tonnies singled out two distinct forms of opposing social organisations, the 'Gemeinschaft' (community) and the more modern 'Gesellschaft' (society). Significantly, Tonnies' paean for the lost innocence of the

Gemeinschaft did not capture the imagination until the years after the havoc of the First World War. The Gemeinschaft is a knitted, organically integrated social unit, dependent upon oral exchange and mutual interests. The Gesellschaft is an atomised society, composed of individual interests, commercial contracts and loose connections. Tonnies maintains that the historical development from Gemeinschaft to Gesellschaft is a fated transition towards utilitarianism, alienation and goal-oriented behaviour. Chillingbourne is a model of tightly knit human relations, founded upon feudal structures, with Colpeper as its local squire. It is entirely consistent, then, that the villagers get their news at six o'clock when the pub opens, that Woodcock should presume that Alison must know the Lord Mayor of London on the same basis that he knows the local magistrate, and that Colpeper should have heard, through a reliable village grapevine, that the salvage boy's father has lumbago.

Tonnies goes on to distinguish between two distinct mindsets which are associated with his two forms of social organisation: the 'Wesenwille' (a natural, impulsive or 'inspired' will), which corresponds with the relations associated with the Gemeinschaft, and the 'Kurwille' (an unspontaneous, intellectual and pragmatic will), which depends upon rationality and prudence and is tied to the economically developed conditions of the Gesellschaft. The two ways of thinking are associated with contrasting modes of production: the Wesenwille stresses the importance of craftsmanship ('the means'), whereas the Kurwille focuses on factory production and the 'ends', the fragmented division of labour and the receipt of the pay-packet. The mystical nature of *A Canterbury Tale*, and much of the Romanticism in the Archers' canon, belongs to the Gemeinschaft and to the impulsive quirks of the Wesenwille. They explore the 'vocational' and the irrational: the creative artists of *The Red Shoes* (1948), the Order of St Faith in *Black Narcissus* (1947), the inspired teacher in *A Canterbury Tale*, even the messianic Nazi in *49th Parallel* (1941). They resist rationalisation in *A Matter of Life and Death* and *The Small Back Room*. In *Blimp*, the wartime expediency of the Kurwille is advanced, although however much it wants to endorse Spud's pragmatic drive, realistic behaviour and goal-oriented determinism, and to dispel the attitudes of the old world order based on good manners, etiquette and form, it can only do so reluctantly. As a piece of wartime propaganda, it expresses a modern approach to war, but its sadness at the loss (or temporary retirement) of Candy's values is palpable in its sentimental attachment to the old man. Its Old Tory bones are dressed in conveniently up-to-date attire.

Tonnies views the development from Gemeinschaft to Gesellschaft as an inescapable historical transition. He denounces nostalgia as regressive, and urges a modern surrender to the inevitable. Nostalgia often expresses itself in an idealised and unrealistic desire to return to the organicity of Gemeinschaft and *A Canterbury Tale* seems reluctant to answer Tonnies' call to embrace modernity. Instead, it is ideologically dedicated to the encouragement of a shared sense of national identity, based upon values which pre-date the urban, industrialised structure of modern society. It craves a cosy re-imagination of half-timbered Englishness. The emphasis given to childhood in *A Canterbury Tale* strengthens a nostalgic affinity between infancy and Arcadia. The relationship between wide-eyed, innocent Bob and the village children (with their riotous mock-battle) is a reminder that the pastoral retreats into what is essentially a playful space.

It is the urbane Peter who remains most immune to the spirit of the village. Peter the Londoner and Bob from Oregon are the antithesis of each other, as their inverted sergeant's stripes neatly signify. A metropolitan figure, Peter admits that he had not even noticed the existence of the countryside before the war, although he has enjoyed the air in Hyde Park,

4. Ludic spaces: Sgt John Sweet and village children find pastoral release in *A Canterbury Tale*. (BFI Stills, © Carlton International Media Ltd)

suggesting that at an unconscious level he possesses the soul to render him ultimately susceptible to the film's charms. While Alison's connection with the Kentish landscape, with the Pilgrim's Road and her memories of her fiancé, are all vague expressions of longing, for Peter such longings are expressed through his artistry, in his long-harboured wish to play a church organ. Peter's destructive platoon of Bren-carriers setting out to 'capture' Alison with her horse and cart demonstrates his cavalier disregard for the landscape. The film views all mechanical technology suspiciously. Speed connotes brutality, a lack of perception and false values. This is in keeping with its romantic reification of the past and its endorsement of organic materials, ancient crafts, workshops and farming, most clearly evidenced in the Hortons' blacksmith and timber yard. Characteristically, Colpeper has an aversion to modern machines: although he uses his slide projector, he is unable to make it work himself; and he gently criticises Bob for his love of cinema. This nostalgia for a pre-industrial time can be traced to a distinctively Victorian cultural counter-current: such medievalism is, after all, a defining characteristic of William Morris's Arts and Crafts Movement. Old Horton is part of a celebration of working yeomanry which ranges from Wordsworth's Michael, through Adam Bede to Gabriel Oak. Old Horton's small-mindedness is initially mocked, and he is caught out by Alison's more enlightened mentality, but their failure to communicate is an indictment of the unnatural polarisation of a population into dichotomised urban and rural spheres, rather than as an attack on Horton's own values – for Bob is able to talk with the old man, who is shown to be both sympathetic and generous to him. Bob (whose background in lumber and love of the landscape connects him to the Kentish locals through a shared rural vocabulary which ignores national boundaries) is able to assimilate himself most easily with the village community. His opposition to Peter is not, therefore, a matter of national geography. While the values which the film champions are allied with Englishness, through Bob they are internationalised, and naturalised, and are offered as an implicit alternative to the constructed 'artificiality' of an ideology such as Nazism. Although Nazism itself relied heavily on its own 'Volkish' ideology and romanticised its own rural characteristics, in Britain Germany was perceived as an urban dystopia. Martin Wiener notes this simple distinction: 'Whereas Nazi Germany was being portrayed as an industrial society run amok, England was seen as just the opposite: humanely old fashioned and essentially rural, the world of Mrs Miniver and P.G. Wodehouse. Consequently the war was seen as a test of the new world versus the old.'[15]

Alison dramatises most fully the polarisation between rural and urban lifestyles. She and Prue, who takes her on as a farm hand, condemn urban existence as dispiriting and unsatisfying: they speak of the city environment as 'a long street and every house a different kind of sadness in it', and Prue's failure to marry is directly attributed to the division between town and country (this damnation of urban life closely echoes George Orwell's *Coming up for Air*, another tale of pastoral retreat first published in 1939, whose hero George sees his street as 'a prison with cells all in a row, a line of semi-detached torture chambers'). Notably, Alison's surname – she is a 'Smith' – does more than cast her as an Everywoman: it betokens a family pedigree of pre-mechanised craftsmanship which connects her unconsciously with the Hortons, even though she feels she has no rapport with them as a result of generations of divergence. Yet, working in a department store, she has at least been able to imagine her picnic baskets in use and her deck-chairs in beautiful gardens: a suburban diminution of the pastoral urge. With the passing references to Alison's off-screen London store, the film gestures towards a debased consumerist economy. Remaining unseen, this world lacks vitality, and while Alison's shop-floor longings for the country are to be applauded within the film's rhetoric, the commodification of the pastoral she refers to is clearly another instance of the film's rejection of the capitalist system. Alison's response to Horton's ridicule of her ignorance of the wheelwright's craft indicates that enforced interaction between city-dwellers and villagers is in the national interest. The Women's Land Army therefore realises the conditions for ideological renewal which the film seeks to establish. Fragmentation is diagnosed; unity prescribed. Through Alison, the film strives to cement the nation together. While Colpeper grabs the opportunity, when soldiers are barracked nearby, to instruct these town-dwellers about 'their' rustic heritage, Alison similarly succeeds in healing the neurotically separated gender division which the magistrate has worked to perpetuate. The goal, as with *Blimp*, is the creation of the nation as a working unit.

CONNECTING WITH KIPLING

Implicit in the phrase 'Why We Fight' is the need to remember, to meditate upon the latent potential and validity of a cultural heritage and, according to Powell, the specific purpose of *A Canterbury Tale* was to explain 'to the Americans, and to our own people, the spiritual values and the traditions we were fighting for'.¹⁶ Rudyard Kipling's poem 'Recessional' (1897) expresses a similar anxiety, warning against the self-satisfied 'frantic boast and foolish word' and anticipating the decline of the Empire: 'Lo, all our pomp of yesterday / Is one with Nineveh and Tyre! / Judge of the Nations, spare us yet, / Lest we forget – lest we forget!' There is an important link between *A Canterbury Tale* and Kipling's later writings. The film's nostalgic ruralism corresponds with the political sentiments expressed in these works (notably *Puck of Pook's Hill*, *Rewards and Fairies* and some of the stories in *Actions and Reactions*, particularly 'An Habitation Enforced'). Ian Christie notes the affinity Powell felt with Kipling[17] and Powell himself recollects a childhood influenced by 'Edgar Wallace, Rudyard Kipling, Rider Haggard and other prolific writers of romance and adventure'.[18] The significance of the connection goes beyond a superficial parallel between the magus-like Colpeper and Kipling's Puck.

Kipling's patriotic agenda and his recourse to domestic evocations of Englishness, particularly after he returned to England to live at Batemans in September 1902, resurface forty years on in the Archers' film. The fringe of the British Empire, to the mythology of which Kipling had contributed enormously, carried a similar symbolic value as the American frontier for the USA. It signified a place where the character of the nation's youth could be tested, the unknown conquered and masculinity proved. To this degree then, imperial literature, the American Western, and indeed the 'How We Fight' battle film fulfil comparable, 'heroic' functions. In the Edwardian era, though, anxiety regarding internal weaknesses, such as the condition of the poor, and a suspicion of urban degeneracy, brought a lack of confidence in the reviving power of the frontier, and led to an ideological recolonisation of the English countryside to bolster the Empire from within. With Kipling's resettlement, as David Trotter has illustrated, 'the South of England replaces the Punjab as the scene for rites of passage which disclose and sustain an Imperial spirit'.[19] Just as Kipling moved from the imperial fringe to its hub, so the cinema of the Second World War, conscious of its home audience, concentrates on the Home Front to make films which distil propaganda of rejuvenation while avoiding scenes of overt militarism or jingoism (it is notable how few films made during the war include scenes of combat). Kipling's centripetal dynamic sought to discover the imperial spirit in the history and landscape of the English countryside, on whose soil it had been engendered. In Kipling's poem 'A Charm', which prefaces *Rewards and Fairies*, a magical quality is invested upon the English soil: 'Lay that earth upon thy heart, / And thy sickness shall depart!' His is an outsider's perspective.

In *Puck of Pook's Hill* (which was first published in 1906) Kipling mythologised the establishment of the English race. Two children, Dan and Una, are performing a piece from *A Midsummer Night's Dream* in their local meadow, when they meet and are bewitched by the spirit-guide Puck. Like many of the characters Puck introduces them to, Dan and Una are knitted into the cultural fabric of the nation's history, so Puck's strategy anticipates Colpeper's initiation of Alison, Bob and Peter through the ritual baptism of the glue attack. The voice of Puck magically links past and present, just as Colpeper's lecture series and slide-shows aim to do, while Colpeper's keen walking and mountaineering, and his love of gardening, perpetuate his role as another 'spirit of nature' and, as the film progresses, Colpeper takes on his own mystical qualities. His impassioned lecture regarding his affinity with 'the old England' mesmerises and inspires Alison, an effect which is cued by the musical soundtrack which accompanies a close-up of her face at this moment, as her closed eyes signify her imagination taking flight. She later experiences for herself the mystical communion with the past which Colpeper had encouraged in his talk. She seems to hear the medieval pilgrims on the Old Road, and suddenly she hears a disembodied voice call to her, 'Glorious, isn't it?' before Colpeper rises from the grass to show himself. Like Puck, it seems, Colpeper materialises and vanishes at will. Colpeper promptly assures her that if they lie flat on top of the hill they will not be seen by Bob and Peter. Later, after speaking to Alison at the Canterbury Garage where her caravan is being stored, he disappears without explanation, oddly and apparently magically.

Colpeper's name is meaningful. It is an occupational name for an herbalist or 'spicer', and is connected to astrology or alchemy. Colpeper gnomically assures Alison that 'miracles still happen' and it is allowed that he may be the force behind the 'blessings' which the young protagonists receive. A momentary intensity is created in the close-up which records Alison's reaction to his assurance about miracles – the camera lingers on her face just long enough to hint that belief in magical powers are being entertained. There was a real Nicholas Culpeper (1616–54), a physician and writer on astrology and medicine. He is featured as a fictionalised character in Kipling's 'A Doctor of Medicine' (one of the tales in *Rewards and Fairies*, the sequel to *Puck*), reinforcing the connection between the texts. In this tale, Nicholas Culpeper tells Dan and Una how he diagnosed the cause of the plague and hence saved a village from contamination. Chillingbourne's Colpeper, also working to ameliorate the health of the nation, is his spiritual descendent. In another tale, 'The Young Men at the

Manor' (from *Puck*), the Norman knight Sir Richard is brought within the Saxon community in England and is recruited to take concerted action against their common enemy. The song he sings revolves around the refrain 'England hath taken me', a happily incorporative sentiment which is close to Pressburger's own immigrant experience.

Kipling's short story 'An Habitation Enforced' (in the 1919 collection *Actions and Reactions*) again details the acquisition of nationality through immersion in rural England. An American millionaire, George Chapin, and his wife Sophie retreat to the English countryside, finding in Rocketts Farm 'the genuine England of folklore and song'. Their induction into the local culture is echoed by Bob's in *A Canterbury Tale*, their initial confusion and hatred of tea drinking anticipating the GIs' difficulties with mirrors and telephones. Sophie's judgement is tellingly like Bob's: England is 'Wonderful, but no explanation'. Settling in the area, the Chapin's buy the estate, acquire baronial responsibilities and, after the birth of a baby boy, discover that Sophie's genealogy can be traced back to the village. Their return to Sophie's roots, and the birth of a boy-child, ensure that continuity is restored. In a decisive gesture towards ensuring the longevity of the estate, George agrees that the bridge over the brook should be made of long-lasting oak, rather than larch. The declamation 'By Oak and Ash and Thorn!' figures prominently in *Puck*, and the care of timber, an organic, honest activity, plays a key role in *A Canterbury Tale* ('You can't hurry an elm'). Just as the birth of George and Sophie's child offers a conventional image of hope to conclude 'An Habitation Enforced', so *Puck* culminates in the optimism of the 'Children's Song', an antidote to the cultural degeneration which Kipling felt jeopardised the Empire. Significantly, the closing credits of *A Canterbury Tale* are played over footage of the village boys playing football: although cued by the film's narrative (the ball is the boys' reward for helping Bob), the images of teamwork and childhood also provide the film with a confident resolution and push home its rejuvenating objective. Yet this hope is rooted in the solidity of history and can be read as deeply reactionary. Like *A Canterbury Tale*, Kipling's praise of honest work and yeomanry (Weland's sword in *Puck* is an example of such craftsmanship) marks an evasion of modernity which is symptomatic of contemporary malaise. Kipling's world-view is, in Preben Kaarsholm's words, 'a deeply depressed and neurotic one…of a society where the trend towards anomie and total alienation can only be countered by an authoritarian traditionalism'.[20] Like *A Canterbury Tale*, it is a regression to Gemeinschaft.

The discovery of Roman, Jacobean and Cromwellian objects in the garden at Batemans stimulated Kipling's interest in English history. Both *Puck* and *Rewards and Fairies* feature such relics. They act as concrete symbols of the co-existence of past and present, and as embodiments of cultural memory. In *A Canterbury Tale*, archaeological artefacts are material fragments of the past, and as such they are treated as fetish objects. An intimate affinity exists between a 'Paradise Lost' which is nostalgically yearned for, and a Utopia which is anticipated, but the past, uniquely and obviously, has already existed, and has left real objects which can take on talismanic value. The stone in the Chillingbourne inn and Alison's old coins represent, for her, a personal memory which is painfully associated with bereavement and isolation. They connote her fiancé, who is missing in action, and are tokens of him rather than of a shared cultural heritage. But by declaring her wish to donate the coins to the museum she marks their transition from the private to the public sphere, and her act of generosity, her appropriate 'team spirit', seems to trigger a round of applause from the crowd of onlookers waiting for Colpeper's lecture (the soldiers are actually cheering the repair of the projector, but her act is nevertheless celebrated). The donation confirms her integration within the fabric of the nation. It establishes her shared cultural identity and, by extension, her progress towards redemption.

The symbolic function of the donation also anticipates Alison's reaction to the news of her fiancé's survival. Like the coins, her caravan, where she once holidayed with him, represents a private memory, a fetishised, coveted, useless souvenir. The film never actually advocates the preservation of the past for its own sake: its nostalgia is not elegiac, and the 'history' which it embraces is an expression of cultural vigour. The jacked-up, moth-eaten caravan, like the privately treasured coins, like Miss Havisham's decaying wedding feast in *Great Expectations*, is a ghostly reminder of a dead past, a burdensome inheritance. With the surprise news of her fiancé's survival it can be shaken off. Alison's desperate cry in the caravan, 'I must open the windows!', is echoed by Pip's similar invocation at the end of David Lean's adaptation of *Great Expectations* (1946). Each act endorses the future (a new dawn coded through the influx of light) and, like Googie Withers' destruction of her husband's haunted mirror in the Robert Hamer section of Ealing's *Dead of Night* (1945), it marks an escape from the stranglehold of a destructive and negatively interpreted cultural memory.

MARKS OF RESISTANCE: ANTI-REALISM / REALISM / DOCUMENTARY

At this stage, it might be objected that the very 'quirkiness' of *A Canterbury Tale*, epitomised in the putative narrative of the Glueman's attacks on local girls, sits uncomfortably with Erwin Hillier's Edenic and resonant images of the Kentish Weald. Initial reviews of the film were divided between praise of the cinematography and performances and, at best, a suspicion of the storyline. Ernest Betts in *The Sunday Express* (14 May 1944) calls the film 'brilliant, beautiful but baffling', but finally asks 'Is this film about Anglo American relations, is it a hymn to England, or what?' Similarly, William Whitebait in *The New Statesman* (13 May 1944) finds that although the film 'is as good as a day in the country' he carried away from *A Canterbury Tale* 'an enjoyment that (he) was loath to examine too closely'. It was thus the narrative to which these critics took exception. Critics in the popular and regional papers generally took less exception to the Glueman story, and praised the cinematography.

The film's commitment to an all-embracing national identity might well be seen to be jeopardised by the perversely distancing eccentricities of the plot. Jarring stylistic or narrative oddities surely disrupt the process of ideological reinforcement which is at the heart of mainstream cinema's national agenda, depending as it tends to on processes of identification rather than of estrangement? The irrational aspects are very much in keeping with the film's subscription to the impulses of the Wesenwille. Nevertheless, the overarching ideological thrust of the film ultimately incorporates the paradoxical nature of its narrative, although it cannot do so smoothly. It is not that the film-makers endorse Colpeper's misogynistic glue-throwing campaign. Instead, the narrative drive of the film actively marginalises and in the last instance dismisses as irrelevant the investigations undertaken to expose the magistrate. Our investment is in the irrational, the spiritual or the supernatural (and in matters which are felt emotionally). The film refuses the discipline of rationalism. The plot's initial enigma, the secret of the Glueman's identity, is quickly answered. We are privileged with the early disclosure of Colpeper smiling with self-reproach for 'showing a light' from his courtroom, having failed to secure his blackout in his rush to avoid capture. The quest for knowledge is thus relegated in favour of a quest for 'Truth'; or, put more candidly, Colpeper's sadistic misogyny is disregarded in the interests of discovering and validating his motives. His earlier chauvinism is sanctioned: his ends justify his means and, anyway, he reforms his character. Kevin Macdonald has noted the debt which the curious 'non-plot' of *A Canterbury Tale* owes to G.K. Chesterton's *The Club of Queer Trades*, a collection of what are nominally detective stories, in which apparent crimes are revealed not to be so.[21] There are no direct parallels but, like *A Canterbury Tale*, Chesterton pits ratiocination (embodied in his narrator Rupert Grant's logical need to decipher what to him are inexplicable events) against the mysticism and inspiration of his brother Basil. In parodies of Sherlock Holmes's deductive techniques, Rupert's astonishment at the behaviour of 'madmen' is comically revealed to be naïve when contrasted with Basil's more ready acceptance of the peculiar.

A Canterbury Tale's similar dismissal of detective work is vividly illustrated in the sequence following Colpeper's lecture. Returning to the blacked-out exterior (to the 'plot' of the film), Bob tells his friends about the evidence he has collected regarding the Glueman's identity. They engage a stammering 'village idiot' in awkward conversation, and this undermines the seriousness of Bob's detective work. Held in long shot until the close of the sequence, the 'idiot' is accompanied by a mocking cuckoo call on the soundtrack. This remarkably staged presentation of a clichéd 'type' of villager alienates us by underscoring the artificiality of the film. A further distancing is experienced by the spectator keen enough to spot that the 'idiot' is played by Esmond Knight, who has been seen in a cameo role as the 'Seven Sisters Road' soldier in the scene immediately preceding this one. The sequence signifies an active, narrative irony (or cruelty) which removes us from the lucid immediacy of the picturesque rural footage, particularly as the sequence takes place on an obvious studio set. Douglas McVay argues persuasively that 'the mocking of the yokel…does possess equivocal, vestigially sadistic overtones, like so many aspects of the Powell canon'.[22] For Wordsworth, this isolated, untutored rustic type might have been a Romantic idealisation of stoicism, honest natural passion and mystic wonderment – delineated simply in the language of the 'Common Man'. In another imagined film, he might have been a lovable cameo for Bernard Miles. Clearly, the incongruously injected tone here is one of metropolitan superiority, and its attitude to the 'idiot' an undeniably patrician instance of cavalier authorship.

Like the Glueman plot, the village idiot sequence sits oddly with the film's predominantly effusive representation of Englishness. Significantly, among the three protagonists it is the 'courtly' sophisticate, Peter, who identifies the stammering old man to us as the 'village idiot'. Echoing *As You Like It*, Peter is the melancholy Jacques of the film, out of place in Kent – although unlike Jacques he does not admit to any dissatisfaction with the court. His cynical disdain isolates him in Chillingbourne. He is the most resistant to the curative properties of the countryside. His Sunday afternoon debate with Colpeper, the embodiment of all the idealistic high-mindedness that Peter claims to oppose, is a vivid illustration of this. It is characteristic of the film that it remains equivocal about its representation of the village (just as its name 'Chillingbourne' contradicts its idyllic appearance). While seduced by the Englishness, it retains enough cosmopolitanism to sound a superior and questioning note, and the tone of the village idiot sequence is an instance of this cosmopolitanism. The tension is between an immediate and subjectively felt attachment and a clinical detachment. Esmond Knight's anonymous and extra-diegetic voiceover in the opening 'Prologue' to the film, which is accompanied by extreme long shots of the Kentish scenery and of a passing locomotive, establishes the distanced, objective perspective (it has a documentary feel to it). Elsewhere, Chillingbourne, and Canterbury, remain seductive. The treatment of the 'idiot' – together with the identity of the Glueman – mark a genuine 'faultline', in Alan Sinfield's sense, in that they expose real ideological contradiction.[23] As cases of textual sadism, they critique, through association, the totalitarianism of Chillingbourne's apparently ancient feudal structure. The connection between Colpeper (symbol of continuity) and the Glueman (symbol of misogyny, yes, but more generally of all ideological coercion – and his glue is very much deployed as social cement) is mystified in the darkness of the blackout, and in the last instance the narrative strives to bring the connection to light. The mocking of the 'village idiot' is done in a fashion so artificial as to foreground and admit the authors' own culpable assumption of dubious authority – yet all the while this critical reading of Chillingbourne vies with the genial presentation of sunny village life. The formal discontinuity here is a sign of the exilic, self-conscious optic through which the Garden of England is being viewed. Pressburger himself, as an alien, was in fact denied a temporary permit to visit Kent during the filming. He was kept, literally, at a distance.

The sturdy yeoman (Colpeper seen in his garden), the jolly blacksmith, the matronly landlady, the barman: *A Canterbury Tale* self-consciously uses hackneyed, popular, 'mythical' types like these, and depends on a familiarity with them. If the village represents a fantasised England, they are the dramatis personae of the nation. To this extent, the village idiot sequence is a self-reflexive confession on the film's behalf that it has hitherto relied heavily on 'typical' representations.

The unmediated realism that characterises much of the presentation of Chillingbourne is here undermined, for until this moment many of the images in the film have been remarkably similar to those we might expect from documentary films of the period. There are strong similarities here to the work of Humphrey Jennings, the most romantic and individual of Grierson's disciples, despite the intellectual, left-wing political orthodoxy from which he emerges. While Powell's patrician, country-shires upbringing concurs with what Kevin Macdonald identifies as Pressburger's 'basically old-fashioned Anglican Tory' vision, Jennings' values, and those of Grierson's documentary movement, remain those of democratic socialism.[24] 'Heritage' England is not the sole province of Old Toryism, and nostalgia is as much a part of the left-wing tradition: each places the community above individuals, each has at times reified the past, and each stands in opposition to brands of muscular libertarianism. What unites *A Canterbury Tale* and Jennings' films is their utopianism. Jennings is primarily an urban poet, and Blake is his spiritual forefather, as Jeffrey Richards and Anthony Aldgate have noted.[25] His films *Words for Battle* (1941), *Heart of Britain* (1941) and *Listen to Britain* (1942, co-directed by Stewart McAllister) incorporate evocative footage of blitzed cityscapes – scenes which compare with Powell's shots of bombed-out streets in Canterbury – yet Jennings fuses these images to pictures of conventional, rural landscapes. In *Listen to Britain*, he returns rhythmically to shots of trees and wheat fields, matched to the sound of Spitfires to evoke, through an audio-visual marriage, a synthesised expression of the country united. These ripe harvest images of late summer suggest a national/natural abundance and fecundity in exactly the same way as *A Canterbury Tale* depicts the late August richness of the Garden of England. Each presents the countryside as a ludic space too. *Words for Battle* has footage of presumably evacuated children playing in boats, a sequence which mirrors the mock naval battle in Chillingbourne, and similar games played by Dan and Una in Kipling's *Puck of Pook's Hill*. Yet, critically, Jennings presents a seamless melding of urban and rural experience. The voiceover in *Heart of Britain* harmoniously merges agrarian and industrial worlds by invoking 'the valleys of power and the rivers of industry' over shots of the Pennines and northern English factories. In *A Canterbury Tale*, a rupture between the urban and the rural is diagnosed, and the narrative is driven by the need to resuture the wound.

With its 'travelogue' characteristics and its idealistic drive towards a united national identity, *A Canterbury Tale* borders on the territory of the documentary movement. The affinity is strengthened with the casting of US Sgt John Sweet to play Bob Johnson. While Sweet is clearly an actor, his presence as a genuine American serviceman belongs to the documentary tradition of using real people as types to achieve a representative authenticity, as seen, for example, in Jennings' feature length drama-documentary *Fires Were Started* (1943). The story of a land-army girl similarly reproduces a familiar format in which the contribution played in the war effort by a particular defence service (or military wing) is profiled. Such portraits logically follow 1930s documentaries, such as Cavalcanti's *Coal Face* (1935), which dignify labour and praise the part played by industry in furthering the nation's fortunes. Although the historiography of 'British National Cinema' has rightly set a distance between the Archers and the documentary form, there are key moments of cross-over. *49th Parallel* (1941) and, more obviously '…*one of our aircraft is missing*' (1942) draw on styles and motifs of the documentary-fiction film. In 1941, Powell produced, directed and photographed a five minute documentary short film, *An Airman's Letter to his Mother*. Narrated by John Gielgud, its text is taken from a letter written by a bomber squadron pilot and published posthumously at the request of his station commander, who 'felt that the letter might bring comfort to other mothers, and that everyone in our country would feel proud to read its sentiments which support an average airman in the execution of his present arduous duties'. The letter expresses a patriotic discourse, advancing noble sentiments of duty and sacrifice, praising the Empire's raising of standards of civilisation: it is steeped in typical values of national wartime ideology. The images Powell selects to enrich the text anticipate the territory of *A Canterbury Tale*. The opening shot is of rural English scenery; a postman then delivers the letter to an idyllic country cottage; inside the cottage we see a dog (Powell's own), a traditional image of loyalty, devotion and companionship. As Gielgud's voice narrates the airman's thoughts, the camera pans slowly around the room, scanning over the airman's belongings. Pictures of T.E. Lawrence, Scott and Nelson are picked out, masculine heroes of Empire and of romantic adventure. Among the books scattered around the room are *Scott's Last Expedition*, *The Pilot's Book of Everest*, *Explorers All*, the collected poems of John Masefield and guidebooks of England. Colpeper's study is strewn with similar guidebooks, walking and mountaineering material, and books on gardening (one entitled *Soil and Sense*). As the airman's letter concludes, the images dissolve to the window, to trees and then to clouds and, as if Powell could not resist injecting a characteristically unrealistic, animated cinematic effect, as the 'Last Post' is heard on the soundtrack the clouds transform themselves into the RAF's winged insignia.

A quizzically guarded interaction with the documentary form is also seen in Powell and Pressburger's wartime 'documentary'-style two-reeler, *The*

Volunteer (1943), starring Ralph Richardson (nominally playing himself) and Pat McGrath as his dresser Fred. Made by the Archers for the Ministry of Information, it is dedicated to the Fleet Air Arm, in keeping with the wartime recruitment documentary style. What marks the film out is its odd mixture of theatricality within the documentary format. There are realistic justifications for this, of course. The film covers Richardson's own acting career. Furthermore, the metamorphosis which military training brings to Fred is the familiar topic of propaganda of this kind, stressing the raw recruit's increasing teamwork, efficiency and acquisition of skills. However, the film also displays Powell and Pressburger's fascination with a 'magic' which is part of Richardson's theatricality but which is also characteristic of their fiction film aesthetic. A marked gap between reality and appearance is coded into the film with the opening footage of Richardson 'blacking up' to play Othello, while the shift into another realm of make-believe is paralleled by the journey into the unknown instigated by the outbreak of war. 'It's the end of one world and the beginning of another,' Richardson reflects. *The Volunteer*'s status as film is scored into its text with a cut to Denham studios. Here the national cinema's response to war is satirised ('At the outbreak of war actors dived into historical costumes and declaimed powerful speeches about the wooden walls of England'), while Richardson points out the unrealistic nature of the medium: 'Odd things happen in film studios: trees blossom in October; you see daffodils and iris on the tables in restaurants.' Nevertheless, mainly through location footage, a paradoxical commitment to documentary realism persists. As Fred is incorporated into his regiment, his individuality is effaced and a group identity is forged. Richardson, looking for Fred, later shouts out, 'There he is! Two thousand of him!' A tracking shot of an audience of uniformed men and women gathered to watch a troop company concert is very much in the style of Jennings' wartime work, and of Ealing Studios' classically group-oriented ethos. However, Powell and Pressburger equivocate between the realistic demands of the genre and their personal attachment to an illusionist cinema rooted in fantasy: back-stage, as Richardson corrects Fred's make-up, a close-up dissolve magically shows Fred's theatrical transformation into character before his performance. This suggests that, for Powell and Pressburger, fantasy is something which can deal with social commitment and political interaction (it is not divorced from reality, as left-wing ideologues might have argued). In *The Volunteer*'s whimsical interplay between two distinct cinematic languages, the ideological division between the film-makers' characteristically romantic outlook and the more sober discourse of 'national cinema' is clearly exposed. The gentle humour and eccentricity of Richardson's persona eliminates the potential friction between the two.

Pressburger's script allows for the possibility of real magic without abandoning the expected language of realism. Richardson's astonishment at Fred's fully trained efficiency on his ship causes him to joke, 'I'd call it a miracle,' to which Fred replies, ''Appens every day here, sir!' Later, a film within the film interrogates links between cinema, propaganda and truth. We see cans of film footage being brought ashore, and this newsreel footage (of Fred's regiment in Algiers and then of his ship in action) is projected to the troops within *The Volunteer*: silent location footage of Algiers harbour is seen within the film, although the status of this 'interior narrative' is manipulated. It is, for example, accompanied by Allan Gray's music soundtrack from the 'frame' narrative. At times the apparatus of the makeshift cinema is foregrounded, while at others we are shown the newsreel in an unmediated fashion, no longer clearly 'bracketed' by the text of *The Volunteer*. Significantly, the frame narrative is dispensed with as the newsreel footage moves on to cover action footage of the ship at war, dramatically magnifying the immediacy and the excitement of the sequence and, in one moment of cinema vérité, the newsreel camera is obviously dropped. The truth status of these scenes is qualified once more in the final sequence when Michael Powell makes his own appearance in the film. In a crowd outside Buckingham Palace, where Richardson and his daughter see Fred being decorated, Powell boldly appears with his camera and takes a photograph, like any other London tourist. The film cuts to a shot of Powell's photograph of Richardson and Fred, placed as a souvenir on Fred's mantelpiece. Powell's presence plays with the objectivity of realist film-making. The multiple levels of cinematic articulation give the film a sophisticated double characteristic. It is the documentary of the Fleet Air Arm which it claims to be; it is also a self-conscious, self-critical exploration of the ways in which cinematic meaning is accrued.

In *A Canterbury Tale*, the same dialogue with the documentary form is at work. Despite the presence of realistic footage, the style of the film shifts to interrogate modes of representation and to make comments about cinema itself. By exploiting properties of light and darkness, it self-reflexively points to connections between the cinematic apparatus itself and the desire of its protagonists. The extended blackout sequences and the transition to the light of Canterbury have a cinematically symbolic significance and, in Colpeper's lecture, where his rhetoric casts its imaginative spell upon Alison, the atmosphere is notably cinema-like. Colpeper criticises Bob's cinephilia, suggesting it would be a pity if all Bob saw in England were movies. Later, Mickey is shown with his cine-camera in Canterbury, again foregrounding the cinematic machinery in the film's text. Elsewhere in the film, Powell and Pressburger celebrate the properties of film. Positively, Colpeper uses his slide-projector educationally, and silhouetted in its beam he is given a mystical property, as befits the idealistic form of cinema he embodies. There is an inconsistency then: on the one hand, Powell and Pressburger are at pains to say 'it's only a film', and their spokesman Colpeper is urging real, curious, touristic, enlightened encounters with landscape and history; on the other, they are as entranced as we are by their imagery.

The opening 'Prologue' sequence of *A Canterbury Tale* blatantly subverts the stylistic properties of documentary realism. Commencing with shots of older texts (a manuscript, a medieval map, a woodcut print of Chaucer's pilgrims), the 'Prologue' then presents a realistic observation of rural Kentish locations, without any medieval markers, yet the scene is shifted back some six centuries to show Chaucer's pilgrims on their way to Canterbury, forsaking the contemporaneity of documentary-style locations. A temporal elision is then made by the well-known match-cut from a falcon to a Spitfire, and from a pilgrim to a soldier, played by the same actor. In itself, this cut exposes the spurious veracity of real location footage. Given that the film questions the nature of 'historical progress' (like *Blimp*, where time is manipulated through a flashback), it is worth pausing to consider the implications of this flamboyant piece of editing. To match the falcon with the Spitfire is to suggest that time is something which can be made magically pliable and is to comment reflexively upon the film medium's very existence in time: without devices such as the split screen or the dissolve, events cannot be shown concurrently; and without clearly coded punctuation demarcating a flashback events can generally be assumed to take place in a strict chronological order. There is thus an implicitly logical linearity to 'classical' cinema. *A Canterbury Tale*'s match-cut functions as a blatant underscoring of narrative/cinematic technique, a naked piece of authorial manipulation which unexpectedly disturbs the viewer's sense of unimpeded engagement with the smooth-flowing text.

Set against the nature of popular mainstream cinema with its 'invisible' continuity editing, Powell and Pressburger's presentation of history is here marked by discontinuities and accelerations. By incorporating their own authorial status so visibly, they mark their text's engagement in an always contemporary discourse with their current audience, and this problematises the objectivity and factuality of the 'history' they seem to present. At the same time, they still celebrate the 'spectacular' nature of cinema (*Blimp*, as we have seen, similarly pirouettes its way through English history). A progressive reading of this disruption of classical linearity nevertheless runs up against a competing conservatism. The falcon-Spitfire montage effect is startling, but it suggests a continuity as well as a disjuncture, conservatively binding past to present in a deeply reactionary way. It is not just that a causal relationship is offered, with the former event leading tidily to the latter (although an historical continuum is certainly suggested). Rather, the slick visual trick achieves a time-bending synthesis between medieval feudal society and the RAF, between then and now, between the spirituality of the Chaucerian pilgrimage and the war effort. At a stylistic level, the film entertains an oddity which criticises empirical certainties, it applauds irrationality, and it endorses the 'magic' potential of the pastoral. It creates an anti-rational climate in which the drive towards ideal conclusions is more readily facilitated.

WE'RE OFF TO SEE THE WIZARD!

The social and psychological divisions in *A Canterbury Tale* are resolved with the ideal optimism of a fairy-tale. As Colpeper learns to accept that his chauvinistic attitude towards Alison is unjustified, an awakened recognition of the countryside brings recuperation and reorientation to the film's three modern pilgrims, and their miraculous epiphanies become a source of wider invigoration to the nation at large. The film ends on an unashamedly utopian note. Alison learns that her fiancé has been found in Gibraltar; Bob receives the redirected letters he has been hoping for from his girl; and Peter, on the verge of joining his platoon on active service, is given the opportunity to play to his comrades on the cathedral organ. Bach's 'Toccata' bursts onto the soundtrack, and Bob, gazing in awe at the cathedral, is able to meld its long history with his own by recognising that his 'own Pa built the first church in Johnson county'. With their spiritual crises overcome through the operation of quasi-divine forces, they are brought together in the climactic cathedral service, where the utopianism compares well with the Blakean vision underpinning Humphrey Jennings' work. Where Jennings' *Listen to Britain* closes on a rendition of 'Rule Britannia' to a montage of factories, wheat fields and clouds, *A Canterbury Tale* concludes with a triumphant rendition of 'Onward Christian Soldiers' and the peal of the cathedral bells. *Blimp* similarly closes in a major key once its crises are resolved – there we hear Spud's off-screen army approaching to an accompanying military march; in *A Canterbury Tale* we are shown the platoon marching through Canterbury's packed streets. Like *Listen to Britain*, *A Canterbury Tale* creates an air of mystical religiosity.

The anticipation of a New Jerusalem in the closing reel of *A Canterbury Tale* matches its nostalgic affirmation of feudal values. The idealised future it foresees is founded upon an idealised past. Canterbury Cathedral denotes continuity and is a relic of pre-capitalist society. Yet at key moments in the text, underscored by Allan Gray's pulsating choral refrain on the soundtrack, this historical symbol is elevated, to become a sign of transcendence. While 'nostalgia' may express nothing more than a discontent with modernity, in its original meaning it expresses homesickness, a want of plenitude and a desire to remystify the world. Significantly, despite the ecclesiastical imagery in *A Canterbury Tale*, its transcendent regime is not couched purely in Christian terms. The agent of redemption, Colpeper, has a quasi-mystical faith but, significantly, we do not see him at the village church service, although he does join the cathedral service in the closing moments of the film. The values Colpeper champions are more pantheistic; and his 'powers' are supernatural. If the critical disquiet meted out to the film is evidence of its apparently awkward and morally problematical apology for Colpeper's nocturnal terrorism (and for the frank implausibility of the Glueman plot), it is perhaps also an indication of some embarrassment felt at the film's appeal to what are essentially utopian and archly romantic absolutes, exceeding even the idealism of Jennings' work, where the 'spiritual' dimension is still rooted in the material certainties of cinematic realism. It is an aesthetic more akin to the promise of the American Dream than it is to conservative English culture.

In fact, *A Canterbury Tale* operates as an Anglicisation of that parable of Americana, *The Wizard of Oz* (Victor Fleming, 1939, US). Just as Clive Candy becomes 'the Wiz' in *Blimp*, so the Canterbury pilgrims mirror the dream-exiles from Kansas, and the unidentified Glueman takes the place of the Wicked Witch (in a scene missing from the released film but present in the unpublished shooting script, early rumours of the Glueman's capture cause soldiers in their barracks to burst into a song reminiscent of the Munchkins' 'Ding dong the witch is dead'). Canterbury holds all the mystical promise of the 'Emerald City', and the blessings conferred upon Dorothy and her companions compare with those seemingly granted by Colpeper. Dorothy's wish, of course, is to find a way home, and 'home' is an acutely sensitive idea for Powell and Pressburger. The magistrate, Colpeper, is an amalgam of both the good and bad witch, and the Wizard himself. *The Wizard of Oz* informs other Powell and Pressburger films. This may derive from the structural similarities with Shakespearean pastoral comedy: as has already been mentioned, plays such as *A Midsummer Night's Dream* and *As You Like It* serve as a rough model for many Archers productions, while the Land of Oz shares the dream-like and magic potential of Shakespeare's enchanted forests. Later, Vicky's 'red shoes' in some ways repeat the function of Dorothy's ruby slippers. Lermontov is called a 'magician', and his isolation, his chaste, yet quasi-romantic relationship with a manipulated heroine and his intense religiosity cast him as a descendent of Colpeper. The first shot of Colpeper in the court-room establishes his authority and sets his distance from the community, while the last shot of him alone in the entrance to Canterbury Cathedral, as Alison walks past in the crowd with her fiancé's father, anticipates the last shot of Lermontov, alone in his box. That Colpeper ultimately walks with the flow of the crowd into Canterbury Cathedral indicates this film's greater commitment to the all-embracing aesthetic of inclusivity which characterises a dominant strand of wartime British cinema.

The concluding images of *A Canterbury Tale* formally return the film to the medieval ambience of its 'Prologue'. To the celebratory peal of cathedral bells and the return of the 'mystical', heavenly, choral refrain, a series of increasingly distant long shots of the cathedral returns the spectator to the bend in the Old Road. Church bells had been silenced earlier in the war, to be used only in the event of invasion or to signify the end of hostilities. They had rung out in 1942 after El Alamein, and by 1944 were regularly heard again (*A Canterbury Tale* shows the village church bells being rung as usual). The peal here can still be taken to have a particularly loaded significance. The series of dissolves from the cathedral service, up through the cathedral itself to its ringing bells, and then to the long shot from the Pilgrims Road, marks a departure from the specific, 'realistic' timeframe of the narrative. It precisely recalls the opening shots of the film, temporally unrooted and dream-like. The image of pilgrimage is a metaphor for optimism, commitment and common purpose, and it retains its divine dimension. The spell of enchantment which the climactic shot of the celestial city of Canterbury casts is blatant exploitation of the audience's appetite for fulfilled fantasy. It is the viewing subject's desire which finally pushes *A Canterbury Tale* into its utopian regime. Over the closing credits, we see men and women going together to Colpeper's lectures, while in the very last shot, played through to the film's last second, is the shot of village children playing football, a return to ordinary, everyday village life which literally 'contains' the transcendentally signified cathedral-spirit. The film's mysticism and medievalism are made immediately relevant, and the final image of childhood proves the film's commitment to the future as well as its fondness for the past.

KILORAN

If their English pastoral deals with sex through displacements and sublimations, Powell and Pressburger's next film, the Scottish pastoral *I Know Where I'm Going!* is more warmly erotic. Released in December 1945, a matter of months after the end of the war, and set in the Western Isles, it is unique among their collaborations as the only female-centred film to chronicle a successful heterosexual union. *A Canterbury Tale* is not utterly sexless, for Alison remembers her holiday with her fiancé, and is promised a reunion with him in the closing reel, but we never see Alison's fiancé, and the film does not revolve around her romance with him. It expresses a note of anxiety, familiar in wartime, about the damaging effects of the conflict on stable relationships. Wartime is central to the film: it is set in Kent (that most vulnerable of English counties) and, in keeping with dominant wartime discourse, it tends to frown on casual sexual liaisons. The war is still present in *IKWIG* (as the film is known), and its romance between Joan Webster (Wendy Hiller) and Torquil MacNeil (Roger Livesey) is pivotal. Its romantic male lead is on leave from the Navy, but otherwise, as its heroine points out, in the Hebrides 'the war's a million miles away'. After his early success with *The Edge of the World* (1937), Powell kept a career-long fascination with Scotland's romantic history. He was interested in the Jacobite Rebellion and longed to make a film about Bonnie Prince Charlie, starring David Niven. He also noted his ideas for a life of Robert Burns. In *IKWIG*, 'older' values occluded by the war are explored, as in the previous film, but the conflict itself is kept at arms' length. Later, *A Matter of Life and Death* guarantees a long marriage to Peter and June, and Sammy returns home to Susan in *The Small Back Room,* but neither of these films concentrates on women, and their positive resolutions denote male success. *IKWIG* tells Joan's story.

Joan is a 'bright young thing', an urban, business-suited materialist, thoroughly modern, with a taste for fashionable, conspicuous expenditure.

Her father is a bank manager and she is engaged to her boss, a much older man whom she whimsically refers to as 'Consolidated Chemical Industries'. With a sense of fairy-tale, she undertakes a quest to claim her suitor. She travels north to Scotland for her wedding, but fog prevents her from crossing to Kiloran, the island where Robert has rented property. Waylaid on the island of Mull, she meets Torquil, who is also trying to get to Kiloran. She prays for wind to shift the fog, and inadvertently summons a storm which keeps her from Robert. She learns of a local curse which prevents any lairds of Kiloran from entering the mysterious ruined Moy Castle, the ancient home of the MacLeans. As she waits for a lull, she meets Catriona Potts (Pamela Brown), an old friend of Torquil's, who offers her hospitality at Erraig House. Catriona is one of the last of the MacLeans: the rest are either dead or have emigrated to New Zealand. During her stay on the island Joan develops feelings for Torquil. Romance is in the air when they attend a local ceilidh. Tempted from her vows to Robert, she uses her wealth to buy the help of a young local, Kenny, to take her away from Torquil and to Kiloran, despite a fierce storm and the dangers of Corryvreckan, a lethal whirlpool (which is also the subject of an ancient legend). Torquil is unable to stop her and so he attempts the crossing with her. He manages to save the boat but the crossing is unsuccessful and they limp back to Mull, having faced imminent death in the waters of the whirlpool. They part with a kiss, and Torquil – the present laird of Kiloran – enters Moy Castle. He finds the curse carved in the castle walls. Joan returns to him and the legend is revealed. Kiloran will never leave the castle a free man, for 'he shall be chained to a woman till the end of his days and shall die in his chains'.

Structurally, *IKWIG* anticipates *The Red Shoes* and *Gone to Earth*. Joan, like Vicky and Hazel, is torn between two men. In *Gone to Earth*, Victorian notions of respectability polarise Hazel's world into saints and sinners with catastrophic results. For Hazel, social rigidity and natural wildness are opposing forces. Geography is everything. Hazel is a border-dweller, and both sides of the frontier stake their claim on her. English respectability and a strict father contend with Welsh magic and a dead gypsy mother. The spirit of the place is riven, and Hazel is torn apart by the division. Separations between 'Art' and 'Life', or 'work' and 'home' take a similar toll in *The Red Shoes*. In *IKWIG*, as Joan dreams her way northwards in a train's sleeper cabin, a voiceover tells her, 'Next station Gretna Green. You're over the border now.' Once in Scotland, the comic, mocking tone of the film's opening sequence is left behind. Even the opening credit sequence, which parodies government documentaries and has a commercial spirit, served to mock Joan's materialism. That tone is left behind and is replaced by one of enchantment. The reason for Joan's happy resolution is that she is entirely enveloped in the remote Hebridean atmosphere, and the 'spirit of place' decrees it: her union with Torquil is foretold by local legend. Nature and fate determine that they should be together, and the mythological folk culture of the Western Isles is in harmony with them. Fog and wind prevent Joan from crossing from Mull to Kiloran, and Torquil's first real declaration of love to Joan comes in the form of a local folk-song, 'You're the maid for me'. She speaks to Robert on the radio (a piece of modern equipment which seems out of place), but Corryvreckan stops her from seeing him. Powell's scouting for locations is put to good use: a roadside telephone box is made nearly useless because of the roar of a waterfall right behind it, a neat symbolic image for the film's theme of imposed modernity overwhelmed by local nature.

This is a sister-film to *A Canterbury Tale*. Both films were shot by Erwin Hillier, a cinematographer with a good eye for landscape and light, put to good use here to create striking, dramatic silhouettes and vividly stormy areas of light and dark – an Expressionist style which could be traced back to his early career in Germany. Both films use music by Allan Gray. Brief refrains from the earlier film are heard in *IKWIG* in the Western Isles Hotel, and the scores for both films feature disembodied choral refrains (looking forward to Brian Easdale's score for *Black Narcissus*). Stylistically, *IKWIG* also echoes *A Canterbury Tale* in being self-conscious about its representation of Scotland. Pam Cook notes the 'rolling tartan hills' which feature in Joan's dream as she heads north on the train, and sees the film, in part, to be a deliberate 'pastiche of images'.[26] This repeats *A Canterbury Tale*'s blurred distinctions between reality and fantasy, with its near-ironic use of stereotypes like the 'village idiot'. Scotland is likewise a hazy confusion of location footage, studio footage, myth, fairy-story and real, psychological drama. Like Chillingbourne, Mull here is alluring and dangerous, real and false, a spectacle *and* an illusion-like cinema. Rear projections, special effects, lighting, and the use of Alfred Junge's solidly designed studio spaces to deputise for real locations, combine to sustain an image of Scotland, and on location a double was used for Roger Livesey, who was appearing in a play in London during the shoot and was unable to be in Scotland. 'Real Scotland' is just within the film's reach, but it is its re-creation which makes the viewer long for its distant reality.

Ideologically, *IKWIG* repeats the earlier film's anti-materialism. Torquil embodies a feudal value system which opposes capital, and the islanders are not poor, they just 'have no money'. Torquil is referred to as 'Kiloran', fusing the man and his island home together through his ancient title. Joan's fiancé Robert is a millionaire industrialist living on Kiloran, having rented the estate from Torquil. He is said to be building a swimming pool, although there is the sea to swim in. He has expensive fishing equipment but the fish ignore it. He has his salmon shipped over from the mainland, so undermines the local fishing economy. Torquil's old friend Catriona, who embodies the spirit of the place with her wild appearance, is married to an unseen Englishman, Potts, who is away in the armed services. Discussing what form of remuneration to accept from the RAF to compensate her for the damage caused by their recent billet in Erraig House, the Englishman would opt for a cash lump sum while Catriona would prefer the house to be made good. 'Money isn't everything,' she later tells Joan.

Robert Bellinger, Joan's fiancé, is never seen, as natural forces keep him out of reach. Early on in the film, Joan and her father do not notice the sinister implications of the arrangements Bellinger makes to transport Joan to Kiloran. They are impressed that Bellinger's black-coated middle-man Hunter has been able to secure her a first-class sleeper cabin at short notice. 'We have our methods, sir,' he replies, with the sort of latent menace we might expect from an SS officer, as he slips the train steward a bribe. Eventually, Joan rejects Bellinger's false capitalist values. The village of Chillingbourne similarly resists the cash nexus: Bob is allowed to stay for nothing at the village inn; Colpeper's kitchen provides all the treats his mother gives to the village children collecting salvage, while Bob, an American outsider, simply gives them money. While Peter fixes on the wages he earns playing a cinema organ, it is clear his ambitions are ultimately musical not financial. Likewise, Horton the blacksmith moans to Bob, 'It's the war – folks go mad,' cursing short-sighted 'capitalists' who 'cut oak at midsummer!' These imagined capitalists share a similar status to Bellinger: disdained, unseen and ethically bankrupt. They are implicitly stained with the crime of profiteering.

Wendy Hiller's performance is strong and polished. She is not as petite as Deborah Kerr – who was initially pencilled in for the role – and is less brittle than Kathleen Byron. She is more rounded, doughty and indefatigable than either. She has more stature than Sheila Sim or Kim Hunter, yet despite these tomboyish elements she is still feminine. She is earthier and less fiery than Moira Shearer. She is English, not Scottish. She says she could dance, but probably she is a better walker (she is often seen striding purposefully). Her face is broad and wholesome, and she is as intelligent as all of them. Joan, despite her professed determination, also tends to fantasise – a generic feature of many female-centred films. On the sleeper from Manchester to Scotland there is an elaborate, jokey dream sequence about her forthcoming marriage. Shot through the transparent cellophane which wraps her wedding dress (the shimmer of which implies tawdry, superficial and commodified tat), the sheets of paper scattering to the floor and the make-believe landscape which make up the dream's mise-en-scène look forward to the surreal 'dream-ballet' of *The Red Shoes*, another musical mime of female desire which veers from the aspirational to the gaudy. *IKWIG*'s more comical, private dream sequence mocks Joan's materialism. It also touches on the theme of geographical displacement, for the familiar folk-song she hears in her dream – 'You Take the High Road' – is a nostalgic anthem for diasporic Scots which imagines Scotland as a barely reachable place. The theme of diaspora is picked up later when we learn about the English families – aristocrats and industrialists – who have effectively displaced indigenous Scots like Torquil from their homes. More than this, though: the Scotland in the folk-song is an imagined space for those who have died in exile – a homely view of heaven.

On Mull, Joan prays for a change in the weather (she is told that in an old house, counting the ceiling beams will make wishes come true – again, 'magic' is connected with the past). When conditions do change we first are clued to her affinity with the place, but she cannot undo the wish, and the winds do not subside. Here, as she is tempted away from her mission by the presence of Torquil, there is an anticipation of Deborah Kerr's role in *Black Narcissus*. She too has a 'superior tone', she too wishes the wind would stop blowing at Mopu, and her imperious independence, like Joan's, makes her resent her dependence on a man who seems more at home with his environment. Joan strongly requests that she and Torquil sit at separate tables in the Western Isles Hotel, an economically unspoken admission that she has feelings for him. The note of desperation in Hiller's performance as she begs the weather to change rehearses Kerr's more brittle, curt and panicked performance, as Clodagh senses the danger of her own desires for Mr Dean. With *IKWIG*, though, Powell and Pressburger still have a 'message', and it is a genuine one about the values of community, locale and friendship. They steer clear of melodramatic, destructive themes, and Joan is tested but, unlike Clodagh, she is not beaten.

Gender relationships are carefully matched in *IKWIG*, but the women characters, particularly the indigenous islanders, have a natural vigour. Catriona is an unkempt nature-spirit of a woman, whose wild looks anticipate but outdo Jennifer Jones's pouting in *Gone to Earth*. Catriona's neighbour, old Mrs Crozier (Nancy Price) still has the spirit to hold court at table when she reminisces to Joan and her other guests about the glories of the Oban Gathering, which was held in peacetime. Fixed in close-up, she describes the yachts, games and the women in tiaras at the ball, but she fixates on how beautifully dressed the men were, 'more dazzling than the women'. She details every aspect of their costumes, her speech as impassioned and trance-like as Colpeper's talk about 'following the Old Road', and as she calls up this magic time we hear bagpipes. It transpires they are real, but she seems to have summoned them. Where her speech differs from Colpeper's is that her vigorous, vivid depiction of the ball is erotic. It centres on male spectacle and on dancing all night, and when she talks about the splendour of the men, it is Torquil, the film's representative virile young Scot, whom we picture, and Joan does too.

On three significant occasions, the film's cinematographer Erwin Hillier catches figures in silhouette as they open doors and walk towards his camera. Hence, although the setting is way beyond the Border Country separating England and Scotland, the microcosm of Mull has its own special, reserved areas, and its liminal places. The first two silhouette shots involve Joan, first when she crosses Catriona's threshold into Erraig House, then later when she comes into the ruined castle of Moy. Her curiosity – a mythical female failing from the Old Testament to fairy stories – drives her to enter the castle. She cannot understand Torquil's superstitious reluctance to follow until he admits that he is the 'Laird of Kiloran', that the curse of the MacLeans applies to him, and that he has never been inside the castle. Later, at a ceilidh celebrating a 60th wedding anniversary, and where playful flirtations are taking place, she tells Torquil that she has seen the interior of the keep, and has read the curse carved on the ramparts. Towering over him from the ladder she is standing on, yet pinned to it by Torquil, Joan plays with his curiosity about this forbidden site. 'Shall I tell you what it's like inside?' she asks. It is hard to ignore the unconscious sexual connotations of Joan's offer. The castle's interior is now a site of private, female knowledge, and the building itself is a metaphor for the female body. But which female? It is associated with Joan, but it is the ancient seat of the MacLeans, and belongs to Catriona. Half-hidden in the mists of the film is the sense that there is an unspoken romantic love between Torquil and Catriona, and in some ways the castle 'is' Catriona. This sense is muted, though, and Catriona is cast more as a controlling magician, quietly directing the fates of Joan and Torquil: Catriona is the one who tells Joan to wish on the ceiling beams; she tells Torquil that Joan is desperate to run away from him; and she is the 'keeper' of the MacLean curse on the house of MacNeil of Kiloran.

The second silhouette of Joan is mirrored exactly when Torquil defies the MacLean curse and ventures inside Castle Moy himself. Once inside, he moves through it, exploring its recesses. On the soundtrack, the lilting voice of Torquil's old nanny (another wise woman) tells him the story of the curse, as she had done when he was a boy. This associates the castle with Torquil's infancy, and explains the tribal taboo on him entering it. 'Once upon a time', we hear, a MacNeil of Kiloran married a woman from the mainland, but she loved a MacLean and ran away to the castle to be with her lover. MacNeil besieged the castle and killed all those inside, save for the lovers, whom he chained together and left in the dungeon to drown. The woman cursed all lairds of Kiloran with her dying breath. The myth is rich in possible connotations, and it certainly shows that Powell and Pressburger are offering no rosy view of Old Scotland as a utopia, for the place is riddled with tales of primeval bloodshed and torture. The myth's illicit affair between the mainland woman and a MacLean could suggest a suppressed lesbian attraction between Joan and Catriona (a possibility which Joan's early exploration of Catriona's ruined ancestral home has implanted). The sense of attraction between Catriona and Torquil (whose surnames – MacNeil and MacLean – are almost anagrams of each other) also opens up the possibility that Catriona, as owner of the castle, could lure Torquil in and chain him to her, as the curse predicts. But the stronger bond is that between Joan and Torquil, and when Torquil breaches the castle walls for the first time he is symbolically losing his virginity (or taking hers) and consummating their relationship. The film can be seen, then, to dramatise both Joan's and Torquil's Oedipal trajectories: Joan's early attachment is to Robert, a man as old as her father (she calls her father 'darling' and dances with him in the opening sequence); while Torquil's infancy is indicated by his memories of his nanny – a mother-substitute.

Torquil's eventual entry into Castle Moy is, then, pungently liminal and, as he climbs the stairs to the ramparts and begins to read the curse, he hears pipe music and knows that Joan is coming back to him. The three pipers were originally booked for her wedding to Robert, but they have been unable to make the crossing to Kiloran. Joan, of course, knows the 'joke' of the curse – namely that Kiloran, having entered, will be chained to a woman – a prediction of their forthcoming marriage. When Torquil looks down from the ramparts to see her, she is marching behind the pipers in a forthright, determined, independent manner, to claim him. This proto-feminist respect for female agency and intelligence is found elsewhere in Powell and Pressburger's work, but the happy heterosexual union here depends on them locating it almost entirely within a mystical but alluring space, and on them placing their heroine in an ancient, feudal community. Beyond the film's closing credits, and by implication after the war (for Torquil is still on active service) the pair will finally reach their mythical goal, the island of Kiloran.

4

Post-war Masculinities: The Pilot and the Back-room Boy – *A Matter of Life and Death*, *The Small Back Room*

'Portrait of a hero being sick at the thought of it.'

Nigel Balchin, *The Small Back Room*

BACKGROUND: ECONOMICS, BRITAIN AND CINEMA

There is ripe cause to read the events of 1945 optimistically, with the war's end and the high hopes of a majority Labour government bringing to fruition the ideals of the Welfare State, progress towards which had already been initiated by the wartime National Government. However, in Alex J. Robertson's view (in a volume aptly entitled *The Bleak Midwinter: 1947*) things were not so rosy.[1] The nation's sense of identity, forged with such apparent consistency during the war years, suffered with the change-over to peacetime, when historical circumstance failed to live up to the rhetoric of hope and promise which had prevailed for so long. Britain saw out 1945 with a colossal balance of payments deficit. With rationing, any pride taken in the Allies' victory was contradicted by the spartan material conditions which were set to continue into the early 1950s. Anglo-American relations, bolstered through the war, experienced a tremor in September 1945, when the USA declared the abrupt and unexpected cessation of Lend-Lease, the system whereby Britain had effectively financed its own war effort on cheap American credit. This move was perceived as hostile in Britain, where Lend-Lease had been seen as early, happy proof of a so-called special relationship with America, though its 'special-ness' was always more keenly felt by the British than by the Americans. John Maynard Keynes was able to rectify the immediate economic crisis by securing a low interest loan from America. However, British reconstruction also depended heavily on US aid provided by the Marshall Plan. Welcome as it was, this aid journeyed across the Atlantic as part of a concerted effort to construct a bulwark against Communist interest in Western Europe (the recent enemy, West Germany, was the third largest beneficiary of American aid after Britain and France). The motivation behind both the loan which Maynard Keynes negotiated and the Marshall Plan was to enable the British to continue to buy American products. Considerable anxiety existed regarding the debilitating implications of this economic subservience. The growing centrality of the US dollar as a unit of currency on the world's economic stage did little to alleviate Britain's dented self-image (and India's departure from the British Empire reinforced this general current). Britain's reluctance to abandon its position on the global stage lay behind the importance placed on the relationship with America: there was a desire to pitch Britain alongside an unquestionable super-power, and only with the eventual humiliation of Suez did the reality of Britain's new world position begin to hit home (even then, the national reassessment was incomplete). Rationing continued. The weather was dreadful; 1947 saw the worst winter on record. If earnings had risen during the war, and if full employment was secured in peacetime, there was little to buy, and much of what was made in the country was produced for export. A sense of dissatisfaction, if not of dashed expectations, was prevalent. In Alex J. Robertson's words, much of day-to-day living remained 'some way behind what people remembered fondly as *real* peacetime conditions, before the war. And the discipline which many had been willing to impose on their frustrated propensity to consume was not so easy to accept once the war was over.'[2]

With Britain's slow, painful adjustment to the realities of its actual world status, and with genuine hardship at home, the utopianism of the Welfare State could be seen to cushion the deprivations of the late 1940s. The establishment of a new education system and of the NHS, together with the modernisation promised by nationalisation, addressed problems perceived in the state of the nation. If the provision of social security did not set about a large-scale redistribution of wealth, it aimed to provide a safety net to eradicate absolute poverty, and in the system of National Insurance it purported to incorporate the working population into a common pool of shared interest. The war years had, of course, seen the abandonment of *laissez faire* politics. The dominant ideology of the 'People's War' aimed to recruit the entire population into a public sphere, and to eradicate the concept of private or individual interest: paradoxically the concept of 'Home' (as a retreat from 'Community') had been put to one side, however much the 'People' were reminded that 'Home' was ultimately what they were fighting to preserve. The Labour government's commitment to extending the boundaries of the State in the post-war period perpetuated this ethos of public involvement in the life of the individual. The government therefore had to tread carefully as it crossed the boundary into traditional bourgeois-liberal preserves. It continued to call upon public duty. Its anti-libertarianism was cast as a democratic commitment towards equality of opportunity.

The British film industry in the late 1940s shared in these conflicts and crises, and the films produced were enmeshed in the same ideological tensions. As always, the British cinema's relationship with America crucially impacted on the texts it produced, and (as always) success depended in part upon macro-economic factors outside its control. Studio space requisitioned during the war was freed up in 1945, and the need for expansion and export (observed across the British economy) was acutely felt within the cinema industry. J. Arthur Rank pursued his ambitious plans to strengthen his foothold in the American market (for example by purchasing the prestigious Winter Gardens Theater in New York). The most significant event to hit the industry in the late 1940s, however, arose from the government's urgent policy to address the balance of payments problem, and here the film industry was notably vulnerable, for in the broadest sense the industry was a drain on sterling. As far as distribution and exhibition is concerned, it relied heavily on American imports, but Britain in the late 1940s was crippled by its dollar shortage. The last thing the economy needed was the seepage of profits back across the Atlantic, and the government therefore addressed the crisis by discouraging all but the most necessary imports. It was a choice, as Geoffrey Macnab sees it, between 'Bogart and bacon' – American films or food on the plate.[3] In August 1947, while Rank was personally in America negotiating distribution deals, the Chancellor of the Exchequer moved to protect the British economy by imposing a massive 75 per cent *ad valorem* tax on all imported films. Hollywood's reaction to this protectionism was to impose an immediate embargo on all new films, halting exports to the UK and effectively denying Rank (and other British producers) access to American screens. The fragile and credit-based nature of the British industry could ill afford such dramatic crises, while Hollywood could well withstand the lack of British distribution and exhibition profits (in any event American reruns and stockpiled releases already in the United Kingdom prior to the imposition of the tax meant that British screens did not run out of Hollywood fare until the end of the year). Seeing a gap in the market, Rank strove to expand his own production by stretching his financial investment to the limit but, as George Perry points out, 'paradoxically, with the field, in theory, completely empty of competition, it became harder to make films in England. The reason was simple. Hollywood's retaliatory action had diminished almost to zero the chances of American release, and it was felt that the British domestic market was insufficient to earn adequate returns.'[4]

While the effect of the *ad valorem* tax was dramatic, it at least offered British production what it had long claimed was needed to consolidate a 'British National Cinema': freedom from the Hollywood factor. The notion of 'national cinema' as something discrete and autonomous runs counter to the realities of a global economy, and the particular reality in Britain is that the industry depended upon the Holy Grail of American distribution deals. Even with protectionism militating against the effects of Hollywood domination, the British cinema's borders were not closed. The import tax was repealed in May 1948. With the British industry over-extended on production, screens were flooded with a backlog of American releases. British films rushed out during the blockade were faced with a tide of American films with which they could not hope to compete. The quota legislation instigated by the 1948 Cinematograph Act (the ten-year spell of the 1938 Act having expired) raised the exhibitors' quota to 45 per cent for first features and 25 per cent for supporting programmes. This further exacerbated Anglo-American trade relations, hampering the British industry's attempts to secure access to American screens. Other well-meaning legislation, such as the system of government loans made available through the National Film Finance Corporation (Alexander Korda took advantage of these funds to produce works such as *The Third Man* [1949]) helped shore up the domestic industry. Transatlantic partnerships continued to be forged – notably Korda's deals with both Samuel Goldwyn and David Selznick. These deals would impact on Powell and Pressburger's work when they left Rank's 'Independent Producers' after making *The Red Shoes* (1948) to return to Korda's fold.

Goldwyn's dissatisfaction with *The Elusive Pimpernel* (1950) and Selznick's with *Gone to Earth* (1950) both culminated in lawsuits with Korda. The British film industry reeled from the economic crises of the late 1940s.

Vulnerable because of its effective dependence on foreign audiences to recoup production costs, it was always likely that the circumstances of the post-war settlement would impact upon it with disproportionate effect. By the time the British economy had turned round with the boom period of the 1950s, changes in leisure patterns, the rise of television and the diversion of surplus private incomes into the purchase of consumer goods meant that the industry had ceded its central cultural position. The status it achieved during the war would not be recovered. Struggling in the face of legislative moves which can at best be described as erratic, and veering between over-expansion and near-collapse, the British cinema industry of the 1940s was characterised by both ambition and dashed hope.

Cinema was still a dominant form in the 1940s (attendance peaked in 1946 at an all-time high of 1635 million visits). Admittedly, part of the problem was that in the main the public chose to watch Hollywood films to escape, as Geoffrey Macnab has argued, from the austerity of their surroundings, 'but by spending money on Hollywood (they) contributed to that austerity'.[5] If we look at British production in the immediate post-war period, the confused and turbulent social renegotiations of the time are powerfully articulated, even if the obvious 'grand narrative' of the war effort no longer provided it with its structuring *Ur*-text. 'Quality films' such as David Lean's *Brief Encounter* (1945) and Laurence Olivier's *Hamlet* (1948) continued to appear, but a very mixed bag of work was actually produced in the period and the critical construct of a 'national cinema' resting on notions of 'quality realism' no longer had the wartime documentary as its bedrock. Neither was its mission to forge a national cinema wedded conveniently to the national imperatives of the war effort. The quality critics' discourse had on occasions closely fitted the propaganda-fuelled cinematic realism of the war years, but the actuality of film production lacked the cohesiveness of that critical discourse, and this situation intensified in the post-war period – staggering as the industry was from financial crisis, marked as it was with internal dissent, and subjected as it was to the slings and arrows of Treasury and Board of Trade intervention.

British cinema powerfully articulated the terms of the war, and largely fell in line with the censorship requirements of the Ministry of Information. After August 1945 those production restraints no longer applied. The British cinema continued to produce war stories, of course, though they were fewer in number, while many documentaries, drawing on styles forged in war, went on to contribute to the public, educational discourse that helped to propagandise national development and reconstruction. Cycles of popular films in the late 1940s continued to address the cultural conditions of the times: psychological thrillers and crime films, such as *Brighton Rock* (J. Boulting, 1947) and Carol Reed's *Odd Man Out* (1947) and *The Third Man* tapped into concerns regarding 'spiv' culture, delinquency and criminal opportunism. The noir-like vein of these works needs to be thought through as evidence of a crisis in the construction of masculinity brought about by the trauma of war, the apparent female emancipation it had ushered in and the diminution of Britain's obvious military-imperial profile. The spate of American noir films in the post-war period likewise relates to that culture's anxiety regarding masculine roles.

Robert Murphy's survey of the period shows what was popular, and the following sketch is indebted to him.[6] In the immediate post-war years, British films topped box office figures: *The Seventh Veil* (Compton Bennett, 1945), *The Wicked Lady* (Leslie Arliss, 1945) and *The Courtneys of Curzon Street* (Herbert Wilcox, 1947) were the most successful films exhibited in the United Kingdom in 1945, 1946 and 1947. *The Third Man* topped polls in 1949, as did *The Blue Lamp* (Basil Dearden, 1949) in 1950. However, this masks the truth of the state of the industry. 'Spiv' thrillers, costume pictures and contemporary melodramas moved into a dominant position by 1947–48, and the overall number of domestic productions rose in the wake of the *ad valorem* tax (from around 60 in 1945–47, to 77 in 1948 and, by the time the backlog filtered through to the screens, to 96 in 1949). Many of these films, though, could only be classed as second features. 'Quality' films such as *The Blue Lamp*, *Brief Encounter* and *The Captive Heart* (Basil Dearden, 1946) together with Powell and Pressburger's *A Matter of Life and Death* (1946) and *Black Narcissus* (1947) did reasonable business, but many other British films in the late 1940s did badly. American work like *Meet Me In St Louis* (Vincente Minnelli, 1944, US), *Duel in the Sun* (King Vidor, 1946, US) and *The Jolson Story* (Alfred E. Green, 1946, US), along with 1948's biggest success, William Wyler's *The Best Years of Our Lives,* continued to do well.

POWELL, PRESSBURGER AND POST-WAR MEN

It was inevitable that some of the familiar, coherent aesthetic which helped to mythologise wartime would begin to fall apart with the return of peace. Much of that group aesthetic was the expedient product of wartime propaganda. Yet its potency did not dissipate overnight, and post-war culture was in part moulded by the immediate past. To use Kaja Silverman's phrase, some of the 'dominant fictions' of the war period were deliberately perpetuated.[7] A 'People's War' ethic propelled the spirit of the Welfare State, for example, and helped to sell it to the nation. Soon, though, the public taste for wartime narratives moved on. As Powell himself conceded in the 1970s (in an interview with Roland Lacourbe and Danièle Grivel for *ECRAN*) when reflecting about the relative box office failure of *The Small Back Room*, 'We were done with the war. We were already in another world. We no longer needed a film full of psychology and reflections on this period which was over.'[8] Some of the myths of wartime were so potent that they continued into the late 1940s and beyond. Ealing Studios, like an echo chamber sounding out the recent past, mocked this tendency, capturing a paradoxical nostalgia for London's war years in *Passport to Pimlico* (1948). Henry Cornelius's film is set in the immediate post-war period, and it protests against the privations of rationing. In its opening sequence, we seem to have taken flight from post-war austerity, as tropical jazz rhythms soothe a pretty young girl as she sunbathes. With leaden bathos, she is revealed to be on the roof of a fish shop, and a BBC radio announcer diegeticises the soundtrack to tell us that we 'have been listening to a programme of lunchtime music by Les Norman and his Bethnal Green Bambinos'. Geographically trapped in a West London locale, the film finds a new imagined community for its Pimlico residents by magically discovering that they are historically part of Burgundy, but the film's real escape is not across the Channel but into memory as it spiritually revisits the community spirit of London's Blitz (the physical evidence of which marks the mise-en-scène). The film is a knowing paean to pluckiness, with its besieged 'Burgundians' rolling up their sleeves and pitting themselves stubbornly against both the faceless bureaucracy of Whitehall and the anarchy of black market 'spiv' culture. Another Ealing document set in the post-war period, Robert Hamer's panoramic realist melodrama, *It Always Rains on Sunday* (1947), centres on Rose Sandigate, a bored housewife and mother (Googie Withers). She is torn between marital duty to her plump and decidedly un-dashing husband George, and the dangerous excitement to be had with her old lover Tom Swann (John McCallum), an escaped convict. She is surprised, shocked and yet irrefutably thrilled to re-encounter him lurking – significantly – in the shadows of their old 'Anderson' air raid shelter. The film is set unremittingly among the drab privations of the late 1940s East End, but the connection made (via an air raid shelter) between memories of the war and sexual excitement is another (illicit) variation on this expression of nostalgia. Away from Ealing, the footage of a deserted airfield which forms the prelude to Anthony Asquith's elegiac *The Way to the Stars* (1945) views the war nostalgically, and the flashback to the airstrip's heroic active service answers an imaginative longing which the ghostly prelude summons up. This is a film which understands its mythologising project.

Discourses of gender and war had been closely intertwined, and images of stoical, self-sufficient, yet socially integrated manhood formed an important element in the collective imagination of the conflict – one of the genuinely dominant fictions of the period. The country's models of social behaviour underwent transformation, with new forms of manhood and womanhood crystallising, while older and apparently outmoded models continued to have some currency. These models provide norms or types, specific instances of which are imprinted in the cultural texts of the time. *Blimp* had asked what the country was fighting for, since 'home' had been eradicated, and 'women' were now fighting alongside the men. These anxieties about gender distinctions continue to be registered in late 1940s culture, and Powell and Pressburger's immediate post-war work cleaves along gender lines. They essayed the female melodrama in three related films between 1947 and 1950 (the subject of Chapter 5), but this chapter looks at some of their male-centred 'war' films of the post-war period. Yet neither *A Matter of Life and Death* (1946) – or '*AMOLAD*', as Powell and his fans abbreviate it – nor *The Small Back Room* (1949) fit tidily into that generic pigeonhole. The war film tends to focus on masculinity, and its exploration of the male group or the 'special', individual male is often premised on the exclusion of women and domestic life (although the ethos of the 'People's War' had led to more popularist, inclusive structures in many films made during the early 1940s). Romantic involvement forms the motivating dilemma in *AMOLAD*, and is central to *The Small Back Room*, where the protagonist's turbulent sexual life is psychologically bound up with his strained relationship to 'honest soldiery'. These films, then, are hybrid romances. The later films, *The Battle of the River Plate* (1956) and *Ill Met by Moonlight* (1957) follow generic expectations more tidily, but are also inflected with characteristic Powell-Pressburger traits.

Charles Ryder, the reactionary protagonist of Evelyn Waugh's *Brideshead Revisited* (1945), gloomily predicts a post-war drabness for England, a frosty period which he labels (after his unimpressive and unimpressed platoon commander) the 'age of Hooper'. Still beguiled by the dazzling, aristocratic Marchmain family, Ryder sees little colour or hope in a future dominated by grey, non-deferential, Everyman figures like Hooper, whom he cynically thinks of as his 'symbol of Young England'. Hooper is a cousin in arms with *Blimp*'s Spud – less feisty, less urgent, but of a similar class and background. In both texts they are minor characters, bit parts in aristocratic dramas, yet, where *Brideshead* clearly displays Waugh's disdain for Hooperdom, *Blimp* gravitates towards Spud, and it closes in a gesture of respect to the younger generation, importantly expressing the nation's ability to reinvigorate itself and to throw its lot in with the future. Where, though, does Spud now go in Powell and Pressburger's post-war period? Has the post-filmic supper which Candy offers to Spud in the film's last sequence been a seductive ploy to tame and to incorporate Britain's great young hope – to give him free life membership to the outmoded Pompeii-world of Candy's Bathers Club? *Blimp* seems more openly, honestly progressive, but the 'common man as hero' nevertheless fails to keep his place on Powell and Pressburger's screens.

Andrew Spicer's survey of masculinity in British cinema calibrates the 'typical men' represented in films of this time to illustrate the historical variability of gender, and usefully identifies some prevalent models of manhood, such as the debonair gentleman, the heroic commoner, the Byronic male, the 'spiv' and the 'damaged man'.[9] Spicer's focus on 'spivs' and damaged men echoes Robert Murphy's observation that the late 1940s saw a 'morbid' cycle of British films featuring crisis-ridden men and often circling pessimistically around themes of crime like the American film-noir genre.[10] There is no easy way to 'read off' signs of a zeitgeist from a set of texts, and it is dangerous to assume any cultural consensus in any period, but it is the case that the late 1940s were a dynamic period of cultural transition from a war footing to peacetime, and the male neuroses at the centre of these films may well relate to the shift in gender roles during the war and to the sense of emasculation which the social upheaval of the period caused. Powell and Pressburger are generally drawn towards 'special men', such as Hardt, Candy and Colpeper, and Peter Carter (David Niven), the debonair pilot-hero of *AMOLAD* is a genuinely idealised image of English manhood. Sammy Rice (David Farrar), the protagonist in *The Small Back Room* (adapted from Nigel Balchin's 1943 novel of the same name) seems at first glance to be unrelated. He is a 'back-room boy', a character akin to the type Spicer identifies as the 'scientist-inventor'. He is crippled, neurotic, masochistic and haunted by a sense of failure: in every sense he is also a 'damaged man' and the film he appears in has many noir characteristics. These two films were released after the war, but their narratives are firmly located during the conflict (*AMOLAD* begins specifically on the night of 2 May 1945, the very end of the war, and *The Small Back Room* is set in 1943). The two films are drawn together by shared allusions to the after-effects of conflict or damage, and to the readjustment to peace. They each set out to repair their men. Peter is a uniformed and glamorous pilot, and Sammy is a civilian figure of the shadowy sidelines, but they have both suffered. Peter seemingly has brain damage; Sammy is an amputee. One has fantasies of Heaven; the other is an alcoholic.

The Small Back Room deals with a disabled protagonist's low self-esteem, but its key themes – sexual relations, heroism, and what is nowadays termed 'post-traumatic shock' – look beyond the mid-war years of its setting to comment indirectly upon the social readjustments of the latter half of the decade. It deals with the after-effects of technologically advanced warfare, like Carol Reed's *The Third Man*, where the effects of Harry Lime's black market medicine trade in post-war Vienna can be read as a metaphorical indictment of 'advanced' chemical warfare during the Cold War. It is fitting, then, that *The Small Back Room*'s central dramatic motif is the threat represented by unexploded German booby-trap bombs: time-delayed repercussions and nervous tension give the film its charged energy. The carnage caused by the belated explosion of the booby-traps mirrors the psychological trauma remembered by Sammy. 'Peace' did not arrive clinically in August 1945. There is no clear binary opposition between the period of conflict and what followed, as the facts of trauma, battle fatigue and cultural/geographical displacement serve to prove. A tense, charged sexual relationship between Sammy and Susan (Kathleen Byron) draws out the links between the man's disability, his own masculine shortcomings and the gender dynamics of the period. *AMOLAD* is set on the cusp of peace, and its protagonist is also damaged. In the opening sequence he leaps without a parachute from his burning plane, 'miraculously' surviving to fall in love with an American girl, June (Kim Hunter), only then to encounter a heavenly messenger sent to claim him for the afterlife. The film anticipates the post-war settlement, and is a key text in arguing for a post-war special relationship between Britain and the USA. It also occupies a metaphysical space between war and peace, between injury and recovery, between the cinematic discourses of war and of romance.

What is crucial is not just the way Peter and Sammy are emblematic of the national culture's troubled readjustment to peace, but the way their narratives of healing, and their recuperative trajectories, stitch up their traumatic histories and send them optimistically into a land fit for heroes.

This would be pleasantly progressive were it not for the stark contrast between the overall thrust of these films and the generally pessimistic direction of the three female-centred melodramas which Powell and Pressburger write, produce and direct in the same period. In the male-centred films, the psychological suffering is related to the armed conflict, and their assured recovery signals a faith in the nation's ability to adjust successfully, but on masculine terms. This is not to overlook the strength and the agency of the female characters, Susan and June, in aiding the revival of their men. In the women-centred films, the cause of the psychological disturbance is very different, and their fates are strikingly at odds with the upbeat reparation granted to the men.

Kaja Silverman's psycho-analytical account of bruised and marginalised male subjectivity takes as its starting point the various obstacles which hamper the male subject's efforts to secure a position of dominance for himself. As she points out, '(his) aspirations to mastery and sufficiency are undermined from many directions – by the Law of Language, which founds subjectivity on a void; by the castration crisis; by sexual, economic, and racial oppression; and by the traumatically unassimilable nature of certain historical events'.[11] Sammy's and Peter's experiences can usefully be explored in these general terms (it is worth considering the use of language and silence in the films, their use of classic symbols of castration, dynamics of class and gender, and so on). More specifically, both films are acutely concerned with the 'unassimilable' nature of the war experience. Trauma is an experience of disintegration. It is a psychological rupture, linked (etymologically) to dreaming because it relates not only to an original injurious event, but also to the way that event cannot satisfactorily be reconciled by imagination and memory. Formally, trauma is a 'broken' narrative roaming between three points: the original historical cause of the injury; the sufferer's flight into a cordoned off imaginary space which represses the memory to cauterise the pain; and therapy, which is found in reconstructing, remembering and reconciliation. In their own, different ways, both *The Small Back Room* and *AMOLAD* negotiate their protagonist's flight from and return to historical reality (signalled in both films by hopeful heterosexual union), and both are therapeutic stories. The 'magic space' of these films is a marker of their protagonists' disintegrated condition.

The sense of rupture, then, is no longer connected to geography, as it was in Powell and Pressburger's earlier films. Rather than tales of exile to strange territory, we have tales of alienation, where the disjuncture is between the imaginary and the real. During the war years there was a commitment to the treatment of physical location and its relationship to individual and social development – a sense of the geopolitical. It may be just a question of shifting emphasis, but after the war, it appears that the dominant, public narrative of wartime Britain no longer afforded a current, viable, utopian space. Neither 'England' itself nor the idealistic aspiration of the war effort has a direct, recuperative currency. Hence, Powell and Pressburger explore more purely subjective spaces. This greater shift towards the private sphere marks a growing lack of interest in the outward, socially incorporative space. Instead they chart journeys into areas of psychological disturbance.

This is where the gender distinction in Powell and Pressburger's films of the period is most striking. The anxieties suffered by Sammy (and to a lesser degree by Peter) are genuinely external in origin, and, while they might be interpreted as symptoms of hysteria, they are certainly not primarily sexual in nature, although that is what the term hysteria very often connotes. Silverman points out that '(Freud) distinguishes...between those neuroses which are motored by a repressed desire, and are hence obedient to the pleasure principle, and those which are produced in response to an external event which reactivates an earlier trauma.'[12] External events, public discourse, objective social reality – this is the 'man's world' Sammy and Peter move in. In their own ways, the private plights of Clodagh, Ruth, Vicky and Hazel in *Black Narcissus* (1947), *The Red Shoes* (1948) and *Gone to Earth* (1950) are closely related to their own 'desiring' nature and, at root, these films are all readable as traditional melodramas of active, aberrant female sexuality, skewed and made neurotic by the pressure to conform socially. Classically hysterical patterns involve a triangulated relationship between the (female) subject, the object of her pleasurable desire and representatives of social order. Permutations of this pattern are there in each of Powell and Pressburger's female-centred films, where none of the female protagonists are allowed to reintegrate successfully. There is another key distinction between their male and female melodramas: none of the women directly represent the 'national' public character, for their dramas are deeply personal. Peter surely is a national emblem, though, and the period setting of *The Small Back Room* connects Sammy to the war effort and by extension makes him representative of a national type of manhood.

The Small Back Room and *AMOLAD* clearly differ visually. *AMOLAD* is a Technicolor romance-fantasy on the broadest canvas, with a tone that shifts between quizzical comedy and allegory. *The Small Back Room* is an intimate, black and white, and broadly realistic 'Kammerspiel'. It penetrates claustrophobic and unglamorous work and domestic spaces, and is a noir-like examination of a man in crisis. It is often a sexually charged film, nosing into a relationship between Sammy and Susan which has uncomfortably sadomasochistic overtones. Yet, beyond these immediate distinctions, both films display formal and symbolic symptoms of their protagonist's trauma. Sammy's body has been violated when the film opens – he has lost a foot, a clear sign of his symbolically castrated state, marking his sense of masculine inadequacy. His obsessive addiction to alcohol is explicitly connected to his disability, and is made dramatically obvious when, at a low ebb, he is tempted to open a bottle of forbidden whisky. In a notorious, Expressionist sequence, the bottle expands massively in size and Sammy, contorted with fear, imagines himself being attacked by it (a 16-foot papier-mâché bottle was made for the sequence – none of the sequence's effects are due to trick photography). It is like something from *Alice in Wonderland* given a nightmare twist: 'Drink me!' the bottle implicitly shrieks. The sequence is formally segregated from the rest of the film, and the classicism of the narrative simply goes to pieces, symptomatically breaking down in a bout of extreme, visual spectacle. While contemporary critics generally praised the film for its intelligence, for the depth and quality of its acting down to the bit-part players, for its mature and realistic treatment of Sammy's relationship with Susan, and for the suspense of its long closing sequence where Sammy, alone, has to tackle one of the unexploded booby-trap devices on Chesil Bank, they were predictably worried by the rudely dissonant whisky-bottle sequence, claiming to find in it signs of Powell and Pressburger's vulgar sense of spectacle, their lack of propriety and their suspiciously Teutonic habits. Typically, Milton Shulman, writing in the *Nottingham Guardian* (22 January 1949) thought Powell and Pressburger benefited when they kept themselves to the 'solid earth of reality' and forsook the 'nebulous realm of symbolism'. He disliked the whisky scene because it abandons any sense of 'proportion' and because he finds in it signs of the film-makers pointlessly making life difficult for themselves and showing off: 'When will this team learn that a great painting doesn't become any better because the artist has painted some of it with his brush between his toes?'

Towards the end of the film, noir elements are downplayed and there is an ideologically crucial shift back towards the war-film style. *AMOLAD* is even more disintegrated, famously organising itself around a pattern of formal dissolves from Technicolor Earth to a pearl and grey monochrome Heaven, or journeying between the two regimes on a fantastically imagined moving staircase as Peter's fate is decided by a heavenly court. Rather than attempting to hybridise the unrelated worlds of fantasy/romance and documentary/realism, Powell and Pressburger make a formal play of their differences. Both films mark out regimes which are 'beyond' reality, one in a noir-Expressionist vein, the other in a sci-fi fantasy vein, and both acknowledge the documentary style of the war film. Their more radically 'broken' narratives point to the ways in which post-war Britain tried to negotiate a transitional period by rethinking its available categories for men, and ultimately by finding healthily reintegrated resolutions for their very different heroes.

In their screen roles, David Farrar and David Niven are in many ways poles apart. Never an actor of great range, Niven came instead to embody and to articulate a rather out-of-date ideal: gentlemanliness – or 'noblesse oblige'. His light tenor and gamin beauty are those of the nobility: he reveals, if provoked, the upright steeliness of a man with backbone, but this grit often shades over into a likeable, smiling insolence. Though we knew he could be naughty (and the actor was a noted practical joker), it was the forgivable naughtiness of a well-liked schoolboy. It is usually his graceful amusement that impresses, rather than his physicality or intellect (to talk of 'grace' might seem antiquated, but old-fashioned words like that seem to fit). He could be the younger son of a minor aristocrat, at times silly but always charming, and in the last instance gallant, gazing upwards with a sparkle in his eyes, a light comedian who, through sensing the necessity of nonsense, is perfect as Phileas Fogg in *Around the World in Eighty Days* (Michael Anderson, 1956, US). He is fittingly dashing in *The Elusive Pimpernel* (Powell and Pressburger, 1950), where as Sir Percy Blakeney he embraces foppishness with gusto. His 'airy' quality is winning, and his poetic virtues shine in *AMOLAD*. He may be well-mannered and eloquent but, as charmers go, his 'classiness' sits easily. Not for him the glib insouciance of Noël Coward, for example. Coward is never convincingly a man of action; he also needs his masks, his seeming cleverness, his cruelty and his wit, all of which are hard-won, vital, camp and defensive. Niven's refinement seems, paradoxically, natural. He is undoubtedly an affectionate figure. Unkindness is not in him, and he is important in our gallery of heroes. But he is never like John Mills, the democratic 1940s 'Everyman'. Mills is the boy next door to everybody and, while that is a nice neighbourhood, we really aspire to live next door to Niven. Is it a question of class? We suppose Niven to be a good host of better parties. Mills is like us; Niven is exotic. Cometh the hour, cometh the man, and during the war Niven stood for some of the most valued of principles, but his quality (or was it just his prettiness?) seemed the stuff of a previous, and probably mythical, time. Niven himself was a Sandhurst-trained army man, who joined the Highland Light Infantry in 1928 and served in Malta for two years before drifting towards America and into film acting. In 1939, when he left Hollywood for the army, he was a star, and managed to complete two propaganda films during the war while also serving in the Rifle Brigade. In *The Way Ahead* (Carol Reed, 1944) the officer he plays is a car mechanic promoted from the lower ranks. It is hard, though, to think of him labouring manually on the bottom rung, but when he is inspiring his troops as they are melded into a tight fighting team of soldiers, he looks and sounds right. He is ennobled by the strong pull of the film's democratic, team-spirit ethos, for that ideology insists that efficient recruitment to the war effort confers grace on all, but if egalitarianism is the aim, then Niven's character is more equal than others. In the opening sequence of *AMOLAD*, it is hard to think of another actor who could mouth Powell and Pressburger's airborne script so convincingly. Bravely putting his house in order, saying his farewells and leaping from his burning plane, he is ridiculously, tearfully beautiful. Notably, it is his voice, travelling to Earth in radio waves, which first attracts the young American girl June, not his looks, and later it is his mind which is damaged, not his body. It is difficult, in fact, to think of the slender Niven in terms of his body at all. We remember the face, and a moustache even more precise and dapper than Anton Walbrook's (which was hiding something). Like Michael Redgrave in *The Way to the Stars*, he is the most celebrated man of war – the pilot who belongs in the clouds.

David Farrar is more prosaic, earthy, baritone: an army man. He is solidly physical, as Sisters Clodagh and Ruth find to their cost in *Black Narcissus*, in which, as Mr Dean, he is pragmatic and broad-chested, dogged British imperialism gone temptingly, loucheIy native. Who but he would visit nuns shirtless (except perhaps Clark Gable)? Farrar is a self-made, middle-class, pipe-smoking man, whether in khaki or demobbed, a product of the Establishment, with a face as strongly and squarely determined as Niven's is determinedly brittle. In many ways he is the progenitor of the tweedy men of 1950s Britain, except that he retains something more: a roguish sexiness utterly unknown to Kenneth More. His brooding contours and mop of dark hair are smoulderingly photogenic in memorable close-ups which carve him out as a romantic figure, isolated from his social environment. But the appearance of physical strength is a sign of a different weakness. Farrar looks such a 'type' of sturdy English stoicism, yet he is very good indeed at expressing its obverse: there is often a raging turmoil beneath his crusty, at times almost donnish frame. This contest between reliable gravitas and inner chaos places him on an uncomfortable faultline in hegemonic British manhood, and Powell and Pressburger know this. It is there in *Black Narcissus*, where Mr Dean's virulent rejection of Ruth and chaste regard for Clodagh both imply emotional inadequacy. In the costume melodrama *Gone to Earth* his philandering squire, Jack Reddin, is all Rochester/Heathcliff swarthiness, but in *The Small Back Room* his ambiguities are more fully exploited.

If it seems far-fetched to pair these two characters and these two stars, note the way Powell and Pressburger, in *The Small Back Room* and *AMOLAD*, chart similar recuperative trajectories (while simultaneously mapping more degenerative, suicidal flight paths for the melodramatic heroines of their 'women's' films), suggesting that these film-makers and their culture strongly – desperately – need to invest in masculine ideologies. Peter and Sammy are yoked to other dominant cultural fictions which give them yet greater cultural kudos. Peter is a poet, an upholder of canonical virtues. He is immersed in 'high culture', and is a distillation of Renaissance values. He is also a fighter pilot – genuinely a war hero. Sammy is a man of science. His work, though, is relegated to the back room of the war effort, and the unit he works for seems amateurish, with blurred terms of reference. Science is not, therefore, regarded futuristically in the film as a white beacon of Enlightenment ideals (the curious non-conformism of Sammy's unit is in fact crucial to the meaning of the film), but Sammy and his colleagues are nevertheless regarded as intelligent, logical, vital, capable both of sparks of genius and acts of bravery which soldiers would recognise as such.

PETER DAVID CARTER

AMOLAD repeatedly asserts the psychological 'truth' of its fantasy narrative. Its opening rolling graphics spell out that the film is 'a story of two worlds – the one we know, and another world which exists only in the mind of a young airman whose life and imagination have been violently shaped by war'. Its plot is a balanced negotiation between war film, love story and quizzical comedy. Peter, a British airman, falls in love with June's voice heard over his radio, and bails out of his fatally crippled aeroplane. Miraculously he is washed ashore alive, meeting June and Dr Reeves. Peter imagines he has a visitation from a heavenly messenger who tells him he was due to die the night he bailed out, and that he must take his rightful place in the other world. The film alternates between Heaven and Earth as Peter appeals against heavenly law. Dr Reeves is killed in a road accident, and is able to defend Peter in a heavenly appeal court, while, on Earth, surgeons prepare to operate on Peter's brain. The heavenly prosecuting counsel, Abraham Farlan, is an Anglophobic American, killed by the British in the War of Independence. Peter and Reeves argue that following Heaven's failure to claim Peter when he was due to die he has since fallen in love and thus has new responsibilities which should keep him on Earth. June's tear, preserved on a rose, is presented as evidence of this love. Unable to resolve the case, the heavenly court descends to Earth, where Reeves commands June to prove her love for Peter by taking his place immediately in the afterlife. She does, and is immediately returned to Peter. As Reeves expected, nothing is stronger than love. Peter survives the operation, waking to find June by his bedside.

As in Frank Capra's *It's a Wonderful Life* (1946, US), which shares *AMOLAD*'s opening sequences of outer space, its metaphysics and a comic heavenly messenger intervening in earthly concerns, the hallucinatory elements here are psychologically driven, and each film has a therapeutic narrative which restores 'balance' to its protagonist. What is more, *AMOLAD* ultimately invests its hope in Peter's *own* ability to deal with his inner demons. As Ian Christie points out, the film has come to be seen as (among other things) a drama of the 'artist as Outsider',[13] with Peter (the poet) resisting incorporation and thereby marking his individuality. In the film's debate between Fate and Peter's self-determination, Peter's own agency is resolutely defended – the individual's appeal against the heavenly court is successful – and, as Christie also suggests, this aligns Powell and Pressburger with the rise of existentialism as a post-war continental philosophy.[14] A ripe motif for this existential self-definition is to be found in the sequence where Peter, last seen disappearing out of his aeroplane, is washed ashore, alive, lost and perplexed. His arrival in this strange 'new' place – which could be Heaven, might be an evocation of classical antiquity complete with Pan, a naked boy piping to his goats, but in fact turns out to be the south coast of England – casts him as a Robinson Crusoe figure, cut off from cultural ties and quizzically noticing his own shadow as proof of his mortal existence.

At the individual level, the faith invested in Peter can, then, be seen to associate the film-makers with progressive continental philosophy. Stress is laid on the logic of Peter's subjective fantasy and on the importance to Peter of his belief in them. We are asked (via Dr Reeves' ongoing diagnosis) to take Peter's Heaven seriously and literally – and by extension to consider the ethical positions about free will and predestination which are argued out before its tribunal. The film also moves away from the individual, psychological storyline to place Peter's personal 'case' in an Anglo-American setting, casting him as an exemplar of Englishness, constructing his identity around the mythic stereotype of the war hero and writing him into a nation's post-war future. It is with a sense of heroic 'grace', of noble acceptance, that Peter jumps from his aeroplane without a parachute. Ripeness is all. He asks June to pass a farewell message to his mother and sisters. He relishes Western philosophy and the English literary canon. He is so committed to public utterance that, with typical English reticence, he has to ask June to write the note to his mother. It is all the more paradoxically moving, then, that he openly declares how much he loves his family. This is a man 'doing the right thing' – 'putting his house in order' – and he later has to insist to the heavens that he was 'ready' to die that night.

While playing out his final heroic scene, of course, he also falls in love with June's voice. In various ways, the film marks transitions like this between wartime scenarios (heroism, patriotism, death in battle, sacrifice) and private, romantic desires. Faces from generic war films people Peter's fantasy – the American Bonar Colleano from *The Way to the Stars* appears briefly as a Flying Fortress captain arriving at Heaven's entrance lobby, and Richard Attenborough, familiar from *In Which We Serve* (David Lean and Noël Coward, 1942) makes a wide-eyed cameo as a dead serviceman. These ghost figures indicate where *AMOLAD* is pervaded by the persistent mythology of wartime, while its colour sequences, where longevity is eventually promised to both Peter and June, are far more concerned with the future. By colliding these different sets of values – through narrative and style – they are wittily intellectualised, and held up for comparison, although the emotional register of Peter's earthly romance with June can leave us with little doubt that the film will resolve itself by settling for a Technicolor Earth.

Theological and metaphysical questions are raised by the status and function of the film's vision of Heaven, but its apparent origin in Peter's psyche forces us to interpret it in worldly terms. Its apparent modernity (Alfred Junge's sets and drawings resemble those for Korda's science-fiction film, *Things to Come* [William Cameron Menzies, 1936]) suggests a planned futuristic State, yet its rigid order alludes to totalitarian regimes (Soviet or Fascist). The global purview of this Heaven also captures the supra-nationalist ethos of the nascent United Nations. Its clerkly regimentation and officialdom, audibly signalled by the ticking, metronome precision of Allan Gray's soundtrack music, also catches the tone of post-war Britain, with the government's commitment to equality of opportunity, to full employment, and its new system of National Insurance (as the film points out, everyone has a 'file' on Earth). Raymond Durgnat is, though, too concrete when he argues that Peter's reluctance to enter this 'Socialist Utopia' signifies an innate Toryism to the film.[15] In his radio conversation with June, Peter admits in a carefully balanced aphorism that he is 'Conservative by instinct, Labour by experience', a topical reference to the 1945 change of government, and it is worth dwelling on how this relates to the film's larger argument about free will, individuality and social contract. It is possible to see Peter's admission as a continuation of one of the lines of reasoning made by Powell in and about *Blimp*. In 1942, Powell defended that film by arguing that Englishmen were 'by nature conservative, insular, unsuspicious, believers in good sportsmanship and anxious to believe the best of other people'.[16] While he hoped that those 'virtues' would be 'un-changing', he saw that in 'total war' they could become fatally divorced from *realpolitik*. Hence, the film's painful but necessary ideological readjustment towards a more socially progressive vision of the 'People's War'. Admitting that there is a distinction between Powell's use of lower-case 'conservatism' and Peter's upper-case 'Conservatism' three years later, there is nevertheless a thread connecting Powell's sense of natural old-fashioned attitudes and Peter's recollection of his Tory instincts.

Peter's new-found Labour affiliation is the effect, it seems, of historical processes. Like old Candy in *Blimp*, he has won a new awareness. Peter, though, has intelligently seen through his innate Toryism while still in his relative youth. Clearly, it would not have been unusual in Britain for an intellectual writer to mark an allegiance with leftist politics in the 1930s and 1940s. Peter's status as a war hero, though, affirms the sense that the discourse of wartime mythology led smoothly towards sympathy for Clement Attlee's government, even though that sympathy cost Winston Churchill the premiership. This rejection of the wartime Prime Minister may, in part, explain the slight inflection of regret in Peter's admission, although his dissatisfaction with his instinctive Conservative values may actually pre-date the war and the 'experiences' he alludes to may be as much to do with his sense of social injustice in the 1930s as with any sense that the war effort demanded the utopian New Jerusalem of the Welfare State. The election of the majority Labour government in 1945 was no radical gesture. Its consensus politics arose from the wartime coalition, and while the social legislation passed in the mid- to late 1940s may well have been a small revolution, the structure of society remained intact. Peter identifies with the aims of the post-war government – he is knitted into a new egalitarian social formation, which can at least claim, in its universality, to endorse the sense of social coherence once associated with 'One Nation' Toryism.

Why, then, does the film distance itself from the 'Welfare State' of Heaven? The answer is in Dr Reeves' statement to the heavenly court: 'I am pleading, sir, for the rights of the individual against the system.' When Peter says he is 'Conservative by instinct, Labour by experience', he defines himself as a voter, parliamentary democracy's paradigm unitary, thinking subject. The conventions of classical cinema also favour instinctive, individual, unusual personal virtues ('hero status'). Peter retains much of this existential, special quality, but his new politics also ally him with the common man, the hero of Labourism. This is what makes him such a genuinely transitional (or ambiguous) character. The reason why this Labour supporter resists the colourless, planned logic of his Heaven is because, as the film makes clear, he is, by instinct, an 'uncommon man'. It is left to Richard Attenborough, the unnamed pilot and familiar wartime Everyman, to embrace the functional orderliness of Peter's 'Other World' in his brief cameo, when he declares 'It's Heaven, isn't it,' to the officer angel (Kathleen Byron) who has shown him and Bob Trubshaw (Robert Coote) the clerical work needed to keep this metaphysical regime running smoothly. For the common man in 1945, job security, cleanliness and equality may well have had their appeal, and in this sense the film has an undoubted tone of social progressiveness, yet, ambivalently, the infinite rows of grey office desks also speak of alienation and the bleak, glacial humour of Kafka. Despite *AMOLAD*'s formally un-classical appearance (and the foreground patterns and repetitions in its narrative), its more classical operations urge us to identify with Peter as an individual, and to celebrate his stand against the 'system'. Just as *Blimp*'s propaganda function (its sense of history) shows how individuals are recruited into a social order, while at the same time its liberal, sentimental, personal register (its sense of memory and desire) expresses a utopian reservoir of unassimilated 'human' emotions which exceeds the social and cannot be fully incorporated (as Chapter 2 argues), *AMOLAD*'s romantic storyline charts a resistance to the system.

The rights of the individual co-exist with the film's self-conscious inquiry into the nation's place in the world, its view of Englishness and, more widely, of national identity *per se*. The omniscient eye of its animated prelude falls towards England through the 'pea-souper' fog in the Channel, and the voiceover insists that this 'is a *real* English fog'. It is significant that it hits upon the island via this strategically vital route, the defence of which figured so strongly in the war. Descending to Earth, an audio-montage mixes Morse code, foghorns, radio voices (including Churchill's), while the voiceover sets up a chain of references by imploring us to 'Listen to all the noises in the air. Listen. Listen.' There is a nod here to *A Canterbury Tale*, which opens with a manuscript map of the Pilgrim's Way – another aerial view of southern England. The shooting script of that film had alluded to Shakespeare's *The Tempest* (which Powell later planned to film) by emphasising that the village of Chillingbourne at night should be 'awful and mysterious, full of strange shapes, stranger sounds, menacing shadows'. *AMOLAD*'s England is yet another version of Prospero's cell, 'full of noises'. By shifting from monochrome to Technicolor, and to and from fantasy, it also perpetuates the link to *The Wizard of Oz* (Victor Fleming, 1939, US) which was set up in *Blimp* and continued in *A Canterbury Tale*. The opening sequence of *AMOLAD* also conjures memories of Humphrey Jennings' and Stewart McAllister's short documentary masterpiece *Listen to Britain* (1942). A preamble to that film explicitly commands us to 'listen to Britain', and an audio-visual montage then commences which binds the nation together by taking snatches of BBC broadcasts and knitting them together with images of the country to create a coherent fabric of sound and image. The opening noises from *AMOLAD*'s England are topical and familiar, and they show Powell and Pressburger's occasional proximity to Jennings' neo-Romantic documentary work. *A Canterbury Tale* had been a more sustained exploration of these affiliations, using extensive location work, but the 'traditional' rural ethos survives into *AMOLAD*. It was partly filmed on the Devon coast, and features images of village life seen through a local GP's camera obscura. Peter himself has harkened to the English Renaissance by quoting Walter Raleigh and 'Andy Marvell' to June in his opening scene. More particularly, Shakespeare's pastoral comedies are acknowledged in the incorporation of *A Midsummer Night's Dream*, the spectacle and performativity of which also invites us to see *AMOLAD* as a 'modern masque', as Ian Christie has usefully proposed.[17]

We hear a brief moment of Mendelsohn's music for the play, and then see an amateur production of it being rehearsed by American soldiers. Various themes are at work here. The play's magic-fantasy-pastoral narrative of heterosexual union informs the film, and is consistent with this strain in the Archers' work. These themes are then overlaid with a set of American perspectives. In a baronial-style banqueting hall (a studio set solidly fashioned by Alfred Junge), preparations for the play are being made. A portrait of a Renaissance lady dominates the room: a reminder of the courtly, chivalric ideals which Peter has inherited, and the literary canon of which he is both a descendent and a distillation. The portrait has grandeur. There are intimations of 'Gloriana' herself about the lady, but she is an enigma to a young American girl from whose point of view we inspect the painting. Her non-plussed attention (somewhere between fascination and confusion) is a reminder of Bob Johnson's naïvety in *A Canterbury Tale*. Where the confrontation between Reeves and Farlan in the heavenly court case towards the end of the film refers to Lexington, Boston and the Anglo-American war of the 1770s, the supposed age of the painting, dating from the early modern period of England's naval supremacy and early imperial adventures, erases historical change by evoking a period before the independence of the modern USA. Peter, of course, is spiritually at home with Renaissance culture, and is seeking to undo the divorce between the two nations by marriage to Boston-born June. The blank gaze of the American girl looking at the portrait signifies the distance between the two cultures, while, ambivalently, the possibility of her connecting with the portrait through a process of identification (the vanity of the portrait-sitter mirrors the girl's own vanity as she checks her stockings; the portrait displays the sitter's femininity and Peter soon notices the girl's own preening…) allows for the wider possibility of harmony and understanding across both time and space.

A group of soldiers are rehearsing the 'Pyramus and Thisbe' scene for the director (a plummy-voiced local vicar), whose disapproval of an overly enthusiastic performance causes him to shout out 'Bottom's not a gangster!', an allusion to James Cagney's generally celebrated role as Bottom in the Max Reinhardt/William Dieterle film version of the play (1935, US). As well as showing Powell and Pressburger's undifferentiated willingness to allude both to modern cinema and to Renaissance 'high culture', the various geographical bridges in play (not just Anglo-American, but also reaching to Austria-Germany with Mendelsohn, Reinhardt and Dieterle) are characteristic of Powell and Pressburger's insistent internationalism. As a personification of the nation's literary *and* military elite Peter represents the soldier-poet. Like Walter Raleigh, Philip Sidney, Lord Byron or Rupert Brooke before him, this fusion of literary and martial endeavour forms a gentlemanly ideal, and is a deeply conservative, class-bound, heroic mode. Dr Reeves makes explicit the film's connection between nationhood, clear-sightedness and literariness when he pays Peter the loaded compliment: 'I like your point of view and I like your *English*.'

Yet the film is ceaselessly anti-xenophobic. Faith in English culture is balanced with openness to foreigners. In the court case which brings the film to a resolution, the American Abraham Farlan is a loathsome bigot. The shooting script describes him as having 'a blimpish hatred of the English', and describes that in their first encounter, he and Reeves are presented 'as they imagine each other to be'. The confrontational court procedure therefore positions them to see each other as stereotypes. Cultural insults are traded: the commentary of cricket at Lords is tedious nonsense to Farlan; American bee-bop crooning is nonsensical mass culture to Reeves (this marks Reeves' specific elitism: Powell and Pressburger had endorsed 1940s American jazz in *Blimp*). When Farlan and Reeves confront each other without prejudice, they see each other more humanely. National difference is acknowledged, but awkward historical embarrassment is spirited away when Farlan's first international jury, representing various peoples victimised or dispossessed in the name of British imperialism (Irish, French, Boer, Russian, Indian, Chinese) are exchanged, at Reeves' insistence, for an identical multi-racial group, this time all of them subsumed as American citizens under the flag of the stars and stripes. A series of dissolves replaces each original jury member by an American equivalent (the same actors playing both). These easy dissolves between nationhood suggest the geographical fluidity of national identity, a fantastically easy acquisition of new identities which salutes the inclusiveness of the American constitution, with Farlan's strident rhetoric about American freedom ('America, sir, is the only place where man is full grown') fulfilling the film's pro-American requirements.

A brief closing scene takes place in a hospital recovery room. Peter comes round from the anaesthetic to find June waiting by his bedside. A nurse (a more material 'angel'?) opens the curtains and, with a touching expression of teamwork, Peter smiles and says, 'We did it.' The gesture of opening curtains repeats a familiar motif from *A Canterbury Tale* and, more specifically, from David Lean's *Great Expectations* (1946). Alison ripping down the curtains on her moth-eaten caravan and Pip letting the sunlight pour into Satis House both ritually rehearse the end of the blackout and an optimistic readiness to face the post-war future. Close-ups held tightly on Peter and June at *AMOLAD*'s closure tell us that their heterosexual partnership is our image of (inter)national hope as well as being their own personal utopia.

AMOLAD was originally devised earlier in the war as a propaganda piece to bolster Anglo-American popular relations, and the romance plot between Peter and June still succeeds in doing this. During the war, and up until its closing stages, the American presence in Britain was not universally popular. This was what the film sought to redress. Arriving on screen for the Royal Film Performance in late 1946, as the chill of the Cold War was beginning to bite, its meaning had shifted. Sue Harper and Vincent Porter's republication of a Soviet review of the film pinpoints precisely how the effect of propaganda can deviate from its intent.[18] As they report, the Soviet critic viewed the film as a desperate and hostile attempt to yoke British interests to the USA, and to propagandise the establishment of an Anglo-American power bloc. The official British response to this was one of denial: the Russian critic is alleged to have misread the film disastrously. Harper and Porter suggest that the foreign policy of the Labour government was committed to maintaining good relations with the Soviet Union, while also remaining cosy to the USA, and that the release of the film at this time put their bipartisan approach in jeopardy.[19] This is a perceptive comment, yet the economic conditions of the late 1940s had clearly exhibited Britain's reliance on credit and aid from the USA.

5. Post-war, post-op reparations: David Niven and Kim Hunter embrace the future in *A Matter of Life and Death*. (BFI Stills, © Carlton International Media Ltd)

It was, though, the experimental play with visuals and narrative form which perplexed many critics (trade papers were understandably more impressed by the technical achievements). Matters of cinematic style cannot be considered without reference to history, and *AMOLAD*'s realist, as much as its anti-realist, elements are bedded down in national and international cultures. Those elements which derive, however loosely, from either the British documentary style, or from neo-Romantic art or from fantasy-based cinema are all bound up with its representation of wartime masculinity and its treatment of national identity. *AMOLAD* is in many ways Powell and Pressburger's most spectacular work: audacious in design, conceptually ambitious and dramatically idiosyncratic, it anticipates their later forays into formal audio-visual experimentation and meta-cinema, where the cinematic medium itself, and its modes of representation, are put under scrutiny. *AMOLAD* is a magician's bag of effects, with unexpected dissolves, freeze frames, the removal of all sound, film playing backwards and famously surprising point-of-view shots (from behind Peter's closing eyelid, or from Dr Reeves' camera obscura). John Ellis, in a highly perceptive piece, notes that the clash of cinematic discourses is what structures *AMOLAD*. He goes further to point out that the two discursive dialects employed here are particularly meaningful in the context of British cinema in the mid-1940s. '*A Matter of Life and Death* begins to disrupt the process of subject positioning by providing more than one point of intelligibility,' he argues, 'by providing two regimes of coherence for the subject: that of a narrative love-story, and that of a more "documentary" mode of exposition and explanation.'[20] The monochrome 'Other World', with its authority, and its sense of order (located not least in the voiceover which opens the film) endorses a set of values associated with the documentary movement of the war period. The love plot disrupts this order: it is individualistic and, what is more, it is premised on sexual attraction. While Ellis rightly identifies these two regimes as alternative modes of address (embodying mindsets which are synthesised only through the film's balanced appeal to both reason and justice in the heavenly court case), it is worth pointing out that in those 'classic' British feature films which exhibit the influence of the documentary movement there is often a struggle between objective/realistic/social/public aspects and the more individual, melodramatic elements. The social types peopling documentaries are fleshed-out, individuated and made sites of identification, often leading to awkward shifts in register from social-public discourse to private storylines of individual psychology. The realist story-documentary (the hyphenation

Post-war Masculinities: The Pilot and the Back-room Boy   151

admits the yoking together of distinct forms) was perhaps best explored by Humphrey Jennings' film about the Auxiliary Fire Service, *Fires Were Started* (1943), with Basil Dearden's fictional AFS film, *The Bells Go Down* (1943), made for Ealing and starring James Mason and Tommy Trinder, standing comparison as a feature film which covers similar turf. While admitting the ideological differences between the documentary form and narrative realism, it is still possible to see both *Fires Were Started* and *The Bells Go Down* as synergistic marriages.

AMOLAD is one of the first films where Powell and Pressburger ask their audience to reflect on the nature of cinema spectacle by providing them with a conflict of representations. For *I Know Where I'm Going!* they built a convincing whirlpool, but it exists within a realistic regime (however much the film is imbued with myth) and we are expected to believe in its literal truth. The moving staircase in *AMOLAD* demands a greater suspension of disbelief and proudly parades its 'illusory' nature. Like a cinema spectator, Peter is diagnosed by Dr Reeves as 'having a series of highly organized hallucinations comparable to an experience of actual life, a combination of vision, of hearing, and of idea'. These hallucinations are accompanied by an imaginary sense of smell – in Peter's case he thinks he can smell fried onions when his visions appear. He is neurologically damaged, then, and his experience is one of synaesthesia, of slippage and correspondence between his senses. Powell and Pressburger later experimented with sound, music, colour, movement and drama themselves to create their own 'highly organized (synaesthetic) hallucinations' in *The Red Shoes* and elsewhere. Here, Dr Reeves' observation implicitly invites us to see the parallel between Peter's diegetic visions, and our own cinematic ones, and to see the reflexivity at play. The effect, though, is not Brechtian. Promoting the spectator's awareness of the medium is not set to destroy the illusion, as politically modernist Film Theory would be advocating by the 1970s, when the spectacle of mainstream cinema was seen to be ideologically corrupt. Instead, the aim is to parade cinema's ingenuity – and to celebrate it. In *Film as Art*, Rudolf Arnheim, the early psychological theorist of film, posited the notion of 'partial illusionism', in which viewers recognise the 'artificial' nature of their vision and in which the film medium never becomes transparent.[21] This is exactly the form of non-radical, idealistic spectacle which is often underscored in Powell and Pressburger's films. Poised between art-house and popular cinema, their set-pieces send eddies through the smooth current of the narrative (if only through fetishised excess). These moments of spectacle rarely operate as anti-illusionist,

Brechtian estrangement effects, because rhetorically they demand that we believe in the illusion, and their films remain securely rooted within an idealistic-romantic mindset. Powell and Pressburger assume that the collaborative spirit in which they were made has been embraced by the viewer, whose own transfiguring imagination is brought to the cinema to intercede between the worlds of film and reality. The medium itself comes to be romanticised. Raymond Durgnat, writing on Powell in 1970, recognised this quality. One of the first critics to reassess the Archers' work, his contribution nevertheless pre-dates the notoriously belated acknowledgement of Pressburger's involvement in the works. Thus, '[Powell's] films…relate to…a spectacular cinema which asks the audience to relish the spectacle as such, to a school of "Cinema" which is always exquisitely conscious of not only its cinematic effects but its cinematic nature'.[22]

SAMMY RICE

The Small Back Room's attitude to men, heroes and scientists can be cast into sharper relief by comparing it to a later film which schematically covers a similar terrain. Six years after *The Small Back Room* (and two years before he sent David Niven's Phileas Fogg around the world), the English director Michael Anderson released *The Dam Busters* (1954), a tribute to both Barnes Wallis, the inventor of the 'bouncing bomb', and to Guy Gibson, the wing commander whose squadron successfully used the invention to destroy the Ruhr dams. Like Powell and Pressburger's films *The Battle of the River Plate* and *Ill Met by Moonlight*, it is one of a spate of British genre war films which, during the 1950s, heroised, mythologised and sentimentalised carefully extracted narratives of the conflict. *The Dam Busters* is worth mentioning here because of the schematic way in which it handles its two central male characters, one a representative of the 'boffin' class, the other of the 'officer' class, implying that their complementary skills were what made the project to wreck the German dams so successful. In effect, the film splits its heroic function into two apparently equal protagonists, Barnes Wallis (Michael Redgrave) and Guy Gibson (Richard Todd). Wallis is nervous, twitchy and bespectacled. Wading into the sea with his trousers rolled up to collect bomb shrapnel after one of his test drops, he is an eccentric 'holy fool'. As he admits, 'there's such a thin dividing line between inspiration and obsession'. While Wallis has a full-time job working for Vickers, we first see him in his garden trying to solve

Post-war Masculinities: The Pilot and the Back-room Boy 153

a scientific problem by recruiting his children to help with his experiment. Science equals playing (it is a 'fine old game'). His development of the bouncing bomb is extra-curricular, and his health is jeopardised by the workload he takes on. He is frustrated by a Whitehall committee culture whose deadening machinations are an obstacle to him, and he has a doctor, his GP (to most audiences, the most familiar representative of the scientific classes) with whom he can talk through his ideas. The image of science here is unthreatening: it is romanticised, individualised and made a matter of amateur enthusiasm. Wallis's eccentricities are signs of genius – he is a prophet in our secularised culture and, although faith is invested in technology and the practical problems of weapon production and labour shortages are discussed, the institutions of government are critiqued for their short-sighted failure to invest wisely in Wallis's time and knowledge. The film observes, then, some of the more familiar patterns of the biopic genre, pitting Wallis against an establishment which will, ultimately, recognise him. Science, in an atomic age, is better conceived, it seems, through the cliché of the slightly dotty but fundamentally harmless and eventually justified 'boffin', unhampered in his experiments by faceless bureaucracy. The stereotype carries with it a danger, though: with this much latitude granted to the individual scientist, personal ethics and social conscience are at a premium. The need to make science godly, and to cast the scientist as a holy priest, has a corollary – that it might grow devilish. Hence the demonised figures of science run mad, and the ambiguities coldly explored in Alexander MacKendrick's satire, *The Man in the White Suit* (1951).

The Dam Busters' pilot, Guy Gibson, is the film's other protagonist, handsome, solid and caring. He and his dog Nigger are devoted to each other, yet, as befits Gibson's heroic function, he has no family responsibilities in the film and can wholeheartedly commit to the campaign. As Robert Murphy reminds us, Gibson was actually married,[23] but the utter effacement of sex from the war film is typical, and is an echo of the Imperial epic's separated worlds of domesticity and heroics, where the soldiery is a displacement of heterosexual energy and yet is proof of masculine prowess. Gibson is able to synthesise bravery (the dangers of flying at 60 feet are mentioned) and intellectual curiosity – he is keen to learn the theory behind the bomb and, famously, he himself then hits on the idea of using twin spotlights to measure his flying height. As he selects his elite crew (Oxford athletes, a Coney Island beach guard, etc.) to form his squadron, he begins to take over the narrative from Wallis. The film's key transitional period is when the first test drops are carried out at Chesil Bank (coincidentally, the location Powell chose for the end of *The Small Back Room*). Wallis, impotent once the raids over Germany have commenced, admits where real narrative agency rests: 'I'm beginning to think the job of inventing [the bomb] was small compared with the job of dropping it.' As the film closes, Wallis walks one way, Gibson the other, but the focus is on Gibson, his sense of duty, and the sacrifice of the squadron's missing men. Clearly, the film has decided to worship its more obvious hero – the practitioner, not the theoretician; the front line of attack, not the back-room boy.

Nigel Balchin's novel, *The Small Back Room*, declares its satirical purpose by opening with a Swiftian epigraph from Gulliver's voyage to Lagado, where professors laboured to extract gunpowder from ice, and sunshine from cucumbers. Sammy's first person narrative then commences in a very different tone: deadpan cynicism. 'In 1928,' Chapter One opens, 'my foot was hurting all the time, so they took it off and gave me an aluminium one that only hurt about three-quarters of the time.' Balchin was a trained scientist and a successful industrialist. He worked as a psychologist for the War Office, and then as the Army Council's Deputy Scientific Advisor, where part of his job was to comment on the usefulness of new inventions to the war effort. His insights into the realities of Civil Service operations, psychology and scientific knowledge give a sense of hectic realism to his psychologically vivid novel. It views bureaucracy disdainfully, while its view of science is largely pragmatic and sympathetic. The satirical edge is sidelined, and instead we are given a character study of a protagonist whose unlikely sense of failure, whose sense of frustration and whose self-pity is so deeply imbued that hope seems misplaced. He is a loser.

The film's narrative is a streamlined yet faithful rendition of Balchin's novel. Robert Murphy points out that 'in marked contrast to the wartime films, [it] shows the war effort as bedevilled by cynicism, vanity and personal ambition'.[24] Certainly, the dark tone of this film sets it apart from films like *In Which We Serve*, but nevertheless it is still governed by the dominant fictions of manhood which characterise British war films. The narrative is straightforward. Sammy Rice, crippled, and with a long-standing drink problem, works for Professor Mair's (Milton Rosmer) research unit, a loose organisation fronted by the ambitious oleaginous salesman, R.B. Waring (Jack Hawkins). Sammy, who is dating Waring's secretary Sue, is consulted by an army man, Captain Stuart (Michael Gough), about an unfamiliar booby-trap device which the Germans are dropping. No unexploded devices have yet been found. In a sub-plot, Sammy is involved in testing a new Reeves gun, which the army does not like, but which Waring has sold, prematurely, to the Ministry of Defence. Plots are afoot around Whitehall to rationalise all research work – red tape is encroaching. As stress mounts in Sammy's relationship with Sue – caused by work, by Sammy's inferiority complex and by his drink problem – Stuart finds two booby-traps intact. Stuart is killed defusing the first; Sammy successfully defuses the second. In a coda, Sammy is given a properly funded unit to head as research is put on a proper footing. He is also given a uniform, and Colonel Holland, a pragmatic military man, makes a 'victory speech' which endorses the need for an efficient, professional campaign. Sammy returns home with Sue.

Homeliness is otherwise missing from this film. Sammy is often to be found in his local bar, a rowdy place, often full of men in uniform. Here, he gets drunk and starts fights. The barman is played by Sid James, and the walls behind the bar are decorated with framed photographs celebrating the barman's macho boxing career: he is one of the many men who are more physically able than Sammy. The bar is never a safe haven. It is merely an alternative to 'home'. Throughout the film, space (especially interior space) is disturbed. When Sue telephones Sammy's home to find him for Stuart in the opening sequence, his empty flat is first seen when a roaming camera trespasses and roams unsettlingly about it. The eponymous 'small back room' is Sammy's workplace, but his small home – a claustrophobic refuge – is another. Sammy and Sue's regular night out at the 'Hickory Tree' restaurant is rudely invaded by an old girlfriend of Sue's, an instance which draws attention to Sammy's inability to dance. After a cramped, tense tube journey with Sue (with his foot causing him agony), their sanctuary at his flat is interrupted by the telephone ringing to summon him to Bala in North Wales, where a young gunner (Bryan Forbes) has been badly injured by one of the booby-traps. Returning to the 'small back room' where the unit does its research, Sammy talks to his assistant Corporal Taylor (Cyril Cusack) about the booby-trap, and also about Taylor's domestic problems (explicitly, in the novel, his wife is seeing other men – here, this is muted, tellingly, to 'trouble at home' involving his wife). Throughout this conversation, feet endlessly and noisily tramp overhead, the outside world seen through a roof grille. A committee meeting is later drowned by drilling outside. Sammy's drunken trashing of his flat is halted by his telephone ringing again, this time to call him to Chesil Bank to deal with an unexploded bomb. This repeated pattern denies any sense of ease. The ringing telephone is a sign of intrusion, yet the silent telephone is a sign of alienation. Open spaces – the Reeves gun tests at Stonehenge and the climactic sequence on Chesil Bank – contrast with the cramped interior scenes, and underscore their claustrophobia.

Writing primarily about *The Small Back Room*, John Ellis draws a character sketch of Emeric Pressburger from this uncomfortable spatial and psychological tension. Noting Pressburger's 'uneasy status' in Britain, Ellis suggests that he 'loved the place; yet he feared absorption just as much as he desired acceptance. As a result he gave us a series of awkward fictions, exposing raw feelings and ambivalences whose existence the British would rather not acknowledge.'[25] It is perceptive to read *The Small Back Room* as exposing British sexual and social mores, and the Archers' representation of Britain as homely, unhomely, wonderful, outmoded, infuriating, parochial and neurotic may well express Pressburger's alien status. Ellis's account foregrounds similarities between *The Small Back Room* and earlier Powell-Pressburger films which might otherwise go unnoticed.

Professor Mair's ill-organised and cramped place of work is an *ad hoc* institution, a little amateur, but as likely to hit upon an inspired solution to whatever problem it encounters as it is to explore fruitless lines of inquiry. Captain Stuart is first surprised to find the unit signposted by a tatty, handwritten notice, and no one seems to know what it is actually called, what its terms of reference are, or to whom it reports. Mair himself is a white-haired, avuncular academic. While this typifies a familiar cliché of scientific research (anticipating the eccentricities of Barnes Wallis in *The Dam Busters*), the sympathetic treatment of an anti-establishment, non-corporatist outfit (Mair has gathered intuitive men of genius like Sammy around him, while Waring is just a sycophantic salesman) is also an inflection of Powell and Pressburger's fondness for non-incorporated, or marginal, positions which are associated with that most praised of virtues – freedom. There are echoes here of *AMOLAD*'s resistance to its over-systematic Heaven. The quirky ethos of Mair's outfit, and its oppositional stance towards super-rationalism and towards Waring's amoral marketeering, mark its commitment, like Colpeper's Chillingbourne, to other forms of knowledge. Science here, like Colpeper's sense of 'history', is mingled with the craft of magic. There is a reminder of *I Know Where I'm Going!*, where local, Scottish anti-materialism wins over the spirit of profiteering industry (whose embodiment, Joan's fiancé, is banished to an off-screen space), and in the coda to *The Small Back Room* Colonel Holland's 'big speech' has an echo, too, of *Blimp*. Mair's outfit, charming and affectionately viewed, has to be regarded as useless in 'total war'. Holland is meant to persuade us of this, and we should be reassured that the move towards greater rationalisation which he promises will be based on his own common-sense pragmatism, not on Waring's dubious politicking. These ideals sympathise, coincidentally, with Powell's own views about film-making and creative freedom in the mid-1940s: 'I don't like the word art. My view is that the cinema is a craft and while it remains a craft, it's all right – no one need be frightened, but once it becomes an industry…' (from a radio interview on 26 January 1945).[26] Powell would come to use the word 'Art' more happily. At this stage, he is still keen to think of his workplace as a manageably small community. 'The Ministry', which ghosts through *The Small Back Room* and is peopled by Machiavellian bureaucrats, has a deadening effect on the unit's creativity and is not to be trusted. In a brief comic interlude, 'The Minister' himself is wheeled in (played by Robert Morley, but credited, cabaret-style, as a 'special guest' – a joke emphasising how little he belongs to the film world). He is a bumbling fool who is suitably impressed by the display of 'magic' experiments and illusions which the unit puts on for him.

Mair's outfit is as remote from the mainstream as Sammy is from the dominant fiction of wartime manhood. Neither the novel nor the film explains why Sammy's foot is missing, although the connotation of his involvement with weaponry (and, in particular, with the unexploded booby-traps) strongly implies a connection between the amputation and a previous bomb incident. Many commentators, such as Robert Murphy, assume, understandably, that the foot has been blown off.[27] The film elides the information given in the novel that the foot was removed as long ago as 1928 and, given the way the film explores Sammy's apparent inability to measure up to the ego-ideal of the 'war hero', the link between this disability and the conflict is clearly encouraged. Powell and Pressburger do not shy away from Sammy's disability – early sequences feature close-up shots of his hidden false foot, and a sense of his gnawing discomfort is sustained – but the literal self-loathing of Balchin's Sammy is downplayed, as is his sense of failure. When asked, at Chesil Bank, if he was ever a surfer, David Farrar's Sammy remembers a time when he used to be: in the novel, the question is tellingly unanswered. An early screenplay in Powell's handwriting has Sammy fling off his troublesome false foot after Captain Stuart's first visit. The explicit sight of either a stump or a prosthetic limb is censored from the final film, and throughout, David Farrar's good looks are more striking than the image of the character which Balchin paints. On film, then Sammy is slightly closer to the physical ideal.

Most of the published studies of adaptations (of 'literary works') into film are troubled by – or fixate upon – the same old chestnuts. The pre-existence of a written text invites an assessment of the 'fidelity' issue, which is premised upon a loaded notion of the original work ('of art'), and the usual, commonplace conclusion which these studies alight upon is that films are culturally/historically different, but that the differences are, in their own ways, either irrelevant or interesting. Either way, the faithfulness/looseness of the adaptation is given a value-laden consideration. It is uncommon now to assume that a text – written or filmed – might have just one 'true' meaning, as Brian McFarlane points out,[28] while well-rehearsed ideas of intertextuality, and wider concepts of the postmodern, would seem to have made redundant the sort of language in which adaptation is often discussed. McFarlane's is one of the few attempts to approach the subject objectively, theoretically and formally. He draws on Roland Barthes to distinguish between what he calls 'transferable' and 'adaptable' elements, the former being those elements which can be displayed on film, the latter those for which 'different equivalences' need to be found.[29] Narratives, he argues, can be broken down into 'distributional' and 'integrational' elements. Distributional elements ('linear' storyline activities, i.e. things which are 'done') can be transferred more or less directly to film. Integrational elements (or 'indices') convey the atmospherics of psychological identity, place, etc. McFarlane divides them into 'informants' (pure pieces of data, such as place names) which are transferable, and 'indices proper', those diffuse, vague senses of character which require adaptation.

In *The Small Back Room*, some key informants – places – are changed, and the fact that a straightforward transfer was possible indicates the importance of geography to the film-makers. The testing of the Reeves gun is shifted from Graveley Bank ('a bare bleak place with a tearing east wind that never stopped blowing…guaranteed to leave me feeling like death'). to Stonehenge. This cinematically arresting location has picturesque qualities, but it also imprints an ancient, mystical English landscape onto the film. It has what the painter Paul Nash liked to call *genius loci* – spirit of place. Stonehenge, like Cerne Abbas and Avebury, is the sort of talismanic location to which neo-Romantic art, such as the Anglicised Surrealism of Nash, was drawn. The association of neo-Romanticism was discussed earlier with regard to *A Canterbury Tale*'s visionary pastoralism, and I have argued that Paul Nash's paintings are in sight when we look at Alfred Junge's sets for *Blimp*'s First World War sequences. The symbolism of Stonehenge – its Englishness, timelessness, its religious-mystical properties and its geometric, mathematical purpose – clearly expresses the themes of *The Small Back Room*'s narrative, although it is fair to say the camera does not dwell overly on its 'spirit of place'. It does, however, form part of an ongoing and consistent neo-Romanticism in Powell and Pressburger's work and allies them with a leading aesthetic movement across the arts in 1940s Britain (a movement which, in cinema history, is occluded by the focus on 'quality realism'). Powell and Pressburger make other geographical changes. Lowallen, an unspecified location 150 miles from London where the gunner has been badly injured by one of the booby-traps, is changed to Bala (and the novel's General Hospital becomes a makeshift tent where the gunner is dying). We see here another sign of Powell and Pressburger gravitating towards the Celtic fringe.

The most significant relocation takes the final defusing sequence from Luganporth to Chesil Bank, Dorset. In the novel, Luganporth is four hours by train from London, but is otherwise un-placed for the reader by Balchin. It is a sandy beach, 'a God-forsaken bit of coast' in Stuart's words. Chesil Bank excited Powell (volume two of his autobiography, *Million Dollar Movie*, devotes 500 words to describing it), and he was convinced early on that the shifting, pebble spit should be the location for the defusing sequence. His handwritten draft screenplay says of Chesil: 'It is a setting peculiarly English: its vast desolation, set against the trim Dorset landscape, is exhilarating. It has the quality of Elizabethan poetry, but Michael Drayton rather than Shakespeare.' Powell's schooling in Renaissance literature is often displayed, in echoes of Shakespeare coursing through his and Pressburger's annotated screenplays, for example (not least in *AMOLAD*). Here, he does not expand on his reference to Drayton, but the choice of this relatively little-known writer associates Powell with the myth-making of the British landscape. Drayton (1563–1631) wrote historical, religious and topographical verse. His principal work, 'Poly-olbion' (written between 1613 and 1622) is a collection of thirty 'Songs' which chart his journeys around England, featuring descriptions of landscape, local culture, legends and fragments of history. One of the impulses behind Powell's location work echoes Drayton's (and is reminiscent of Colpeper's): his tourist's gaze wants to photograph, celebrate and advertise these magic places. One of the few sets of extreme long shots in the film establishes a 'spirit of place' at Chesil, and at the nearby Abbotsbury Castle. Chesil Bank is also a ripe symbol. In the handwritten draft screenplay, Lieutenant-Colonel Strang says to Sammy: 'It's a strange place. It's unique in Europe. A sea-wall constructed by the sea, against itself (he broods). The Law of Compensation.' Chesil Bank's pebbles crunch and shift underfoot and with the waves, and its audible instability heightens the suspense of the sequence, evoking Sammy's own neurotic insecurity; Strang's dramatic phrase (omitted from the film) suggests a dynamic balance of self-defence and self-destruction, a topographical rendition of Sammy's contorted psychology (and more prosaically the natural sea-defence also has clear ramifications during wartime). And Chesil is another liminal place, not entirely England.

'Indices proper', in McFarlane's template, cannot be transferred directly. The novel's first person narration controls its atmospheric tone, but Balchin's sophisticated use of irony tells us more about Sammy than he is conscious of (his humility blinds him to his good points, for example). Cinema tends towards objectivity, and restricting narration to a single point of view is rare. Conversely, entirely omniscient narration, where a 'meta-language' of authorial commentary marshals and interprets characters' thoughts, words and deeds is difficult to sustain cinematically (for example, through extra-diegetic voiceover). Such elements tend, then, to be figured in the significant use of soundtrack, editing etc. *The Small Back Room* adapts the first person narration into what seems to be objective cinema, and the novel's psychological intensity is adapted into melodramatic camerawork and mise-en-scène. In Raymond Durgnat's telling phrase, 'the film's *style* paraphrases [Balchin's socially critical stoicism] by atmosphere'.[30] The tone changes with Sammy's solitary challenge to defuse the unexploded bomb. Claustrophobic sets and harsh lighting are abandoned for the open natural space of the beach; earlier warped close-ups of Sammy's tortured face, his aching ankle or his threatening telephone are now inflected differently, conveying instead Sammy's physical effort rather than his despair, or inspecting the bomb itself in cold, fetishistic detail. Sammy's occasional use of a field telephone provides an online commentary, and the realistic register of the sequence shifts the film away from its noir-melodramatic-Expressionist style towards the discourse of the traditional war film (anticipating Colonel Holland's propagandising coda). Importantly, it is through this discourse that Sammy is ultimately justified and repaired. The language of the war film signifies good masculine health.

Where the film re-plots distributional elements it does so to emphasise the 'booby-trap' storyline (thus isolating a clearer linear narrative), and conveniently to shift Susan, who co-habits with Sammy in the novel, to another flat just across the hallway. Excisions and alterations like this clearly have an effect – Balchin's world is more confusing and agitated – but they do little more than beat the narrative into the broad contours of a standard fictional film. Some alterations are more significant. Sammy's young nephew Dick, a decorated airman of the Guy Gibson / Peter Carter type, is left out of the film altogether, and then the events of the crucial defusing sequence are changed. These are the changes which impact most on Sammy's masculinity. Dick is 'rather a prize specimen – big and handsome and winning medals and so on'. He is already decorated with a DFC ribbon and is up for a DSO. In the novel he is a self-conscious image of perfection, a two-footed, handsome, 25 year old against whom Sammy finds himself wanting. His appearance in the novel is brief: Sammy hears that Dick has been killed just before he sets off to Luganporth, and he reflects morbidly in a note to Susan that if he too is to be killed, 'it'll put (him) alongside Dick, which is good enough for anybody'. Where Balchin taunts Sammy with this idealised justification for his inferiority complex, Powell and Pressburger prevent us making that invidious comparison, which is in Sammy's favour. Without Dick, Sammy can honestly tell Lieutenant-Colonel Strang – who is overseeing the crisis at Chesil – that with Stuart dead he is the man for the job as he has no family, because his unit knows all about the risk, and because, as far as he is concerned, 'Heaven can wait'. The speech is bravado, but it shows Powell and Pressburger allying Sammy with life rather than death. The first two of his considerations, about his family and employers, are lifted from Balchin. The third is an addition – a reference to Ernst Lubitsch's *Heaven Can Wait* (1943, US), of course, and an echo of *AMOLAD*. It is consistent with the other changes made to give the film a more positive, life-affirming slant: masochism transformed to heroism.

The sequence on Chesil Beach where Sammy is tested is the focal point of the narrative, and again Powell and Pressburger depart from Balchin's un-heroic cynicism to engineer Sammy's ascendancy. In the novel Sammy changes into shorts (socks covering the attachment of his false foot). The film omits this possible exposure of his disability: during the dismantling, Farrar takes off his jumper and hat in an angled medium close-up which emphasises his physique. Strang's offer to help him wrench open the bomb is refused, and Sammy then needs all his brute physical strength to get into it. With the bomb successfully defused, he says to Strang: 'Sorry, it was a personal matter.' He then collapses onto his back and a point-of-view shot of sky and seagulls undoes the tension and hints at transcendence. Characteristically, the novel refuses this utopian resolution. Sammy's strength fails him and he starts to sob. Strang appears next to him. 'He was wearing shorts and his chest and arms were naked, and looking up at him like that made him look enormous…I looked at him for a moment standing there with his big shoulders and the thick black hair on his chest and I knew I'd lost.' Sammy's galling adoration of Strang's physique shades into the masochistically homoerotic. Critically, he needs Strang to turn the wrench for him. Raymond Durgnat has suggested that it is Sammy's 'nerves' which fail him.[31] Not so: it is his muscles which give out. Powell and Pressburger conservatively beef up Sammy's filmic incarnation to raise him to a heroic pedestal. His ability to make his body work is then recognised by the military. This is unsurprising, for men's bodies have often been seen as instruments and masculinity has been judged according to what men's bodies can actually 'do'. In a railway farewell scene, Sammy looks down at Strang on the platform and says, 'I think I'll go put my feet up' (a linguistic slip which restores his symbolic two-footedness) and Strang replies, 'If anyone ever has any doubt about what you can do with your hands, your arms, or any other part of you, send 'em along to me.' The novel closes in a minor key, with Sammy still not liking what he is, and unable to be what he likes. He is alone in a cold wind, reflecting on Stuart and Dick, feeling trapped and alienated at work, covering his sense of failure with wry irony, and wanting to go home to Susan. The film's upbeat resolution is utopian in comparison. Powell's handwritten screenplay shows where Sammy's credentials lay for him: 'He looks just like any happy man with two feet…No longer outside the world, but in it: no longer talking to a man in uniform, but with him, as an equal.'

The Small Back Room was not a popular success, and Powell himself usually admitted that in his enthusiasm for Balchin's novel he gauged public opinion wrongly by making a war film at the end of the 1940s. It is still a taut, incisive and unique exploration of male failure during wartime. Kathleen Byron's intelligent and understanding Susan, whose shrewdness enables her to tolerate R.B. Waring's patronising management skills and allows her to compliment Sammy despite his bouts of destructive self-loathing, is a modern, cosmopolitan woman. Sue's bond with Sammy reverses the dynamics of Byron's 'pairing' with Farrar in *Black Narcissus*. In that unrequited yet similarly sado-masochistic relationship, Byron's ill-fated Sister Ruth is hysterically neurotic while Farrar's Mr Dean (despite the complications of his character) is strong and pragmatic. For *The Small Back Room* Farrar is the pained and sweat-browed sufferer. Therapy, heterosexual union and a return 'home' are his rewards for proving his manhood to the armed forces.

THE TWILIGHT OF THE GODS?

The Second World War film was important and popular in 1950s British cinema, although films such as *The Cruel Sea* (Charles Frend, 1952), *I Was Monty's Double* (John Guillermin, 1958), *Ice Cold in Alex* (J. Lee

Thompson, 1958) and *The Dam Busters* long suffered from critical neglect. In Andy Medhurst's view, the genre was simply written off for being 'formally conservative and…ideologically irredeemable'.[32] It was considered archaic until the mid-1980s onwards, when, following Medhurst, writers such as Christine Geraghty, Neil Rattigan, Robert Murphy and James Chapman began to revise and finesse our understanding of the genre and its various sub-genres. Chapman argues plausibly that the genre stumbled 'somewhere between the poles of "realism" and "tinsel"' and also notes that it fell chronologically between the high pinnacles of 1940s cinema and 1960s new wave.[33] The new critical insights have focused on the genre's treatment of masculinity and on its attention to 'special men',[34] and have considered how the 1950s saw a shift in the centre of gravity of these Second World War stories away from the communal, democratic 'all-in-this-together' ethos which seemed to prevail a decade earlier towards a more class-bound view of society. Neil Rattigan's reading is that the (upper-) middle classes, who had seemed to lose their centrality in the popularism of the 'People's War', were now reinstated by a genre which demonstrated Britain winning the war (the 1950s films tend to feature victories), but winning it without the significant input of the working classes.[35] It is a well-made argument: there was a falling apart of one of the chief myths of wartime, but a simultaneous writing of another national myth which allowed military-diplomatic failures in the 1950s such as the Suez Crisis to be mythologically countered by an ideological investment in another, more virile model of social and martial endeavour. A longer view, though, would observe the continuity between the 1950s war film and older modes of adventure storytelling – *Boy's Own*-esque yarns of masculine heroism, such as those which provided Korda's Imperial epics with their material. Those tales customarily focused on the public school/officer class, and the 1950s war film restores that emphasis after the propagandising popularism of 1939–45. Raymond Durgnat once stated (with a characteristically tantalising simplicity) that the 'war film is the European Western'[36] – a point echoed by Chapman and taken further by Geraghty. Like Westerns, the war film makes a spectacle of action and tests masculinity, although Geraghty pinpoints two important distinctions: the war film is technologised, and pays attention to machines, not men; and it uses landscape differently, emphasising cramped conditions on ships, submarines, aeroplanes and POW camps, and often constructing the natural landscape as an enemy (for example in *The Cruel Sea* and *Ice Cold in Alex*). There is no rapport between man and environment, and that rapport is a defining characteristic of the Western.[37]

Powell and Pressburger's contributions to the war film, *The Battle of the River Plate* and *Ill Met by Moonlight*, are their most generically 'determined' films. Each of them shows features which are typical – they are each based on real events, with remarkable men as their protagonists. They can also be classified along auteurist lines, for while they are by no means as ripely idiosyncratic as the Archers' work at its most extreme, they repeat and rework familiar Powell-Pressburger motifs: friendship across national borders; foreign (and neutral) territory; the solitude of leadership; and the masquerade of national identity. While *The Battle of the River Plate*, with its uniforms, ships and explosions, repeats the key features of the war film (and was enormously successful at the box office), *Ill Met By Moonlight*, with its characteristically dramatic use of natural scenery, is a different sort of film. Dirk Bogarde's role as the Byronesque Major Patrick Leigh-Fermor (writer, traveller, classical historian, man-of-action – and unsurprisingly a man whom Powell greatly admired) is drawn from a type not unlike Peter Carter in *AMOLAD*. His successful kidnapping of a German officer, Major General Karl Kreipe (Marius Goring) on Crete is an adventure tale set in wild mountainous landscapes and dealing with the Cretan resistance to the German occupation. As Ian Christie has noted,[38] it forms an interesting late addition to the Archers' tales of militarism, but the script is leaden. Powell and Pressburger disagreed vehemently over the film. Pressburger argued the need to present the facts; Powell wanted to romanticise them. Correspondence from Powell at the time catches his characteristic enthusiasm. He notes the spectacular Cretan scenery, nods to the mountaineering films of Luis Trenker (who had appeared in, and filmed, the Alpine location footage of *The Challenge* [1938], one of Pressburger's early British scripting successes). Echoing *'...one of our aircraft is missing'* he praised the way the Resistance left an inspiring record of human achievement, and hoped that the project would give them the opportunity to combine a 'March of Time' approach with 'wild romance' and 'imaginative flights of fancy'. However, the realised film clings to realism. As they were making it the pair also disagreed over whether or not to sign a multi-film deal with Rank (Pressburger was keener, for pragmatic grounds, while Powell was wary). *Ill Met by Moonlight* would be the last film made by the Archers.

Spool back a year, though, to consider *The Battle of the River Plate*. Powell's memoirs make the point that while he had always wanted to make a naval film (he has his own, excited *Boy's Own* agenda here), it was not until he and Pressburger were given Captain Patrick Dove's published memoir *I was a Prisoner of the Graf Spee* that Pressburger's imagination was sparked.[39] Dove, who is played by Bernard Lee in the film, assisted Powell and Pressburger in making it. Dove was Captain of the MS *Africa Shell*, which was sunk by the mighty German pocket battleship the *Graf Spee*. He developed a respect for his captor, the *Graf Spee*'s Captain Langsdorff (Peter Finch), and this respect would form the key psychological interest in what was otherwise a documentary restaging of the Battle of the River Plate. The *Graf Spee* is engaged in battle by HMS *Ajax*, HMS *Exeter* and HMNZS *Achilles* and limps damaged into Montevideo harbour in neutral Uruguay. Allied vessels converge on the river mouth and a diplomatic dispute ensues regarding the status of the ship and the sanctity of neutral waters. When the *Graf Spee* is forced to leave Montevideo after having been granted a brief period to make itself seaworthy, Langsdorff, facing probable defeat, evacuates his crew and scuttles his own ship.

The film has dated. It is hard to enthuse about footage of warships now, however spectacularly shot (and Powell, who was highly effective in his dealings with the Admiralty, managed to capture a lot of impressive footage). The film is at its most interesting in those brief moments where it displays its relationship to earlier Powell-Pressburger films such as *The Spy in Black* (1939), *Contraband* (1940) and *The Life and Death of Colonel Blimp* (1942). The Dove-Langsdorff relationship may be underdeveloped, but the two are united through the code of seamanship, which each man respects. Even though Langsdorff is engaging in piratical behaviour, his ultimate act is seen to be one of valour. Dove calls him a 'gentleman' and their first meeting on the *Graf Spee*, when they eye each other curiously and cautiously from opposing wings of a wide, VistaVision long shot, is reminiscent of the first shot-reverse-shot visual exchange between Clive and Theo in *Blimp*, where notions of gentlemanly conduct are also examined. Camera distances signal the difference between the two films, though: the up-close, engaged characterisation of *Blimp* has become a solid long-shot tableau which makes little use of Lee and Finch.

The Spy in Black had also opened with a comment about gentlemen at war. Like *Contraband*, the meaning of neutrality is examined: there, a neutral Dane, Captain Anderson, is forced to enter British territory; here, opposing combatants are forced to enter neutral Uruguay. National loyalties and identities are important, but may be faked. The *Graf Spee*'s supply ship flies a false flag, and its true identity as the German prison ship the *Altmark* has been literally painted over. We have seen disguises, labels and false badges of belonging before, in *Contraband* and in '*…one of our aircraft is missing*' (1942). Langsdorff is proud of these metamorphoses. His own ship has its aliases, the *Deutschland* and the *Admiral Scheer*, and it disguises itself with these names to confuse neutral ships. Langsdorff playfully (and queerly) runs together this delight in confused identities with a male-centred view of female performance: 'I'm like a pretty girl. I change my hat – I change my frock – Presto! – I am a different girl!' Shortly afterwards the gruff, no-nonsense Dove, who has been given a warm coat to wear by Langsdorff, is wrongly assumed to be a German by the British sailors who are transported from the *Altmark* to the *Graf Spee*.

The film's central interest is in offering shots of naval vessels, and in dramatising the fate of the *Graf Spee*. Personal relationships are downplayed, but the focus is on the officer class, and on the diplomatic corps in Montevideo. After long early sequences all filmed at sea, the film's monochrome canvas of battleship grey and naval uniforms suddenly gives way as the first Montevideo sequence commences in a riot of neon lights, colourful costumes and a local girl singing a popular song in a quayside bar. It is a sudden picture-postcard from an exotic new location, but the film's emphasis remains at sea and with the documentary re-enactment of the battle and its consequences. Powell's customary 'touristic' gaze is barely indulged. Exchanges between British minister Millington-Blake, his French counterpart and the Uruguayan authorities echo the ambassadorial brouhaha that was satirised in *Blimp*'s Berlin sequence, but without the earlier film's gusto. Brief glimpses of the lower ranks are there for comic or token purpose. There is a sense, then, that the film is a class-bound document about 'special men', notably Langsdorff, whose distance, whose brief appearances and whose long absences from the screen magnify his enigmatic 'star quality'. Peter Finch is given very little to do, but he is attractive, charming and full of gravitas. Powell, who was massively enthusiastic about the film, wrote a novelisation of the Battle of the River Plate. *Graf Spee*, which was published in 1956 to coincide with the film's prestigious debut at the Royal Film Performance, anticipates the style of his later volumes of autobiography. It is dramatic, and while it is bound to respect the facts of the historical episode, it reinvents likely conversations and descriptively catches the spirit of the place and time. This is Powell the storyteller, not Powell the historian, and in it he invests Langsdorff with the same sense of superiority that we see elsewhere in the Archers' canon. The film closes with a gentlemanly farewell between Langsdorff and Dove after the demise of the *Graf Spee*. The last page of Powell's written account records how Langsdorff 'tossed the Nazi flag on one side and wrapped himself in the German flag before putting a bullet through his brain … Millington-Drake's intuition was right: it was the Twilight of the Gods.'[40] The film makes no mention of the suicide. The absence of this psychological dimension from the film, its failure to address either the specificities of the conflict or Langsdorff's commitment to the German/Nazi cause, signal how far the generic constraints of the action-war film have impinged on the film-makers. Andy Medhurst has observed that the genre tends to strip its subject matter of historical weight and to treat its conflicts mythically so that politics are replaced by adventure.[41] Millington-Drake's allusion to Wagner in the film and the novel is a prime instance of this process.

Unlike the hybrid war-romances *AMOLAD* and *The Small Back Room*, neither *The Battle of the River Plate* nor *Ill Met by Moonlight* deals with the theme of masculine 'reparation', although it is worth noting, as a brief coda, Powell's later film, *The Queen's Guards* (1961), made without Pressburger. Structured around flashbacks from a Trooping of the Colour ceremony (where the spectacle of massed scarlet uniforms seems like a homage to Powell and Pressburger's earlier aesthetics, and a throwback to the Korda epics of the 1930s), its dramatic crux is in the relationship between a young officer, John Fellowes (Daniel Massey), his over-bearing militaristic father (Raymond Massey) and his dead brother, a 'hero' killed in the war, whose beloved status in the family has impaired John's own self-esteem. The film was not a success, and is not well written, but it is interesting insofar as it allows John Fellowes to escape the iconic image of militaristic heroism set up by his brother's reputation, to establish his own credentials as a soldier, and thereby to put to rest the ghosts of the previous conflict.

5

Post-war Femininities: Mopu, Madness and Melodrama – *Black Narcissus*

It's an impossible place for a nunnery.

This time she answered blandly: 'Difficult but not impossible, Mr Dean. Nothing is impossible with God.'

Rumer Godden, *Black Narcissus*

BACKGROUND: LATE 1940s BRITAIN AND 'WOMEN'S FILMS'

When peace came, the high hopes of the majority Labour government bore fruit in the ideals of the Welfare State. In the face of Britain's painful readjustment to the realities of her actual world status, and genuine hardship at home, the utopianism of the Welfare State sought to cushion the deprivations of the late 1940s. The new education system, the National Health Service and the planned modernisation of newly nationalised industries all set out to eradicate problems in the state of the nation. While the provision of social security emphatically did not set about a large scale redistribution of wealth, it cast out a safety net to protect the people from absolute poverty, and the system of National Insurance purported to incorporate the working population into a common pool of shared interest. Things, though, were not so rosy. Lived conditions fell short of the rhetoric of hope which had prevailed for so long. The clear sense of national identity fostered by wartime propaganda suffered with the change-over to peace.

Rationing continued, and the weather was dreadful – 1947 saw the worst winter on record. Earnings had risen during the war, and full employment was secured in peacetime. There was still little to buy, and much of what was made in the country was produced for export. A sense of dissatisfaction prevailed. The war years had seen the abandonment of *laissez faire* politics. The recruitment of the people as a fighting force brought them into a public arena, figuratively eradicating private spaces and individual interests. In the post-war period, the Labour government's commitment to extending the boundaries of the State perpetuated this ethos of central involvement in the life of the people. The government had to tread carefully as it extended its interest into what were once liberal-bourgeois preserves such as the home and the family, justifying legislation in this sphere as a democratic commitment towards equality of opportunity.

The conscription of women had both respected and implicitly prioritised their roles as mothers. Women with small children had been exempt from conscription. The shift into full-time paid work, which many women did find genuinely liberating, was always circumscribed by the stress laid on its temporary nature. It was 'for the duration', and this failure to normalise the gender shifts of wartime ensured that patriarchal structures remained in place. Women had never achieved parity with men, and during the war debates had raged regarding equal responsibility, status and pay. It is too simplistic to argue that British women were redomesticated in 1945, but some pressure was exerted to return them to exclusively motherly and wifely duties. The position was actually one of flux, and at times blatantly contradictory messages were given out. The Labour election saw a raft of social legislation, and whatever its idealistic ambitions, this enshrined official policy regarding gender relations. Beveridge's *a priori* assumption was that women would be economically dependent on their husbands, and this conviction, as Jane Lewis points out, was written into the Welfare State.[1] A perceived rise in juvenile delinquency was associated with the 'problem' of mothers working. Anxiety even existed regarding the birth rate, which had fallen dramatically in the early 1940s, although it was soon to rise with the post-war baby boom. The Royal Commission, set up in 1945 to investigate population trends, reported that parenthood should be encouraged, and the thrust of its findings suggested that women's problematically increasing engagement in paid employment needed to be addressed. If women's paid work was not actively discouraged by the government – and there was never a concerted effort to get working women back into the home – the terms of the Royal Commission Report (1949) did re-emphasise their parenting duties. It was argued that family stability depended upon full-time mothering. This was the bedrock upon which the sound socialisation of the nation's young was built.

Paradoxically (and incompatibly), women were also still seen as workers. Domesticity may have been admired, but the nation needed female labour. The problem was economic. Reconstruction demanded expanded production, which in turn required a larger workforce. The end of the war had not seen the immediate withdrawal of women from the labour market and, despite the anxiety over women's wavering commitment to their 'natural' maternal function, in 1947 the Ministry of Labour was paradoxically forced to call for more women to enter paid employment. Women represented the only significant reserve population to be recruited. Echoing wartime rhetoric, this fresh appeal was pitched in terms of segregated jobs for men and women. Again, women would not be taking men's work. Assurances were made that the labour shortage was temporary. Again, women were called upon in a crisis, this time to help the nation's export drive, and to reduce its national debt. In Elizabeth Wilson's words, the appeal to women was set out in moral terms of 'duty, selfishness, patriotism'.[2] What can be deduced from these cross-cutting ideological messages is that a genuine cultural resettlement was underway, and that it was fought out with particular energy on the terrain of the traditional family, with moral panics set against a general anxiety about the State's intrusion into the hitherto private regime of the household. British films of the late 1940s were one of the stages on which this resettlement was fought out.

Melodrama is a symptom of contradictory cultural signals and some melodrama is often said to be a 'woman's thing'. Pam Cook notes that the sub-genre of the women's film 'is differentiated from the rest of cinema by virtue of its construction of a "female point of view" which motivates and dominates the narrative, and its specific address to a female audience'.[3] This is largely true, although there are also male melodramas with male protagonists, in the work of Minnelli (*Home from the Hill*, 1959, US) and Ray (*Rebel without a Cause*, 1955, US), for example, where men struggle within traditional social constructs of masculinity and family. But melodrama's association with passivity, victimhood and disenfranchisement has generally drawn it towards the plight of women under forms of social arrangement which work to women's detriment. Not all women's films are so negative. Positive examples had been a feature of the war years. Frank Launder and Sidney Gilliat's *Millions Like Us* (1943) is a portrait of various family members on the Home Front but predominantly deals with a group

Post-war Femininities: Mopu, Madness and Melodrama

of women conscripted into factory work, and their *2000 Women* (1944) follows a group of women prisoners-of-war in occupied France. While these films contain melodramatic and fantasy-like elements, moments of dreaming and expressions of desire, they are squarely founded on documentary-fiction principles. Women's films were still prevalent at both the 'quality' and the 'mass entertainment' ends of the post-war cinema and Powell and Pressburger's work of this period, much of which specifically addresses issues of gender, needs to be seen within this context. Their *Black Narcissus* (1947) presents a group of female characters, and focuses on the tensions which lead to the group's disintegration. Where the dominant mythical theme of the war years was the focus on narratives of aspiration, here we have a tale of dashed hope, a story of frustration centring on the dissolution of a group, not on the forging of a shared communal identity (as had been the case in propaganda films such as *The Gentle Sex* (1943), Leslie Howard's documentary realist drama which follows the transformations of a group of women recruited into the army). *Black Narcissus* is a highly subjective account of one woman's sexual repression and another's fatal desire. Although its narrative shifts us to an uncertain time in recent imperial India, it is rooted in debates about women in British society, and in the gendered implications of the end of the war.

Within a few years of *Black Narcissus*, Powell and Pressburger also made *The Red Shoes* (1948) and *Gone to Earth* (1950). Each of these films charts an hysterical, triangular love plot, in which a deviant female, torn between impossible options, plunges to her death. The recurrence of the motif indicates its importance to the film-makers, but also shows how much they connect with some of the melodramatically generic conventions of the time. Each of their post-war female-centred melodramas pushes towards a higher or more intense level of existence, whether it is spiritual transcendence, mythical communion, sexual fulfilment or a confused medley of all three. The Sisterhood's faith, interrogated by the sublime atmosphere of the Himalayas, and Ruth's passion for Mr Dean in *Black Narcissus*; Hazel's folkloric superstitions in *Gone to Earth*; Vicky's ballet (ambiguously both a striving for an artistic ideal and, given the sexual meanings of the red shoes and the focus on her dancing body, an expression of female sexuality) in *The Red Shoes*: each of these marks a desire for plenitude which will be quashed. It is as though faith in the utopianism once articulated in the various propagandist nuggets of rhetoric in the war films, or resolved in the vital sexual union promised at the end of *I Know Where I'm Going!* (1945), or symbolised in the permanence, the size and the phallic rectitude of Canterbury Cathedral in *A Canterbury Tale* (1944) can no longer be maintained. Only in the restitution of Peter and Sammy in the male-centred *A Matter of Life and Death* (1946) and *The Small Back Room* (1949) is there any final sense of utopian social aspiration. This chapter focuses on *Black Narcissus* as a 'women's film'. *Gone to Earth* has a similar set of themes and style. *The Red Shoes*, despite its kinship with these films, can also be linked aesthetically with *The Tales of Hoffmann* (1951) and it illustrates its directors' views on 'Art'. As such, it is dealt with in more detail in Chapter 6.

With plunging necklines, female display, histrionic performances and exotic narratives centred on female protagonists, the costume melodramas produced by Gainsborough Studios in the mid-1940s have (unsurprisingly) attracted critical attention in recent years. These cheaply made costume films were highly popular, were critically derided at the time and have since been seen to articulate something of the turbulent gender relations of the war and post-war years. The studio's famous logo – a portrait of a painted 'Gainsborough lady' nodding with an ambiguous 'come hither' look to camera, with a decorous, faux-classical musical accompaniment – invites us into a playground version of history. The frame of the portrait, though, signifies the parenthetical nature of that playground: it marks off the world of these films from reality. The flirtation with the exotic here leads Pam Cook to say, rightly, that the costume films 'deal in fantasies of loss of identity. They suggest that identity itself is fluid and unstable,...a hybrid state or form. And they suggest that national identity is not pure, but mixed.'[4] Fantasy spaces are created where passionate heroines enjoy a release. A change of clothing is often the occasion for this. Barbara Worth (Margaret Lockwood) switches into highwayman's garb in Leslie Arliss's *The Wicked Lady* (1945) and Maddalena Labardi (Phyllis Calvert) has a gypsy alter ego, Rosanna, in Arthur Crabtree's *Madonna of the Seven Moons* (1944). In *The Man In Grey* (1943) Lockwood is pitted against saintly Phyllis Calvert; in *The Wicked Lady* her demure opposite is played by Patricia Roc. This world of crude polarities is echoed in *Black Narcissus* (Deborah Kerr and Kathleen Byron can effectively be read as flip-sides of the same character). Because these films promote pleasurable desires, they signal a healthy and liberal sexual potential within British womanhood. This sense of liberation, however fantastical, is allied to the change in women's roles during the war years. It is a destabilising energy, activated by real social upheavals and by the utopian rhetoric of war.

Cross-dressing into her highwayman's outfit, *The Wicked Lady*'s Barbara seems like a principal boy, given the camp, pantomime feel pervading the film. Barbara's manly attire critiques the passivity and subservience culturally associated with the outward show of femininity, but her status as a heterosexual woman is always to the fore. James Mason, as her highwayman lover, is unequivocally an object of desire. Tales of his criminal activity are the topic of excited female gossip, and Barbara's house guests are clearly titillated vicariously by imagining the scenario of his pistol-wielding robbery. This is not to say, of course, that Gainsborough's costumed romps are blind to contemporary issues. Divorce, adultery, female ambition, motherhood: themes like these play out the prevailing ideological tensions of the period. As to the progressiveness of the films, the cycle's deviating heroines are marked by hysterical neuroses and are ultimately punished for their transgressions, notably in *Madonna of the Seven Moons*, where Maddalena suffers from split personality. In part she is a chaste, respectable wife and mother; in part she is an unrestrained gypsy fleeing to Florence to cavort with swarthy Stewart Granger, with an eyebrow-raising frankness for so suburban an actress as Phyllis Calvert. Barbara's changes of costume in *The Wicked Lady* are another index of instability. Heroines such as these – even the notably evil and self-serving Barbara – capture audience attention more than the demurely moral and middle-class characters against whom they rebel. And in each of these films, there is a romance plot, imbued with sufficient signs of genuine feeling to carry audience sympathy too. All this suggests that, until the appointment of the more conservative Sydney Box as Head of Production at Gainsborough in late 1946 (after which female desire in the studio's work tended to be repressed and a more realistic tone came to dominate), the major output of the studio endorsed an ethos of *carpe diem*. This contradicted the call to duty which characterised national discourse during wartime. The studio's shift to a greater conservatism by 1947, as noted by Sue Harper,[5] marries with the atmosphere of the period, inasmuch as female ambition was reined in (or at least rechannelled) by official doctrine encouraging motherhood and domestic duties. However, as I have said, this ideological doctrine competed with urgent economic calls for women to leave home and take part in paid work, and the genuine schism to be detected here in the ideology of the time works its way through to the more crudely polarised split-heroines and black-and-white morality of the Gainsborough storylines. Gainsborough's thrills, though, come at a price. The brutal narrative punishment which is exacted upon these wayward, desiring heroines flags up just how sensitive this issue was. Generally, the fantasies are indulged only to be brutally closed down in the final reel.

Stark divisions and invidious choices are to be found in other, more realistic films of the period. Despite the praise meted to it on account of its 'realism' – which might mean nothing more than the sense, as Richard Dyer puts it, of its not being 'gesturally big' like Hollywood, or not being like contemporaneous, critically deplored hits such as *The Wicked Lady*[6] – the most significant other British 'melodrama' of the period is David Lean's 'quality' production, *Brief Encounter* (1945), which charts the extra-marital longings of Laura Jesson (Celia Johnson) for Alec Harvey (Trevor Howard). In her voiceover, she describes herself to us as a 'romantic school girl, a romantic fool', but her longings are nonetheless real, and the flights of fantasy she allows herself – such as her dreams of being in Paris at the opera, or in Venice – are as exotic as those enjoyed by Gainsborough's heroines. However, the overall impression is of restraint, but it is not a restraint which the film endorses. Laura's frigidity and her sense of entrapment are tragically clear, and the film aestheticises the tensions and agonies which are excited by Laura's potential crossing of moral boundaries. Rather than 'being' restrained, then, it is 'about' restraint, and balances masochistically on the knife-edge of temptation.

What is curious about *Brief Encounter* is that it erases wartime altogether. Although it may not be obvious now, it is set in the 1930s, in a pre-war innocence far removed from the mid-1940s. Just as the 'period' status is never made clear, its sense of geography is similarly hazy, as it shifts from a Home Counties urban locale to an undisguised Carnforth Station in Lancashire, and then to some obviously Pennine countryside which speaks of a romantic grandeur far removed from Laura's Thursday shopping trips to 'Milford'. The much-lauded realism of the film is overstated. The implicit journey back to the 1930s spirits away the privations of rationing. Chocolate is for sale, as is brandy at pre-war prices. Importantly, this shift also allows for a reactionary curtailment of female desire. Laura's romantic/sexual aspirations are stifled. It is as though the emancipatory benefits of wartime mobilisation had never happened, and that period's proto-feminism is denied. Her fears that her flirtation with Alex will cause her to neglect her children's welfare resonate with the post-war concern about bad mothering. As she idles a Thursday afternoon away with her quasi-lover, the sight of children playing pricks her conscience, and when her son suffers a minor injury during one of her absences, the accusation of neglect is implicit.

Brief Encounter's immediately decodable message is conservative, so much so that the popular audience in 1945 famously chose to watch

Lockwood and Mason riding coach-and-horses through 'quality realism' rather than sitting with Johnson and Howard lunching in Milford's 'Kardomah' café. Ambivalent, negotiated readings are available to us, though, because the differing discourses at work in *Brief Encounter* vie for attention. The clipped cut-glass precision of Noël Coward's dialogue underscores the class-bound inhibitions explored in the film, and it is possible simultaneously to admire its perfectly grammatical poise and to regret the way it strangulates passion. The screenplay evokes emotion, but does so indirectly. The Rachmaninov score used in the film, however, is candidly, nakedly late Romantic. It does not 'accompany' the dialogue so much as 'compete' with it.

How, then, can films as different (visually, and in terms of cultural kudos) as *The Wicked Lady* and *Brief Encounter* both be thought of as melodramas? Like 'realism', 'melodrama' is a slippery term, and for it to have any useful meaning some criteria need to be laid down for it. The notion of competing internal discourses – such as the mismatch between *Brief Encounter*'s visual, verbal and musical tracks – is integral to melodrama, because the form deals with ideological conflict, and with the failure to construct an over-riding, persuasive, dominant narrative. It may well construct what purports to be coherent, but it simultaneously nods towards the cracks in what it builds, and in this it enacts a possibly progressive and sophisticated double mission. Such a category of film-making was singled out by Jean-Luc Comolli and Jean Narboni in 'Cinema/Ideology/Criticism', a much-cited editorial from *Cahiers du Cinéma*, delineating categories of films according to the degree to which they comply with or resist dominant ideology.[7] Their fifth category accounts for works which 'seem at first to belong firmly within the ideology and to be completely under its sway, but which turn out to be so only in ambiguous manner'.[8] Such films are fragmented by their own internal criticism, with the dominant ideology simultaneously presented and undone by the text. This potential to lay bare social conflicts has given melodrama a progressive reputation, and this is the impetus behind the feminist and neo-Marxist rediscovery of 1950s Hollywood melodramas from directors such as Douglas Sirk, Vincente Minnelli and Nicholas Ray.

One way to incorporate this form of internally layered double meanings is through the use of irony, and it is not surprising, therefore, that the characteristically ironic Sirk is the director whose reputation most benefited from the critical activity these critics advocated. His *Imitation of Life* (1959, US) offers a fractured narrative and a contradictory closure of deeply qualified catharsis. It seems to conform to the values of the dominant social order, and to shore up the institution of the family, while in fact it cynically undermines the pretences of that very system. Fetishised images of American success and utopian signs of achievement are presented, but faith in their veridical nature is simultaneously negated. The refusal of the narrative to iron out this contradiction marks its departure from traditional classic realism. With Sirk, it is a measure of his partial commitment to Brechtian techniques (or is it camp?) – alienation devices which work by separating out elements of production rather than by melding them together, by laying bare the artifice of the work. *Brief Encounter* flows along Sirkian lines, ironically pitting Rachmaninov against 'received pronunciation', and its tragic structure of feelings derives from the yawning chasm between the late Romantic score and its protagonists' internalised inability either to achieve or to express the feelings and desires which the extra- (and intra-) diegetic soundtrack so glaringly recommends.

At the level of narrative, *Black Narcissus, Gone to Earth* and *The Red Shoes* are thematically similar to *Brief Encounter, The Wicked Lady* and even *Imitation of Life*, as all of them touch an ideologically sensitive nerve by recycling clichés about the inappropriateness of women's sexual desire and/or their professional ambitions. Where Sirk pulls apart the cracks of bourgeois ideology, Powell and Pressburger's melodramatic language is differently inflected, striving instead to amplify their crises with a brand of quasi-nineteenth-century 'operatic' or 'symphonic' melodrama which aims for amplification through excessive visceral impact, and when Powell writes in his memoirs about his ambitions at this stage in his career he talks in terms of musical composition and unity. As such this trio of films can be seen as backward-looking phenomena. Indeed, Raymond Durgnat, recalling the Victorian stage, dispiritingly judges *Black Narcissus* (along with *The Elusive Pimpernel*, 1950, and *Gone to Earth*) to 'represent Powell's *Lyceum* streak'.[9]

If the Sirkian mode (anticipated in Lean's *Brief Encounter*) is a kind of ironic counterpoint, orchestrating dissonance to subvert the conformity of his broadly realistic milieu, the Archers depart just as fundamentally from the constraints of realism to create a close harmony of visual and aural codes, sustaining intensity by avoiding any relapse into the more ordered regime of realism. Sirkian melodrama's defining structure is antithesis (discordance); Powell's is stylistic synthesis (concordance), the coming together of a variety of super-charged modes of expression to tell tales about hysterically fraught and often gothic situations. Hence the concluding sequence of *Black Narcissus* is, in Powell's words, 'music, emotion, image and voices all blended together into a new and splendid whole'[10] and hence his sense that because he chose not to film it in its Indian setting he was 'left free to compose a sound-track which would be an organic whole of dialogue, sound effects, and music, very much in the way that an opera is composed'.[11] His talk of unity is entirely within an old-style Romantic discourse dating back to Richard Wagner and beyond in its ideas of totality and wholeness.

There are cinematic precedents for Powell's ambitions too. As early as 1929, in a piece entitled 'The Cinema of Tomorrow', the French director Abel Gance drew similar musical analogies. 'A great film,' he had written, 'has to be conceived like a symphony…in time and a symphony in space', and through the use of synchronised triple screens, superimpositions and sound (and anticipating both colour and three-dimensional effects) the hopes he expressed were for the widening of 'the field of our spiritual vision…the creation of visual harmonies, the transporting of the spectator's imagination into a new and sublime world'.[12] The orchestral metaphors here are no mere poetic allusion. Norman King has argued that as well as insisting that cinema had to 'become a visual orchestra', music for Gance was ultimately 'a determinant of the image, providing a basis for tonality, movement within the frame, and cutting between frames'.[13] Powell's ideals, which he begins to aspire towards at this time, are anticipated by Gance's prediction of '[t]he aesthetic synthesis that the cinema of tomorrow will achieve…The great symphony of sound and vision'.[14] Powell had his own pantheon of cinematic heroes, such as Gance, D.W. Griffith and Fritz Lang, an idol ever since he saw the overtly fabulous *Die Nibelungen* (1924, Germany). The films he champions comply with his own aesthetic principles: the use of unified design (he ranks the art director second only to the author on a scale of creativity);[15] the preference for the visual, and hence an initial suspicion of synchronised sound, which he felt bound cinema more closely to reality; the ambition to create the 'composed' film organised around musical principles; the repeated belief in the indivisibility of the arts; and a collaborative working practice which recalled the detailed pre-shooting conferences of Lang and F.W. Murnau. As well as bowing to his early mentor Rex Ingram, to Gance and to Griffith, he himself admits, 'I had the German film-makers to guide me and reassure me and lead me finally to *The Red Shoes*, *The Small Back Room* and *The Tales of Hoffmann*.'[16] Some of his stylistic ambitions regarding the use of colour and music, however, are first deployed on *Black Narcissus*.

Powell's thoughts about viewing cinema 'holistically' echo Sergei Eisenstein's commitment to the construction of cinematic unity. Recalling

Wagnerian notions of the Gesamtkunstwerk, Eisenstein wrote of an ideal total cinema 'that contains a maximum of emotion and stimulating power' and he was critical of views of film which saw it exclusively in terms of *either* montage or content, admitting that, 'We should have occupied ourselves more with an examination of the nature of the *unifying principle* itself.'[17] Powell only briefly acknowledges Eisenstein in his memoirs, but Eisenstein's essays 'Synchronisation of the Senses' and 'Colour and Meaning' imply a deep sympathy between the two men. Powell composed his 'organic whole of dialogue, sound effects, and music' in *Black Narcissus*.[18] Eisenstein writes that for *Alexander Nevsky* (1938, USSR) 'Many hours went into the fusing of these elements into an organic whole'.[19] His concept of 'vertical montage' – where image-track, soundtrack and music are charted as if on an orchestral music score – allows him to map out this formal synthesis and to visualise correspondences between these different kinds of film language: 'To remove the barriers between sight and sound, between the seen world and the heard world! To bring about a unity and a harmonious relationship between these two opposite spheres. What an absorbing task! The Greeks and Diderot, Wagner and Scriabin – who has not dreamt of this ideal?'[20] Rimbaud and Rimsky-Korsakov are also mentioned in his wide-ranging survey of the quest for absolute connections between harmonies, colours and images, and he concludes that '"synthesis of the various sensations" is one of the fundamental indications of a romantic work of art'.[21]

In 'Colour and Meaning', Eisenstein draws on forms of colour symbolism to examine whether the meanings associated with parts of the spectrum are arbitrary or intrinsic. He reverts to the idea of synaesthesia, defined as 'the production from one sense-impression of one kind of an associated mental image of a sense-impression of another kind'.[22] Although he finally concedes that no catalogue of absolute relationships can be fixed, the search remains a romantic one. His appreciation of colour as a system of signification which can interact with other signifying systems anticipates Powell's interest in relationships between the components of film language. Eisenstein and Powell celebrate the material nature of their medium, discussing technological developments, colour stock, synchronised sound, lighting techniques, trick shots (and how best to combine them all), while still mystifying the film-making process through metaphysical references to totality, unity and 'organicity'. This is a measure of how far their own discourse is ambitious, forward-looking, yet often rooted in the aesthetic forms of the nineteenth century.

Powell's keenness for so-called 'pre-composition' is the nearest he gets to declaring a cinematic creed. The 'composed film' – where the entire film is shot to a pre-recorded soundtrack – has a German pedigree. Many of the operas/operettas which Pressburger had worked on at UFA were filmed this way, while Powell mentions having been intrigued by the German Friedrich Feher's *The Robber Symphony* (1937), a film which was entirely pre-composed.[23] Frederick Feher, an émigré to England from Germany (and incidentally one of the stars of *The Cabinet of Dr Caligari*) wrote, directed, composed, orchestrated and conducted *The Robber Symphony*. An experimental work, it was a box office failure. While Powell never saw the film, its relationship between music and film sparked his interest, and being antithetical to customary modes of cinematic realism which prioritise the visual image, its pre-composition satisfied his 'subconscious desire to experiment,...to reverse the order of things'.[24] Like his enthusiasm for the ill-fated 'Independent Frame' system, a cost-driven mode of production which sought to use extensive story-boarding, mattes, rear projection, special effects and the 'doubling' of star players wherever possible rather than expensive location shooting, his excitement about composed film shows his antipathy to 'British National Cinema's' more formally conservative, realist style. The studio-based production of *Black Narcissus* gave Powell all the creative expressiveness he wanted without the cost restrictions which 'Independent Frame' would have imposed.

COLOUR, MUSIC AND HYSTERIA

Having stretched their wings with the formal experimentation in *A Matter of Life and Death*, it might have been expected that the Archers' next film, *Black Narcissus* (an adaptation of Rumer Godden's 1939 novel about a group of nuns in India, 'going into the wilderness, to pioneer, to endure, to work') would be more traditional. The spirit of Godden's novel is psychologically realistic (the author drew on her own life experiences in India to capture the local colour), although her style of writing shades over into internal, subjective narration as the difficulties of colonial and communal life begin to pray on her central character, Sister Clodagh. Godden's prose is like a curious offspring of Rudyard Kipling and Virginia Woolf, and her tale is mediated through the shifting consciousness of the nuns, but primarily through Clodagh's. Powell chose to film *Black Narcissus* entirely at Pinewood, with some brief exterior work done at Leonardslee in Sussex, using the skills of his long-term designer Alfred Junge to construct a set for the Palace surrounded with background paintings of the mountains, and employing special effects wizard 'Poppa' Day to create matte paintings, rather than travelling to India and splicing very different location and studio footage together afterwards. The artifice of Junge's designs is clearly visible, and the studio aesthetic Powell opted for is acutely meaningful, helping to sustain the atmosphere of the film. Powell's memoirs give various reasons for his decision to film in England. He was committed to being in England (not least for the Royal Command Performance of *A Matter of Life and Death*), and he suggests that he did not feel up to dragging his crew, then settling down to family lives after the war, off on an expedition to India.[25] Just as telling a reason was the decision made by Independent Producers to leave Denham Studios to settle into Rank's efficient, high-tech studio complex at Pinewood.

Is this a sign of the rogue Powell's recruitment into the organised machinery of the industry? In *A Matter of Life and Death* he and Pressburger had sympathised with Peter's reluctance to enter the rational world of Heaven. This dislike of rationalisation (and concomitant embrace of perversity) is also there in *A Canterbury Tale* (1944) and *I Know Where I'm Going!*, and it would emerge again in the eccentricities of Professor Mair's unit in *The Small Back Room*. Denham Studios was Sir Alexander Korda's sprawling, ambitious development, thrown up erratically, and the Archers loved its Hollywood-like feel and its great history. Pinewood was orderly, planned and formal, and Powell's discomfort with this – despite the studio's efficiency and the fact that the Archers made some of their best films there – is palpable. He recalls 'a certain civil service mentality in the permanent staff, which jarred with the gaiety and confidence of [their] unit', and sounding very like a maverick grandee of the industry he echoes the anti-establishment spirit of some of the Archers' films. 'In this strange business of ours,' he writes, 'there is something after all to be said for lavishness, improvisation and a certain amount of waste.'[26] The decision to make *Black Narcissus* entirely at Pinewood marks Powell out as a studio director, striving for a level of control which location work would deny him, but given his repeated keenness for location and for authentic 'spirit of place' the decision is a key transitional moment in the Archers' trajectory, initiating a more formal inquisition of film spectacle *per se*. They would still capture effective location footage – in *The Red Shoes* and *Gone to Earth* – but we should also see *Black Narcissus* as picking up from *A Matter of Life and Death*'s meta-cinematic qualities and leading towards the utter

Post-war Femininities: Mopu, Madness and Melodrama 181

eradication of 'realism' and 'the real' in *The Tales of Hoffmann*. For *Black Narcissus* we enter the protagonists' disturbed inner worlds: an India of the mind, not of external reality.

Mopu, the remote setting for *Black Narcissus*, is a strange and exotic alien space, but it is not so much a geographical location as a plastic rendering of the protagonist's interiority (an externalisation of feelings, typical of Expressionism, of noir, and of melodrama). Sigmund Freud's 1924 essay 'The Loss of Reality in Neurosis and Psychosis' sketches an imagined space in which the (specifically neurotic and female) subject restages reality satisfactorily: 'This is made possible,' Freud writes, 'by the existence of a *world of phantasy*, of a domain which became separated from the real external world at the time of the introduction of the reality principle.'[27] A similar metaphor occurs in Joseph Breuer's account of the hysteric Anna O, whose day-dream retreat from reality is referred to as her 'private theatre'.[28] Victor Burgin has more recently accounted for the alternative reality of the unconscious as a 'mysterious area of transaction,…that space in which fantasy stages its mise-en-scène of desire'.[29] This is the magic arena of *Black Narcissus*. Images in the film of palace doors opening – notably majestic double doors sweeping outwards to reveal the rocky precipice and the palace bell – connote transitions from one imaginative space to another. Significantly, the arrival at Mopu is inaugurated by Ruth, the most hysterical of the Sisters (in her first appearance in the film), opening those doors to ringing the bell ecstatically.

Powell and Pressburger are known for their use of saturated colour. Red, especially, is a defining motif, and the association comes mainly from their work with Jack Cardiff, one of Technicolor's greatest craftsmen. Cardiff, the director of photography on *Black Narcissus*, had worked for the first time in that capacity with the Archers on *A Matter of Life and Death*. He worked previously in a minor function on *The Life and Death of Colonel Blimp* (1942), where Georges Perinal's relatively light, pastel palette is decorative, and colour is used expressively to contrast the dark, muddy khaki of the First World War sequences with the periods before and after it. In *A Matter of Life and Death* there are sensitive uses of colour – in the gaudy rhododendron blooms which cause the heavenly Messenger (Marius Goring) to remark that he is 'starved of Technicolor' in Heaven, and in the rose which holds June's tear and proves her love for Peter. For *Black Narcissus*, for which he received an Oscar, Cardiff worked with Powell and Junge – and challenged the restrictive supervision of Technicolor, who rigidly oversaw the use of their system – to sustain an atmosphere of the fabulous, using fog filters and coloured lighting (such as blue for shadows) to create exaggerated effects. Cardiff would stay with Powell and Pressburger to film *The Red Shoes*. Brian Easdale, who composed the music, also worked with the Archers for the first time on *Black Narcissus*. He had lived in India, and he knew Rumer Godden. Powell found in Easdale a composer with whom he could collaborate as effectively as he could with Pressburger. Easdale sympathised with Powell's wish to absorb music into the flesh of the film, rather than simply using it as dressing. Allan Gray's music for *Blimp* is memorable, but it is pastiche, a set of tunes and motifs used to cue satire or sentiment, and to place the period settings. With Easdale, Powell decided to film the closing sequence of *Black Narcissus* by shooting it (with a stopwatch) to a piano track of the composed score, giving authority to the music and focusing on movement. The experimentation here anticipates the ballet and opera films to come.

The symbolic use of colour and music in *Black Narcissus* marks a development in the Archers' style and also marries with its chief themes: gothicised neurosis and hysteria; masculine power; and the articulation of female desire. The plot of the film closely follows Godden's novel. A group of nuns headed by Sister Clodagh (Deborah Kerr) journey to the high Himalayas to open a school and a hospital at Mopu, an old Palace – once a harem – given to them by the local General, Toda Rai (Esmond Knight). They try to make progress without the help of the British agent, Mr Dean (David Farrar), a dissipated but attractive cynic who has 'gone native', and who warns them that Mopu is 'no place to put a nunnery'. Mopu is ominously perched on the edge of a precipice, and the wind never tires. The nuns are disturbed and distracted: by the remote mountain atmosphere; by the presence of a native 'wise man' silently meditating in their grounds; by Angu Ayah (May Hallett), an old servant woman who longs for the old lecherous days of the harem; by Kanchi (Jean Simmons), a dissolute local girl brought to the Palace by Mr Dean, by Dilip Rai (Sabu), the exotic and beautiful nephew of the General, who will mock the nuns chastity when he runs off with Kanchi; and by Mr Dean himself. Clodagh remembers a failed romance in Ireland which led her to flee to the religious order. After her initial disapproval of Dean, she finds she needs his help, and a chaste relationship develops between them. A younger nun, Sister Ruth (Kathleen Byron), who is always known to be a 'problem', obsesses on Mr Dean. She leaves the Sisterhood to pursue him, and when her love is rejected she returns to the Palace. Warped by sexual frustration she tries to kill Clodagh, but in the attempt she falls from the precipice to her death. The nuns leave the Palace and retreat back to Calcutta, leaving Dean behind.

Apart from *The Spy in Black* (1939), which Alexander Korda had already had adapted into a film treatment from Storer Clouston's novel when Powell and Pressburger were brought into the project, and which Pressburger then changed freely, *Black Narcissus* was their first adaptation from a source novel, and in content it is faithful to Godden. A few minor changes, underscored in the film, clue us into the themes which the film emphasises. An early sequence makes much of the fact that the Sisters' Order of St Faith requires them, uniquely, to renew their vows each year. The need to monitor their commitment highlights its very fragility. Giving advice before the journey to Mopu, Godden's Mother Dorothea encourages Clodagh to 'enjoy' herself. Clodagh is surprised by this – her task as she sees it is to endure. Dorothea also tells her not to be afraid to say if she wants to come back. Emphatically, in the film Dorothea (Nancy Roberts) tells her instead to 'work them hard' and the film then stresses that an ethic of industry will be a way of warding off the threat of dissolution which the colonial outpost represents. Clodagh's aspirations are examined, and we are asked to question whether her religious zeal is a sign of her own ambition, and whether it is also a symptom of her flight from a humiliating broken romance in Ireland. The pure 'mission' of the Sisterhood is seen to depend on how rigorously they police their borders (literally and psychologically), on how they attempt to control the area within the Palace (this is why the 'wise man's' presence is so troubling) and on how they remain focused on their cause. As a discrete unit, the Order of St Faith is an agent of British imperialism and to Clodagh part of their sense of 'order' depends upon maintaining boundaries and observing polarised distinctions. Needless to say, she is frustrated. These minor interventions made to the film's storyline emphasise the provisional nature of the Sister's cause, and suggest (in an echo of Conrad's *The Heart of Darkness*) that attention to work will be a necessary defence mechanism, a displacement or a way of repressing the 'otherness' or the pleasure which threatens to encroach on them. Clodagh fails to hold herself together, for as tension mounts Powell and Pressburger push the melodramatic hysteria so far that *Black Narcissus* takes on the guise of a horror film. Clodagh's repression provokes a schizoid fission, and Ruth splits off to embody the more frigid Sister's monstrously released libido. The confrontation between the two, which is more dilute in the novel, is drawn out into a direct conflict between Clodagh, all ego, and Ruth, her double and her opposite.

The coding of colour is pervasive and highly expressive, taking on solid emotional and tonal associations. The relationship between blue and red forms a visual texture, thematically knitting the film together. For example, at Calcutta in the opening moments, the Mother Superior's office has a blue fan and floor, and contains a lone red chair. Such details seem naturalistic, but throughout the film blueness and redness become 'values', pitted against each other. One of the nuns inspects a red apple, unconsciously evoking Eve and the fall from Eden, another parable of women's sinful curiosity. Whites and sky-blues connote traditional purity – in the scenery and in the nuns' habits. Reds connote the reverse. The contrast between carnal reds and ethereal blues visualises the Sisterhood's Christian efforts to drive a wedge between the body and the spirit. As an ironic emblem of the Order's inability to keep these colours apart, a statue of their named saint is painted in a combination of red and blue and, when Kanchi arrives, she too is wearing both colours. An aquamarine 'blue room' in the Palace is bordered in crimson, and the Himalayan background scenery is tinted so that at dawn its whiteness flushes with pink, just as the purity of the Sisterhood blushes with sexuality. Joseph Anthony (Eddie Whalley Jnr.), a young servant boy, links this visual effect to the film's theme of blossoming when he tells Clodagh that the locals call the effect 'the flowering of the snows'. To mirror Ruth's mad rampage at the film's crescendo, red light later floods the Palace completely.

Redness taps into a range of familiar connotations: viscera, corporeality, sex, immorality – hence the presumably undeserved reputation of red-heads, and the ripe cliché of the scarlet woman. It means fire and danger and also release – we paint the town red. There is also an association with madness – seeing red. Nineteenth-century accounts of female hysteria relate it to menstruation, a 'horror' of adult female sexuality, and records of hysterical colour-blindness report that when all other colours are gone, red remains. An intense relationship between Ruth and her signifying colour is marked early on. Her habit is splattered with blood when she first encounters Mr Dean, and he is wearing a crimson shirt. But some of this colour coding operates at an almost subliminal level to give an unconscious unity to the film. To return to Eisenstein, he had demanded that 'consistency in a definite tone colour-key…must be given by an imaginary structure in a strict harmony with the work's theme'.[30] Rumer Godden's novel refers to Ruth's 'wild tempers (feeling) like something dark and wet, flooding her brain, like blood',[31] and this image is recollected in a point-of-view shot of Mr Dean from Ruth's eyes during her climactic confrontation in his forest house.

Red Technicolor dye is haemorrhaged across the screen at the height of Ruth's panic, when 'Sister Clodagh' is mentioned, and she loses consciousness when the screen goes blank. To emphasise the decisiveness of this moment (it marks Ruth's shift into paranoid psychosis), a contrasting electric blue blank and silent screen is then presented. It is held long enough for unfamiliar viewers to sense a jarring break in the cinematic apparatus – to fear that the film, projector, video or transmission has gone faulty – before the narrative recommences and images fade back into view. This highly coded visual language radically departs from the form of Godden's prose. At no point in the novel's equivalent scene does Ruth black out (or 'red' out). And when she visits Dean she is wearing her nun's attire. Nowhere in the novel does Ruth wear a red dress, one of the film's most bluntly effective pieces of mise-en-scène and one of British cinema's most notoriously meaningful costumes.

More on the wider, political significance of this theme of polarities (and hybridities) later, but first we need to focus on psychological issues to consider the film's Freudian imagery. Powell and Pressburger's melodramatic trio of post-war 'women's films' conform to a pattern: namely the 'hysterical scenario', in which a heroine, characteristically denied the scope for self-expression, is faced with an impossible choice between two equally unacceptable positions. In *Black Narcissus* it is between spirituality (the Sisterhood) and sexuality (with Mr Dean as the object of desire), and this polarisation is effectively dramatised in the splitting of the protagonist figure into two 'bodies': Clodagh and her 'alter ego' Ruth (the cliché of the frigid Madonna and the reckless whore). Femininity has long been connected with passivity and silence, and Powell and Pressburger at least deviate from this, for many 'strong women' feature in their films and in the post-war melodramas women characters 'strike out' to express and to act upon desire. Ruth's rebellion expresses single-mindedness of purpose, courage, an independent spirit and sexual freedom, even though her rebellion connotes madness. In breaking free of the bonds of a rule-dominated, organised religion, she enters a natural 'wild zone' (in the film's closing sequence we see her fighting through the jungle to get to Dean, startled by threatening animal noises and beating native drums). Yet what makes this proto-feminist gesture so genuinely hysterical is that in escaping the constrictions of Christianity, in rejecting Law and the Order, she is actually running *to* a man. It is a simultaneous rejection of, and longing for, patriarchal authority, for however much the all-female community of nuns is preserved, and however much Clodagh insists that Jesus Christ merely 'took the shape of a man', the young General and Mr Dean each point out that, nevertheless, he 'was a man'. Receiving nothing but rejection, Ruth shifts into madness. She becomes a monster. It is hardly a positive fantasy of liberation.

Black Narcissus tells of a struggle to sublimate and charts how unexpressed mental processes find a displaced outlet in neurosis. Freud writes in his *Three Essays on Sexuality* that such repressed energies 'strive to obtain an expression that shall be appropriate to their emotional importance – to obtain a discharge; and in the case of hysteria they find such an expression…in

6. Kathleen Byron crosses the threshold into psychosis in *Black Narcissus*. (BFI Stills, © Carlton International Media Ltd)

somatic phenomena, that is in hysterical symptoms'.[32] Sister Briony diagnoses that spots breaking out on the Sisters' arms are due to the water at Mopu, but they are early indices of mental distress projected onto the surface of their bodies. As Elaine Showalter (1985) has shown, patriarchal culture has readily associated active or vocal women with insanity, and for struggling transgressively to make a space for herself Ruth is punished, soon to be followed over the ledge by Vicky in *The Red Shoes* and then by Hazel in *Gone to Earth*. As an aside, by the time of his own late work, *Age of Consent* (1969, Australia) Powell is flushed with generosity, for here he allows Cora (Helen Mirren), his sexualised young heroine, to bloom. In a late 1960s culture which has passed through its sexual revolution, and which comes to idealise its youth, *Age of Consent* reverses the values of *Black Narcissus* for here he sends the young heroine's puritanical elderly grandmother over a cliff to her death. In the earlier film, the old grandmaternal figure, Angu Ayah, mocks the high ideals of the nuns and lasciviously shares Mr Dean's fascination with the days of the harem.

The classic texts of Joseph Breuer and Sigmund Freud, such as the studies of Anna O and later of Dora, can be seen as emancipatory accounts of heroic struggles against an impossible status quo. Likewise, these films arguably dramatise female rebellions which indict the social order. In Anna O, Breuer found a patient 'bubbling over with intellectual vitality (who) led an extremely monotonous existence in her puritanically-minded family'.[33] Her neurotic symptoms are an escape from her domestic confinement – a visible, semiotic code expressing the frustrations she is unable to communicate through consciously articulated speech. Her seizures are a creative rebellion. The restraints demanded by the Order of St Faith in *Black Narcissus* produce a psychological instability which is writ large in the sumptuous mise-en-scène. Desire, frustrated elsewhere, is discharged in Technicolor. Geoffrey Nowell-Smith's reading of melodrama is relevant here:

> The undischarged emotion which cannot be accommodated within the action… is traditionally expressed in the music and, in the case of film, in certain elements of the *mise en scène*. That is to say, music and *mise en scène* do not just heighten the emotionality of an element of the action: to some extent they substitute for it. The mechanism here is strikingly similar to that of the psychopathology of hysteria.[34]

With the protagonist's relationship to reality disturbed, melodrama's mise-en-scène operates as an allegory of hysteria, in which the latent suffering of the 'silenced' patient is channelled into another form – is shifted into visual/musical metaphor. It is the unspeakability of what the visuals express which causes the distortion. In the strict moral code of the Sisterhood, sex is unmentionable, of course. Complaining to Mr Dean about Kanchi's assumed sexual laxity, Clodagh can only say of her that 'she is...what she is', glossing tautologically and awkwardly over the messy truth. Later, Clodagh's confrontation with Ruth regarding Mr Dean exemplifies the workings of conversion hysteria. Called to see Clodagh, Ruth's mannerisms as she enters her Sister Superior's study are an index of her nervous state. Her rigid movements are well-nigh robotic. The two nuns sit facing each other across Clodagh's desk, in significantly mirrored shots which emphasise the doubling between them. Clodagh first counsels Ruth sympathetically, enquiring what is wrong with her, for she looks so ill, but Ruth's response is that she 'can't speak of it – to anyone'. As they square up to each other, repeated shots of Ruth from a height near that of the desk emphasise the bell handle in front of her with barely coded phallic symbolism. Girding herself to broach the painfully unspoken topic of their conversation, Clodagh likewise fingers a pencil anxiously, and this is accentuated in one of the film's occasional and very significant extreme close-ups, with the same shot tilting up towards Ruth as Clodagh's voice tentatively and euphemistically ventures her suspicion that Ruth has 'let (herself) fall into thinking too much of Mr. Dean'. The dark truth has now been said; and the implicit admission of repressed sexual desire precipitates a tense exchange between the pair. In this brief sequence, obvious connotations have been rendered spatially, and have been grappled with euphemistically. As the confrontation closes and Ruth leaves, an orchestral accompaniment adds a melodramatic flourish before a brief diminuendo and a fade to black restore some sense of calm.

All of a sudden, a full orchestra blasts a brass fanfare at us as a brief montage of brilliant rhododendron flowers fills the screen. It is an unexpected moment. The flowers are redolent of female sexuality, of the exotic Indian sub-continent and of decadence. Sister Philippa's planting of flowers rather than vegetables in the Palace garden has already been flagged as a sign that her spirit has wandered from the Sisterhood's pragmatic work ethic. More than this, though, the flowers gush with the contorted sexuality of the preceding sequence, and they initiate two similarly charged moments: the arrival of Sister Ruth's dress in a parcel (she changes into this dark red dress when she abandons the Sisterhood in her mistaken pursuit of Mr Dean); and a curiously warped and sado-masochistic episode in which Angu Ayah commands the young General to finish whipping Kanchi, who has been found stealing, and 'become a man!' The blossoms' vibrant colours then percolate through to the film's last reel, eventually to nourish the symbolic redness of Ruth's dress and lipstick – sin and sex incarnate.

Since the scripted narrative touches on the cultural silencing of women's desires, we can theorise how far the extra-diegetic music in the film also serves as a displacement of the female voice. Classically constructed films typically use sound – particularly extra-diegetic music – to buttress the regime of the visible. The relationship may be sympathetic or contrapuntal, but the visual regime has authority and is allied theoretically to values which are empirical and patriarchal. Here, the music dominates (there are few words) and what we see is organised according to a governing principle which is fundamentally musical. Music is non-verbal, and it can also be thought of as non- or pre-logical: certainly it is often associated with the realm of the 'feelings'. In Mary Ann Doane's words, 'the ineffable, intangible quality of sound – its lack of the concreteness which is conducive to an ideology of empiricism – requires that it be placed on the side of the emotional or intuitive'.[35] Eisenstein himself noted this relationship, and went further to suggest that music is inherently polysemic. Music, he writes, 'is remarkable in that the images created by it flow continuously...Music has preserved this emotional plurality of meaning in its speech, the plurality of meaning which has been displaced from language that seeks precision, distinctness, and logical exhaustion.'[36] If precise, logical 'language' has masculine characteristics then musical language comes to be connoted with the feminine. Julia Kristeva's notion of the 'semiotic' – a disruptive 'pre-signifying' and feminine energy working within language – performs the same function which Eisenstein allots to the musical code. In her model, this 'semiotic' is committed to the anarchy of the pleasure principle, and is bound up with the Freudian unconscious. The Symbolic regime tries to harness this energy; but the semiotic resists this regimentation and constantly threatens to burst through the policed border of the Symbolic, harrying its sense of order. A carnivalesque force, the semiotic is given a privileged role in some forms of discourse: Kristeva singles out moments of transgressive holy ecstasy, madness and poetry, at its most subversive in the writings of the avant-garde. She also suggests, specifically, that music is 'constructed exclusively on the basis of the semiotic'.[37]

Music is linked to a feminine energy in *Black Narcissus* as it is the renegade Ruth's encounter with Mr Dean which initiates the 'composed' section of the film. The tense rhythm which accompanies her murderous return to Clodagh clearly broadcasts the throb of her quickening pulse.

Orchestral music has expressed irrationality and licentiousness already in the film: during the early montage which accompanies Mr Dean's scene-setting letter to the nuns in Calcutta, we hear 'ghosts of a bygone age' – the spirits of the old General's concubines – calling musically to Angu Ayah, and harmonic outbursts later in the film retain some of their supernatural connotations. The persistent drum beat which punctuates the closing sequence of *Black Narcissus* has also been cued earlier, to ominous effect: it is heard as a vigil for the ailing (and unseen) young General, heir to Toda Rai, and its cessation marks his death. These connotations aptly spill into the final section as Ruth is possessed by morbid tendencies. Outbreaks of choral chanting match the sudden cut to Ruth in her red dress when first seen by Clodagh. The same dramatic outbursts later reinforce extreme close-up shots of Ruth's psychotic eyes in the closing moments of the sequence, while a gradual orchestral crescendo marks Clodagh's increasing vulnerability as she is uncannily felt to be watched by someone in the chapel. This entire sequence is largely lacking in dialogue, like other key sequences in Powell and Pressburger's films, such as the defusing scene at the end of *The Small Back Room* or the ballet in *The Red Shoes*. The demotion of diegetic speech superficially returns cinema to its silent days, for despite his eventual enthusiasm for the 'organic whole', Powell was initially suspicious of synchronised sound, acknowledging that long sequences in some of his films are 'essentially silent' and that in his films 'images are everything'.[38] The key dramatic function here is to display the murderous effects of Ruth's thwarted sexual desires. Such desires are literally unspeakable, but they can be scored musically, and daubed onto the mise-en-scène.

Mr Dean is the film's chief masculine presence. As David Farrar's voiceover reads his introductory letter to the Sisters in the film's opening Calcutta sequence, his sensible pragmatism is reflected in the accompanying montage sequence which shows scenes of everyday life from the General's estate. An issue of gender is at stake here. In this, their most female-centred film, a man is granted the superiority of what is in effect almost an extra-diegetic voice – for we have not yet seen Mr Dean, and his voice has yet to be 'rooted' in the narrative. This man represents the masculine world which will crowd in on and disrupt the Sisters' sanctuary. For some time, a close-up of his letter is shown as he begins to recite the clearly visible, typed script. This apparently redundant repetition marks Mr Dean's control of both the written and the spoken word, and his autobiographical opening ('My name is Dean') stakes his claim to this power. His spoken and written words then conjure images of the General's estate. This footage –

establishing shots of the 'Himalayan landscape' and close-ups of natives working on the land – is in a documentary style, married to a male voiceover which is well-nigh a parody of (or homage to) 1940s Griersonian paternalism: 'The people are like mountain peasants everywhere: simple, independent. They work because they must. They smile when they feel like it and they're no respecter of persons. The men are men: no better and no worse than anywhere else. The women are women; the children, children.' It sounds and looks like a disinterested travelogue commentary, or an anthropological documentary, albeit that the obvious studio set parades its artificiality. The film does not abandon this documentary style altogether: as the Sisterhood begins to settle at the Palace, a further brief montage of toiling locals mirrors these first impressions. Later, Joseph Antony is seen teaching English to the local children, innocently training them in a significantly male-oriented discourse by naming weaponry for them: 'Can-non; War-ship; Bay-o-net!' As the Sisterhood drifts into distraction, and alternative, impractical impulses come to dominate, Joseph Antony's lessons then centre on identifying Sister Philippa's decorative flower beds instead. Mr Dean's baritone voice, however, emboldened by alcohol before a Christmas carol service, will still hold its power, if only to the admiring young General, Dilip Rai, to whom it is 'so nice and loud'.

The information gleaned from Mr Dean's voiceover is a touchstone of reliable narration in a film which is otherwise devoid of objectivity. His narrative parenthesises the dream-like atmosphere which dominates the rest of the film. In a parallel gesture, when the documentary style 'location' montage initiated by Mr Dean's voiceover cuts back to Sister Clodagh and the Mother Superior in Calcutta, we are shown a scattering of black-and-white photographs of the General's estate which the nuns are examining. These 'scientifically verifiable' photographic images clearly lay claim to a truth status, despite the fact that what they represent is Alfred Junge's fabricated studio set. They quiz the veracity of the visible, and by extension they address issues to do with Western empirical traditions – issues which are animated by Powell's very decision to 'interiorise' Rumer Godden's novel. The 'realism' of the montage sequence and of the photographs (geared as they are towards capturing the real) is entwined with empiricism, while the modernist current in *Black Narcissus* aims towards subjective interiority. The external world is demoted or excluded as we move into the magic space of the Sisters' interior world.

The proud and ambitious Sister Clodagh rails against Dean's fatalistic resignation, and against the imperviousness of the Himalayan environment to the Sisterhood's efforts. The sequence which visualises the contents of Dean's letter for us differs from the style of the rest of the film. Although the realist-documentary mode is left behind as *Black Narcissus* comes to inhabit Clodagh's (and Ruth's) distorted point of view, the two forms are in implicit dialogue. A highly symbolic audio-visual texture replaces Dean's more realistic montage, yet ultimately the subjective world is confounded, as Dean's assessment that the Palace is 'no place to put a nunnery' is proved to be correct. The qualifying point may also be made, of course, that while the images seen in the early montage sequence are triggered by Dean's words, and are guided by his voice, they derive in fact from Clodagh's own reading of the letter, and given the highly fantastical nature of the mise-en-scène at Mopu, the status of this first impression of the Palace, its environs, and even of Dean's voice itself, may not be so assured as it first appears – for even this seemingly impartial sequence of film is polluted with the unreliable taint of the Sister's imagination.

If distinctions between documentary and fantasy are characteristically undone here (as they were in *A Canterbury Tale* and *The Volunteer* and as they are elsewhere in the Archers' work) then similarly any neatly conceptualised boundaries between West and East are also put under scrutiny. The realities of Indian life are represented more authentically in Godden's novel. The charge may well be made that the script for *Black Narcissus* and Powell's decision to re-create India imaginatively in a London studio subscribe to a crude 'Orientalism': a naturalistic storyline is beefed up into a Eurocentric fantasy, with Mopu being no more than a screen onto which Western anxieties are projected. Insofar as the studio set is coloured by Clodagh/Ruth's increasing neuroses, some of the accusation stands. The Orient is used to offer an alternative to the Western values established in the Order of St Faith. That Western regime, with its reliance upon science and rationality, and firmly rooted in the reality principle, is commonly presented as a moral and cultural justification for imperialism. Its Enlightenment discourse sustains the missionary zeal of Empire by permitting the exotic and the foreign to signify that which should be brought under the control of a regimented Western order. As Edward Said has remarked, in this discourse, 'the Oriental is irrational, depraved (fallen), childlike, "different", thus the European is rational, virtuous, mature, "normal"... The Oriental is *contained* and *represented* by dominating frameworks.'[39] Traces of this can be seen in the way *Black Narcissus* views both the peasantry and the young General (typically, Sabu is infantilised and exoticised), but some qualifying comments are necessary. First, the most significant 'Other' which the text animates is Sister Ruth herself, Clodagh's pursuing *doppelganger*: this is the most dramatic splitting in the text, not that between East and West. Furthermore, there is no attempt to 'pass off' the studio set as an authentic re-creation of India, and the attempts of the Westerners to impose themselves upon the Himalayan environment are clearly mocked from the outset. The Orient, then, is neither 'contained' nor 'represented by dominating frameworks'. The text actually problematises the very distinction between East and West, and touches on the undoing of geographical 'Otherness'. Clodagh's Irish flashbacks are as romantic, sensual and saturated with colour as the 'Orient'. Sarah Street's detailed work on the censorship of *Black Narcissus* in the USA. suggests that the excisions to the film made there following pressure from the Catholic League of Decency had the effect of polarising the film's visions of West and East. Clodagh's Irish flashbacks were cut, as were shots of Ruth applying lipstick and Mr Dean violently rejecting her. Street argues that without the Irish sequences, with their erotic potential, the 'dichotomy' between East and West is maximised. This, though, was contrary to the film's original meaning.[40]

Powell and Pressburger were always interested in the Indian subcontinent. Powell visited Burma in 1937 on a research trip with a view to making 'Burmese Silver' for Alexander Korda. That project was abandoned. Pressburger began writing a project called 'South East Frontier' in 1938, based on W. Somerset Maugham's play *Caesar's Wife* and emulating the style of Korda's series of 'Imperial' epics. With Powell's involvement, that project developed into 'The East and the West', and an early sequence of this unfilmed script anticipates *Black Narcissus*'s treatment of the exotic. Set in the late 1920s, it opens with visual jokes about how fashionable the Orient has become in London because of the public's excitement about the visit of the King and Queen of Afghanistan. A modern young lady is seen parading Afghan hounds; fashionable dresses are modelled on Afghan styles; and an up-market Bond Street shop window advertises 'Lipsticks in the new "Amanullah" shade' and 'Rosalind's new Perfume "Kabul"'. By rooting the story in London's West End culture, the script begins to work through the ways in which the East represents a fantasy to the West (rather self-consciously for an 'Imperial epic').

The exotic perfume which Dilip Rai wears in *Black Narcissus*, and which gives the film its title, seems at first to evoke the exotic and the sensual, but he tells the nuns that it was bought from the 'Army & Navy Stores' in London, complicating the merchandising of the exotic seen in the earlier unfilmed project. On horseback, Dilip Rai is heard to cry 'Ride On!' in an American accent, identifying himself more with cowboys than with 'Indians' (this touch is not in the source novel). Mr Dean, the voice of rationalism, seems to have 'gone native', while General Todo Rai, played in heavy disguise by the Archers' stalwart actor Esmond Knight, is known to be a highly westernised sophisticate. Young Kanchi (played by another European, Jean Simmons) carries a Western gentleman's umbrella, while the 'wise man' permanently meditating on the hillside is revealed to be General Krishna Rai, a highly decorated, multi-lingual cosmopolitan who has now abandoned his European lifestyle in favour of Eastern asceticism. The legend of Narcissus is about a collapse of the boundary between Self and Other, and here tidy geographical demarcations are also done away with. Even the rhododendron blossoms which represent the exotic flowering of female lust have a cross-cultural significance, for these staple plants of the English country house garden and canonical images of 'National Trust' calendars (the ones here were filmed at Leonardslee in Sussex) are themselves imported souvenirs of the British in India.

As Clodagh, Deborah Kerr is proud, cold and officious, and her voice is shrill and orderly, but the whiteness of her face is mask-like. In fact, when we first see her in the opening sequence at Calcutta, a curious blocking has the actress turn slightly in profile as the camera cuts to a reverse shot, ensuring her anonymity by keeping her face from view in both shots. Metaphorically, her 'self' is veiled, and appropriately we learn later that she entered the convent to hide from the world. When we do see her, her slightly protruding lower lip is petulant, but it is also fleshy. We have seen Kerr before in her three roles in *Blimp* as Edith Hunter (the Edwardian suffragette, whose toughness Clodagh aspires to), as the easy-going Barbara Wynn who marries Clive, and as the dynamic, no-nonsense Angela/'Johnny'. It is when Clodagh's face lights up in close-up and we dissolve back in time to Ireland that some of Barbara Wynn's gentleness is remembered. Unconscious triggers – the word 'emerald' or the sound of horses – cause Clodagh to 'lose her place' and to drift back to Ireland, and the warmth of these deeply coloured Irish sequences contrasts with Clodagh's pallid Himalayan exile. Ireland is not all good, though. Galloping foxhunting scenes (looking like out-takes from *Gone to Earth*) resonate danger as well as excitement, and in one shot during Clodagh's courtship she runs outside to meet Con and melts for a second into the pitch black nothingness framed by a doorway, just as Con's imminent abandonment of her will annihilate her sense of self. Back on the terrace of Mopu and almost breaking down as she admits her defeat to Dean, we finally get a throb of emotion in Clodagh's voice, but again, and in a very English way (despite the character's Irishness) there is a strangulated impression of self-control vying with her patent longing to cry openly.

When their heads are both wrapped in their religious clothes, tightly framing their faces, Clodagh and Ruth look similar (far more similar than the two actresses actually are). Kathleen Byron's more angular features become apparent as her tenuous self-possession deserts her. There is intelligence in her face. It was used by Powell and Pressburger when they first cast her as an officer angel in *A Matter of Life and Death*, and later, in *The Small Back Room* she is the shrewd and caring Susan, partnered (this time successfully) to David Farrar as Sammy. Because of her quick-wittedness, we believe Ruth when she accuses the generally reserved Clodagh of 'thinking too much of Mr. Dean' herself. As Clodagh's 'double' it is only right that she should declare what Clodagh herself cannot admit. These gothic operations are at home, of course, in a nunnery. Ecclesiastical establishments like this are part of the mise-en-scène of the gothic novel, where they signify ancient, mystical and oppressive order, and where they are haunted by tales of corrupted innocence. Powell and Pressburger wrestle with Godden's text to bring this out. Gothic tales require a demonic 'Other', a monster, and typically this demon is internal in origin, a *doppelganger* like Jekyll's Hyde, like Frankenstein's monster, and like the two 'Marias' in Fritz Lang's *Metropolis* (1926, Germany). The Sisterhood brings with it the germ of its own catastrophe, and its downfall is caused not by its encounter with the East, but by its foolish struggle to separate spirit and matter, and its failure to admit its own flawed, fleshed and human nature. Ruth is the id split off from Clodagh's ego. Her escape from Mopu is redrafted for the film to reinforce their relationship (in the novel she slips away while Angu Ayah fails to watch over her). Clodagh's discovery of Ruth in her dark red dress still has the power to shock, and is accompanied by a shrieking chorus on the pulsating soundtrack. An extreme close-up of Ruth's red lipstick, and of beads of sweat on her brow, battles visually with shots of the bible which Clodagh clutches as the pair sit the night out together, while inter-cut shots of old wall murals show images of the concubines of old who haunt the Palace. Appropriately, Clodagh falls asleep, allowing Ruth to take flight to Mr Dean, vicariously acting out Clodagh's repressed desire. Figuratively, then, the entire sequence in which Ruth declares her love for Dean is dream-like, and it is Clodagh's dream. When Ruth and Dean's exchange is over, a close-up of David Farrar's face dissolves back to Clodagh, on the verge of sleep again, as if to reaffirm the hypnagogic, trance-like nature of the episode, and its true status as Clodagh's vicarious fantasy of a jungle encounter with Dean.

The dream becomes a nightmare. The horror genre dramatises how the failure to repress the unspeakable produces monstrosity out of the self – a return of the repressed. When Dean's rejection pushes Ruth into psychosis, she is made monstrous – a pursuing evil who is seemingly possessed and who returns to Mopu. Some of the camera movement at this stage captures its genuine eeriness. An eye-level shot tracks leftwards, unmotivated, to spy on Clodagh outside the Palace; soon afterwards, another eye-level tracking shot creeps to the right to watch her praying in the chapel. Ruth is at large somewhere, but has not yet been glimpsed. The shots may or may not be Ruth's murderous point of view, but they are ontologically inexplicable and are genuinely uncanny. When she finally emerges, Ruth's hair is wild, her complexion and movements zombie-like, and the fires of hell seem to burn in the Palace. She tussles with Clodagh at the precipice bell, and falls to her death. This eradication of the 'Other', which is typical of horror, allows order to be reimposed and Ruth's transgression to be punished. An abbreviated coda finishes the film. Ruth's grave is seen, and as the nuns leave there is a tender farewell between Clodagh and Dean. She finally begins to learn humility, saying that her inevitable demotion will be good for her. He holds her hand to say goodbye, and this is all we see of the muted possibility of romance between them. The rains come, the Palace of Mopu is lost in cloud, and Dean is left alone as the Sisters leave. Jack Cardiff was proud of a final scene he shot, set back in Calcutta, with Clodagh sobbing and admitting her vulnerability as she is embraced by the forgiving Mother Dorothea. Powell cut that scene, with its positive and redemptive ending, and shifted the sense of catharsis to the dramatic moment of Ruth's death. The coda therefore seems anti-climactic. David Farrar is left as a figure of broad-chested stoicism – the stuff of English manhood – but there is a sense of remote longing in his rain-drenched eyes as they watch Clodagh depart. His expression niggles away at the image of Jack Hawkins-like self-sufficiency which he connotes, and it speaks volumes about the chasm separating this type of man from women like Clodagh.

6

Art and Artists – *The Red Shoes*, *The Tales of Hoffmann*

> I believe in…the one and indivisible Art; I believe this Art to be an emanation of God that dwells in the hearts of all enlightened men; I believe that whoever has steeped himself in its holy joy must dedicate himself to it forever and can never deny it; I believe that all men are blessed through Art and it is therefore permissible to die of hunger for its sake.
>
> Richard Wagner, 'Death in Paris'

THE MAGIC OF ART

For idealists, 'Art' is a passport to a realm of transcendence. Artists are exotic creatures, divorced from bourgeois culture, elevated, and possessed of a superior vision. Art itself is a specially preserved area, spoken of with reverence, written about with an upper-case 'A'. This is the consequence of historical forces, as Raymond Williams observes:

> With the development of the market came the notion of 'culture' as that which resists the base, the mass judgement. And from this comes the notion of art and the artist as favoured, reified, threatened by the social forces of commodification. Art is therefore a 'magic' space, resisting through its appeals to 'culture'. It is specialized, abstracted from the quotidian. Along with this comes the notion of Art as a 'superior reality'.[1]

The romantic view of art is thus bound up with the development of mass literacy and mass audiences, with the decline of artistic patronage, and with the spread of industrial production and market economies. It is no accident that the development in literary circles of ideas of the imagination, the increasing interest in subjectivity and artistic freedom, and the fetishisation of the 'work of art' coincided with economic developments around 1800 which saw writers thrown to the mercy of the marketplace and required to sell their artistic wares: a tense relationship of independence and dependence. Here, the idea of 'Culture' raises itself magically above the commonplace. It can resist hegemonic values, and can sound its critique of society. Its elitism may, therefore, be an indicator of dissidence. The very fact that 'Art' can seem 'unnecessary' indicates the boundaries of bourgeois culture, which prides itself on its utilitarianism and its productivity. To have a sense of the aesthetic is a marker of taste and a marker of class.

In their 'art films', *The Red Shoes* (1948) and *The Tales of Hoffmann* (1951), Powell and Pressburger flaunt their own romantic credentials. 'Art' itself is a symbolic territory for them, as full of strange spectacles as Chillingbourne, Kiloran, Heaven or the Himalayas. *The Red Shoes*, though, is marked by ambiguities: art is supernatural, inspired, demonic, but it is also the product of graft and skill. Its exotic impresario Boris Lermontov (played imperiously by Anton Walbrook) is called a 'magician' but even he admits that 'not even the best magician in the world can produce a rabbit from the hat if there isn't already a rabbit in the hat'. There is a slick deception here: *The Red Shoes* ballet is shown to be the material consequence of factors of production (the celebrated skills of the Lermontov ballet troupe – the 'rabbit in the hat'). As such the ballet cannot be commodified, for commodities by definition deny the factors which made them and present themselves pristinely as spectacular objects in a consumerist system of exchange. However, the filmed sequence of the ballet clearly uses a gamut of cutting-edge special effects and the film's 'cinematic' status remains magical. It dazzles us. There is a tension, then, between the quasi-realist 'laying bare' of ballet's 'back-stage' intricacies, and the secret, mesmeric trickery of which cinema alone is capable. Formally, the film is 'about' the celebration of cinema. *The Tales of Hoffmann* exists entirely in a magical register, and expects us to be amazed even more, for it has no internal benchmark of realism against which to judge its spectacle.

Another ambiguity: these films deal with, and aspire to be, 'high art'; at the same time they are popular products of the culture industry. The Ballet Lermontov represents a 'magic space', in Williams' sense, but the film also fetishises its contained production of *The Red Shoes* ballet, its red shoes and its ingenue star dancer Victoria Page/Moira Shearer. Powell and Pressburger's motivations are enthusiastically, decisively popularist. These may be 'art films' but they are not 'art-house' in the sense we understand today, and neither do they appeal primarily to the special cultural competences of an elite coterie. Both films therefore occupy ambivalent cultural positions. This chapter sets out to explore the concept of 'Art' in these films, and to demonstrate the ways they show how mythic structures, texts and cultural fantasies work to conscript us. It also seeks to explain the rampant colour and music of the films in terms of Powell and Pressburger's developing output and to situate them within British culture of the late 1940s and early 1950s.

The history of *The Red Shoes* suggests that Powell and Pressburger's interest in high-romantic ideals was approaching a zenith at this time. Here, they present art as an ideal. Lermontov calls ballet a 'religion' and, echoing his sacred invocation, Vicky is first seen dancing solo in a converted church hall – it is the Mercury Theatre in Notting Hill, London, which was the early base of Marie Rambert's Ballet Club. In Walter Benjamin's terms, Lermontov's company radiates an aura: its work is special and crafted. Benjamin suggests that works of art which are untouched by mechanical reproduction retain a quasi-religious quality because of their fixed association with a specific place. When Lermontov opens his new production of *The Red Shoes* ballet – the focal point of the film – he has no qualms about the audience of a mere 300 in the theatre to see it, because after opening night 'everyone will be talking about it'. The performance's cultural worth is inversely proportional to the number of people who are fortunate or sophisticated enough to see it. Lermontov, though, is a shrewd businessman. He is quickly hospitable to potential patrons of the arts, and his company tirelessly tours the world, but its unique status at London's Covent Garden Theatre shows that their aura is preserved within a tightly bound, nomadic community of artists, and Lermontov's eye is clearly not on mere profit when he jealously decrees that no one besides Vicky will ever dance the lead role in *The Red Shoes* ballet.

The Ballet Lermontov is held up as a mirror for the Archers' own company, and the film negotiates implicitly between ballet and cinema as art forms. Lermontov is therefore both a ballet impresario and, at times, is very like a film producer. Though Powell and Pressburger make 'commercial' films they are still working towards aesthetic goals: 'art' films for popular appeal. The correspondence between Lermontov's production of the ballet and the Archers' production of the film betrays their views about the status of film, but it is their long central sequence of *The Red Shoes* ballet itself where they stake their faith on cinema's own ability to make magic. Regardless of the evident skills of the dancers, choreographers, musicians and designer, the sequence pointedly escapes the literal space of the theatre stage. Rather than filming a performance, or worshipping the canned and captured skills of their dancers, they provide a surreal series of spectacles which are uniquely cinematic, created by the camera itself or in post-production. The film formally captures the auratic quality of Vicky's dancing at Monte Carlo, and then expresses it through cinema, insisting on its aura however many times the film is mechanically reproduced.

Pressburger originally wrote the script of *The Red Shoes* for Alexander Korda in 1937. That script, which was to have starred Korda's wife Merle Oberon, was never filmed, and the Archers bought it back from Korda after the war to produce it for Rank following *Black Narcissus* (1947). The film tells a mythic tale of the incompatibility of 'life' and 'art', and it differs tellingly from Pressburger's original version. In the film, the internationally famous Ballet Lermontov is in London to premiere a new ballet, *Heart of Fire*, with music by Professor Andrew Palmer (Austin Trevor). His composition student, Julian Craster (Marius Goring), is there to hear; Victoria Page, a dancer, is there to watch. Both their evenings take unexpected turns. Julian hears his own music plagiarised by his tutor, and storms out of the theatre. Victoria's aunt, the wealthy Lady Neston (Irene Browne) lures Boris Lermontov to her post-ballet soirée, where she has arranged that Vicky will dance for him. Lermontov brusquely refuses to suffer an audition over his champagne cocktail, but later he hires Victoria as a chorus dancer. Julian writes angrily to Lermontov about Palmer, and through this contact he too is taken on, as Lermontov's orchestral coach. His ambitions are noticed and Lermontov asks him to rewrite some sections of an untried score for *The Red Shoes* ballet, based on the Hans Christian Andersen story of a young girl whose pride is punished when she is supernaturally 'possessed' by the new pair of red shoes she has coveted. She puts on the shoes and dances, but the shoes will not stop, and they dance her to death. Julian composes an entirely new score and also conducts the new ballet. Vicky is retained for the company's Paris and Monte Carlo seasons. When prima ballerina Boronskaja (Ludmilla Tcherina) leaves the company to marry, Lermontov makes it clear that he demands total commitment to dance and Vicky overhears his contempt for any dancer foolish enough to marry. Lermontov believes in a complete separation of life and art, and ignores 'human nature' entirely. In Monte Carlo, Vicky is invited to Lermontov's villa, where she is given the lead role in the new ballet. After extensive rehearsals *The Red*

Shoes ballet opens to a rapturous reception. Stylistically, the ballet is a contained set-piece of music-dance-cinema, drawing on Surrealism and Expressionism to visualise Vicky's sub-conscious dancing rapture, part thrilled, part terrified. Lermontov learns that Vicky and Julian are in love, and immediately fires him. Vicky leaves the company to be with Julian. Lermontov has twice lost a protégée. We see Julian and Vicky in London: inspired by his love, he is finishing his opera, *Cupid and Psyche,* for Covent Garden. She paws her dance shoes wistfully. When she visits Monte Carlo with Lady Neston, Lermontov tempts her back to dance *The Red Shoes* ballet again. His Svengali-like character is to the fore here, and when Julian suddenly arrives to claim her back Vicky is trapped in a typically hysterical dilemma between two incompatible, polarised wishes (in this triangular structure the film resembles the 1950s *Gone to Earth*). She has been trying on the red shoes just before curtain up, and suddenly they seem to impel her outside to a balcony over which, balletically, she plunges to her death, leaving Julian and Lermontov devastated. The performance goes ahead with just the white disc of a spotlight's beam describing the place where Vicky was to have danced.

The film dispenses with the social realism which marks Pressburger's original script. Palmer's ballet was originally called *Caledonian Market* (an echo of contemporary 'realistic' ballets choreographed by Kurt Jooss or Robert Helpmann). In the film, its name is more mythically resonant – *Heart of Fire* – and its mise-en-scène alludes to classical fable. Incidental characters from the original script are deleted, and this lessens an initial interest in class: Vicky's confidante Lilian (cut from the film) was a working-class girl, a foil to highlight Vicky's class privilege, and Julian was a poor, struggling student barking class resentment (Lady Neston was just 'some rich old cow' to him). Vicky and Julian argued over money when they left Lermontov's company. This sense of material disadvantage survives only in the final film's opening sequence, where Julian and the hordes queuing for cheap seats in the 'gods' are kept separate from Vicky and Lady Neston in their expensive private box. By the late 1940s Pressburger enjoyed greater financial security than he had done a decade earlier. Powell himself never showed an artistic interest in 'working-class realism' or expressions of class struggle: biographical explanations for the new emphasis are therefore available to us. When they were asked to write a novel of *The Red Shoes* in the 1970s, when their film careers were far from flourishing, they fleshed out the social detail again – part of the process of novelisation – and they restored a sense of Julian's poverty. Is it the case that Pressburger's initial identification with the young man struggling to establish a career matured into his and Powell's less easy identification with the powerful producer Boris Lermontov? Whatever the answer, the removal of class from the filmed script complies with their general disinterest in social reality in the film.

The rewriting of the script in the 1940s echoes their adaptation of Rumer Godden's novel of *Black Narcissus*. In both films, 'Bildungsroman' traits in the source material are pared down and the core tale is beefed up into highly mythological and polarised melodrama. Despite the presence of real dancers from the London ballet scene, this is emphatically not realism. A brief, establishing sequence using location footage of Covent Garden Market self-consciously 'stages' crowds of workmen going about their business – one singing 'I went to Covent Garden in the morning', another wolf-whistling 'What a corker!' when Vicky walks past – as if to acknowledge the artifice at the core of the film. Its critical opposition between 'Life' and 'Art' (and its frank preference for the latter) demands that social concerns be manoeuvred out of frame, and that the boundary between the two worlds should be absolute. Consequently, Boris Lermontov is made less 'human'. In his first, unfilmed incarnation he is domineering and exotic, but also emotional enough to be a plausible love object for Vicky. The original script's energy relies on a simple 'love triangle' plot between Vicky, Julian and Boris, and Boris's attachment to Vicky is such that he tries to keep her with his company by compromising and telling her that Julian can stay too. There is no such equivocation in the film, and the possibility of romance between Vicky and Lermontov is a spectre of the original story structure. Lermontov is removed (almost) from human feelings, and is propelled beyond the world's value systems. He is a pure aesthete, the 'high priest of Art', with Vicky torn between being its ecstatic votary and Julian's wife.

At the core of *The Red Shoes* film is the original script's affinity to the 'back-stage musical', a genre premised in reality – the tribulations of staging a show – but which actually articulates myths of success. Vicky is plucked out for stardom; the film's momentum is directed to the 'opening night'; rehearsal snags are overcome; the plot of the contained show reframes and comments on the 'real' back-stage drama; and the 'performance of spectacle/spectacle of performance' matrix becomes the film's chief *raison d'etre*. In the mythic topos of the back-stage musical genre, self-definition, articulation and fulfilment are achievable; career success and heterosexual love enjoy an effortless coalescence. Personality is a keyword and is celebrated. In Richard Dyer's terms, this is popular entertainment at its most utopian: energetic, intense, communal, transparent and abundant.[2] Powell and Pressburger's film still carries some of the baggage of the musical genre. Powell, writing to Pressburger while in the USA scouting for a leading dancer-actress was characteristically quick to note this. 'There are many angles for exploitation on the film for every department but the main thing that all publicity, exploitation, advertising and selling should concentrate on is The Girl. The Red-Head who wears *The Red Shoes*.' Conscious that the film has no big film stars, he also notes, 'We shall never have a better opportunity to show the world that we can do better than Rita Hayworth and Ginger Rogers.' Contemporary reviewers also noticed this. Reg Whitley wrote in the *Sunday Mirror* on 21 July 1948 that 'Moira's Bigger than Ginger Rogers', an impressive cultural shift for someone so recently dancing for the Royal Ballet Company. These observations suggest that by popularising ballet, Powell and Pressburger see no distinction between high and popular art, and that some critics were sympathetic with their views. The film's original trailer capitalises on its marketable generic kinship, calling it a 'musical adventure' which 'catches all the glamour of the South of France in exquisite Technicolor', noting its international stars, selling the beauty of its newly discovered leading lady, and singing up its love story elements – although, to be fair, it also boasts/admits that the film is 'daringly original', couching its sales pitch carefully by pointing to familiar genre horizons of expectations while angling for more ambitious or experimental cinema-goers.

However, *The Red Shoes* is not part of Ginger Rogers' world, despite its ultimate status as a commercial film. It deals with the elite world of ballet rather than popular dance. Vicky's aspirations are straitjacketed, and the uncomplicated utopianism of the musical is contorted here into the tragic values of romantic art. Powell, in his memoirs, states: 'I think that the real reason why *The Red Shoes* was such a success, was that we had all been told for ten years to go out and die for freedom and democracy, for this and for that, and now the war was over, *The Red Shoes* told us to go and die for art.'[3] This is characteristically romantic rhetoric, and it signifies the way the Archers rechannel popular, democratic wartime idealism into new avenues in the post-war period by engaging with, and aiming to popularise, nineteenth-century values often associated with 'high art' (such as those espoused by Richard Wagner's idealistic young composer in his short story 'Death in Paris'). While *The Red Shoes* repeats *Black Narcissus*'s story of dashed aspirations, it holds out a faith in the pure transcendence which dance makes available. Vicky's suffering is justified by the film's appeal to 'high art' values. Transcendence costs (to echo the television series *Fame*, a spin-off from Alan Parker's American 'back-stage' musical film (1980), and right here is where she starts paying.

Lermontov is one in a line of messianic magus figures in Powell and Pressburger's films, although the type is perhaps more closely associated with Powell than Pressburger. From David Barr (Leslie Banks) in Powell's 1934 film *The Red Ensign* to Bradley Morahan (James Mason) in his *Age of Consent* (1969) there exist authoritarian, mystical, mesmeric men. Such men may be embodiments of idealistic longing. They may also blur with Powell's own persona. The very ambiguity of the title of Powell's memoirs, *A Life in Movies*, implies that his own personality is contained by the medium he works in, and however much credit he gives to his collaborators he enthusiastically incorporates their input into a grandiose perception of the director as Orchestrator: 'The camera and its crew are no longer that bunch of people out there, but an extension of my own eyes and arms and head. We are rolling!'[4] Powell's own brief appearances in his films corroborate this self-conscious fascination with the aesthetic personality, the dark side of which is exhibited in his role as Mark's father in *Peeping Tom* (1960). This type of character has its roots in Expressionism – not in its modernist strain, though, but in the anti-materialist, metaphysical line which Expressionism inherited from German neo-Romanticism. The Expressionist movement in Europe declared itself to be an urgent, engaged social polemic marking a break with the past and a rejection of nineteenth-century aestheticism, but its modernist credentials were compromised, and much of what we think of as Expressionist cinema clung to a sense of mysticism. It continued to be fascinated with the aesthetic personality and held an aristocratic view of art. Further back, the gothic had explored a hypnotic nexus of charisma and power, and these are the characteristics channelling into the Powellian 'magus figure'. Men like these often evoke terror because, although they are a locus of order and coherence (Lermontov is the point around which the carnival mayhem of the Ballet Lermontov is organised), they are simultaneously cloaked in mystery, and imbued with tyrannical power. The quasi-magical atmosphere surrounding Lermontov is compounded by the sense of enigma in Anton Walbrook's performance, with his foreign accent, rigid deportment and sense of control.

Like Conrad Veidt, an actor whom his career seemed to shadow, Walbrook never lost his accent. In Veidt's roles for Powell and Pressburger, the accent is a clear marker of his characters' sense of rootedness (an aural equivalent of Captain Hardt's unwillingness to take off his naval uniform and to disguise himself in *The Spy in Black*). As André Aciman puts it, 'An accent is a tell-tale scar left by the unfinished struggle to acquire a new language. But it is much more…An accent marks the lag between two cultures, two languages, the space where you let go of one identity, invent another, and end up being more than one person though never quite two.'[5] A vestigial foreign accent may well express geographical origins; to the listener it may signify a threat, a seduction or a mere difference, and Walbrook, a fluent linguist, seems to have retained his accent to exploit a niche position in British cinema: charismatic outsider (whether charming or demonic). Tortured, 'possessed' characters figure in his British filmography, such as *Gaslight* (1940) and *The Queen of Spades* (1949), both directed by Thorold Dickinson. In Lermontov's case, there is a clear homage to German cinema, a pattern seen in Conrad Veidt's earlier roles for Powell and Pressburger. Lermontov has a Nosferatu-like preference for shadows, and often wears sunglasses outdoors to protect himself. He is referred to as a 'gifted cruel monster' and is said to have 'no heart'. One moment in *The Red Shoes*, where Lermontov smashes his fist into a mirror, alludes specifically to Walbrook's early German success, *The Student of Prague* (Arthur Robinson, 1935), a horror tale in which a young student is pursued by his shadowy *doppelganger* until he shoots at his own mirrored reflection. The multiple meanings contained within the Lermontov role therefore refuse to observe national borders. Walbrook 'continentalises' him, elements of Powell and Pressburger can be seen in him, he was reputedly modelled in part on the Hungarian Alexander Korda and very clearly he is also based on the Russian (yet passionately international) ballet impresario Sergei Diaghilev (whose company, after 1922, had its winter headquarters in Monte Carlo, as Lermontov does). The presence in the film of such notable dancers as Léonide Massine, Robert Helpmann, Moira Shearer and (briefly) Marie Rambert underscores its real affinity to European dance, the entire culture of which owed much to Diaghilev and his 'Ballets Russes' company.

The way the film draws on ballet culture emphasises its construction of art as a separate sphere. The film draws on the history of Diaghilev and the Ballets Russes, which first took Paris by storm in 1909, and refashions it into one of its structuring myths. The popularity of ballet in Britain took hold largely through Diaghilev's visits (the company's first London appearance was in 1911) and through the dancers and choreographers he introduced to the West: Anna Pavlova, Tamara Karsavina, Vaslav Nijinsky and Michel Fokine. Initially, he employed only Russian dancers, but after

1917 he found an international cast including Vera Sarvina, Ninette de Valois, Alicia Markova and Anton Dolin. These artists were apt to change their names for the stage. The convention of adopting Muscovite names gestured respect to Diaghilev's origins; sometimes, though, French names were assumed: Vera Clark became Sarvina; Alicia Marks became Alicia Markova; the Irish Edris Stannus mutated into Ninette de Valois; her fellow citizen Patrick Healey-Kaye first arrived with Diaghilev as Patrikeyev and rejoined as Anton Dolin; Marie Rambert lost her Warsaw name Miriam Rambam; and Leonid Miassine, a Muscovite, became Léonide Massine. Likewise, and elsewhere, the young Austrian actor, Adolf Wohlbrück renamed himself Anton Walbrook (a deft hybrid of French and English) when his cosmopolitan career came to centre on English language cinema and when European politics contaminated his real first name. It is a world of multiple identities. The custom of renaming trades playfully in the exotic and betrays a wish to seem 'sophisticated'. Moreover, it severs the reinvented identities from their origins, giving the ballet world an uprooted, 'bohemian' character and gesturing to a culture of genuine internationalism. It also parallels the myriad displacements which figure in the text of *The Red Shoes*, where Ballets Russes translates into Ballet Lermontov which substitutes for the Archers, where Lermontov connotes a range of men, real and fictional, where characters in the film are re-presented in the 'contained' ballet narrative of *The Red Shoes*, and where the principal male dancer Ivan (Robert Helpmann) plays the multiple roles of the Boy, the priest and a dancing daily newspaper.

Though he was associated with the Russian school of dance, Diaghilev's international team was effectively a troupe of nomads (a form of picaresque social organisation explored by Powell and Pressburger in films such as *49th Parallel*, 1941, and '*...one of our aircraft is missing*', 1942). Rather than preserve traditions of dance, Diaghilev modernised the grand Russian balletic style. In the nineteenth century, Russian ballet culture focused on dancing itself. Diaghilev created fluidly staged combinations of music, design and dancing in a modern fusion which swept away the old classicism. Fokine's choreography avoided classical geometry, and the company presented a combination of innovatory new work – at the cutting edge of European modernism – while it also refreshed the canon of established romantic ballets. Diaghilev's Wagnerian interest in combined modes of expression anticipates the Archers' own striving for 'total' cinema and their interest in dance-opera-drama; his collaborations with Russian painters such as Léon Bakst and Alexandre Benois, Western artists like Picasso, Derain and Cocteau, and composers such as Stravinsky, Debussy, Ravel and Milhaud anticipates the Archers' own recruitment of the best collaborators.

The founding of the Royal Ballet at Sadlers Wells by Ninette de Valois in 1931, and her early success with *Job: A Masque for Dancing* in 1934 (scored by Vaughan Williams) helped to establish ballet as a serious undertaking in Britain and to raise its national prestige. Robert Helpmann, who appeared in '...*one of our aircraft is missing*' and who plays the dancer Ivan Boleslawsky in *The Red Shoes*, arrived at her Sadlers Wells ballet school in 1933 from Australia and was the leading male dancer for the company. Helpmann's reputation was for acting and choreography as well as dancing. Some of his early work on the British stage shows that his ambitions in the theatre anticipated Powell and Pressburger's. The first ballet he choreographed and danced was his adaptation of a masque, Milton's *Comus* (1934), which brought words and dance together to music from Purcell. This was a radical innovation. Much of *Comus* was a traditional ballet, but at two points Helpmann stopped dancing to deliver speeches. The physical difficulty of presenting words and movement (which Helpmann only achieved by arresting the flow of dance and trying to reserve enough breath to speak) would be solved cinematically in *Hoffmann* where soundtracks and imagetracks were recorded separately and were then edited together so that dancers appear to sing while in motion. Helpmann's fourth ballet at Sadlers Wells was a contemporary dance drama called *Miracle in the Gorbals*. Moira Shearer was dancing in it when Powell first saw her and offered her the role of Vicky in *The Red Shoes*. *Miracle in the Gorbals* was influenced by Kurt Jooss's work. Kurt Jooss's ballet company had found a home at Dartington Hall in Devon, in exile from occupied Europe, and its own brand of modern dance-drama drew on the skills of their designer Hein Heckroth, whose work for the Archers reached its own pinnacle in *The Red Shoes* and *Hoffmann*.

Real biography is most graphically folded into the film's text when, during a jokey montage sequence charting Vicky's career after the success of *The Red Shoes* ballet, we see her dancing in *La Boutique Fantasque*, and a close-up of the theatre programme shows its choreography to be by Massine and its scenery and costumes to be by André Derain. In 1919, this had been one of Massine's and Derain's notable successes, and the inscription of Massine's name blurs the distinction between him and Grischa Ljubov, the character he plays in the film. Massine's performance as Ljubov thoroughly underscores the film's link to Diaghilev. Diaghilev had famously terminated Nijinsky's contract as principal male dancer in 1913. Nijinsky had been Diaghilev's lover, and he was dismissed when he announced his marriage to Romola de Pulsky. Diaghilev had by this time already lost an earlier male lover to a heterosexual romance. After Nijinsky's departure, Diaghilev groomed Massine as his leading male on and off stage, and their romantic/professional bond continued till 1920 when Massine began a relationship with ballerina Vera Savina and the pair left the company. This unlucky or obsessive pattern in Diaghilev's love life is heterosexualised in Powell and Pressburger's reworking of the story, and translates into Lermontov's neurotic separation of 'work' and 'life', although what Alexander Doty terms an 'aura of queerness' still permeates through to the Ballet Lermontov.[6] There is no overt sign of homosexuality in the Ballet Lermontov, but the film relies heavily on Walbrook and Helpmann, who were gay, on Massine, whose own wavering sexuality was a matter of record, and on Hans Christian Andersen, who was homosexual.

Some of the histrionic performances – Ivan's preening, Grischa's intense screeching and Lermontov's mask-like yet charismatic persona – introduce a currency of campness, a performativity beyond that which the theatrical setting demands, and the company's senior collaborators, Ivan, Grischa, Livey, Ratov and even Lermontov's silent, sinister 'assistant' Dmitri (Eric Berry), form a tight, homosocial group. Beyond this, the queer Diaghilev-Nijinsky subtext informs Lermontov's contempt for Julian and Vicky's relationship. He is detached from bourgeois culture not only because of his purist's view of romantic art, but because he stands in opposition to heterosexual romance and to the institution of marriage. These twin explanations are expressed in the ambiguity surrounding his attitude to Vicky: she is a vehicle for his artistic ambitions, but he can seem just to envy her romance with Julian. When Julian says towards the end of the film that Lermontov is 'jealous', the impresario shouts back, 'Yes, I am, but in a way that you will never understand!' This cutting denial that he desires Vicky sexually also asserts his superiority by pointing up Julian's limitations, while the cryptic allusion to a secret set of codes beyond Julian's grasp fits in with views of queerness which see it in terms of enigmas, subtexts and subversions of bourgeois face values. 'Art' as high culture and 'queerness' as a radical stance share a set of elitist, prestigious connotations (fused together in the image of the aristocratic gay aesthete, a role most obviously personified by Oscar Wilde). They both resist the 'base'. The Lermontovian system depends on sexual repression, or more rightly on the displacement of sexual desire into artistic rehearsal, practice and performance. Like certain religions, Lermontov requires a vow of celibacy, and like those faiths, this censuring of heterosexual expression creates a special space where male homosexuality, however occluded, can prosper.

'VICKY-PSYCHE-KAREN-THE GIRL' VERSUS THE SYSTEM

The Royal Ballet was a cultural powerhouse by the 1940s, but smaller scale, innovatory work was also being accomplished by Marie Rambert, who founded the Ballet Club at the Mercury Theatre in 1920. *The Red Shoes* shows Vicky dancing for Rambert in *Swan Lake* (and Rambert herself makes a non-speaking cameo appearance). Rambert's 'chamber ballets' could be experimental and modernist, featuring dancers who often left her to go to Sadlers Wells (just as Vicky took up a position in Lermontov's *corps de ballet*) but, as the critic, writer and 'balletomane' Arnold Haskell noted in 1948, the distinguishing feature of Rambert's work was that she developed and promoted the individual qualities of her performers: 'Her dancers were young but never amateurish and they had a quality never before associated with the English dancer, personality. With Pavlova it had been discouraged, with Diaghileff [sic] disguised. Rambert exploited it.'7 Anna Pavlova, whose fame pre-dated her spell with Diaghilev, was more interested in the classical style; Diaghilev emphasised dramatic acting and the development of character 'roles'. Rambert teased out the inner traits of her young dancers. Vicky's interior subjectivity, the basis of her 'personality', is first glimpsed in dizzying, zip-panned point-of-view shots as she pirouettes her way through *Swan Lake* at the Mercury Theatre. Her 'individuality' prevents her from being incorporated fully into Lermontov's system, which calls for the eradication of personality and for dancers to be engulfed entirely in the dance world. There is a gendered slant to this process. Nineteenth-century ballet saw an increasing interest in women and in roles for ballerinas, due to the development of painful, impressively graceful pointe-work technique. One of the unresolved tensions in *The Red Shoes* is whether Vicky's dancing for Lermontov *expresses* her personality (as her performance probably would if this were a musical), or whether it is a sign that her identity has been choreographed out of existence altogether, like the automaton we see her dancing in *Coppelia*. Her name, after all, is 'Page', a *tabula rasa* waiting to be written on, and what is interesting is the way in which her unstable, uncertain position is complicated: avenues which seem to allow her to articulate her feelings actually conspire to harness her energy. Here the film's existential leanings, similar to those anti-establishment sentiments found in *AMOLAD* (1946) and *The Small Back Room* (1949) are to the fore. As she undergoes rehearsals for *The Red Shoes* ballet, Vicky is called an 'old cart horse' by Ljubov, and she is publicly insulted again by Julian, who criticises her from his conductor's podium, 'We understand it, don't we, gentlemen, n'est ce pas? It's quite simple. You see this baton? Well, follow it!' Even though he concedes later that he will follow her tempo as she performs on the 'first night', he could hardly, at this stage, flaunt his male power more symbolically. Lermontov later expresses the film's ambiguity about Vicky's autonomy, telling her that he 'will do the talking' – while she can do the dancing.

The appropriation of the title of *The Red Shoes* from Hans Christian Andersen makes explicit the film's fairy-tale foundations. Vicky enters a world of myths (the roles she dances and the texts structuring the film), which weave together and chart her fate. In this respect, the film recapitulates the process mapped out in *Blimp* (1943), where Clive is offered a gallery of culturally sanctioned heroic paragons to identify with and to internalise. The situation satirised in *Blimp* is one where heroic behaviour has ossified into a tradition: conservatively, and in a postmodern paradox, a hero in the world of Blimpery is one who best impersonates his iconic heroes. In *The Red Shoes*, there is a tension between the modern woman's existential need for autonomy and her recruitment into a rigid structure which possesses her as wholly as the shoes possess the Girl in *The Red Shoes* ballet. In part, this tension expresses nothing more than romantic, artistic anxieties about originality and free expression set against the need to practise, to train and to obey customary laws of form. But myth, as Cynthia Young notes in her Lacanian-Barthesian reading of the film, is a 'powerful tool for subtly reinforcing...cultural, political and artistic ideologies',[8] and role-playing has its dangers. The canon of romantic ballets which we see Vicky dancing repeats powerful ideological messages, often of martyred heroines and female sacrifice. Young shows how Vicky is inserted into this oppressive symbolic order, and she correctly notes how the film self-consciously lays bare its strategy of rearticulating mythic discourses in a truly modernist fashion. Viewed through this optic, *The Red Shoes*' misogyny is brought to the fore, but its investment in Vicky's vitality and agency, its indictment of Julian's patriarchal containment of her energy and its anti-realist, explicitly mediated self-consciousness all complicate readings which argue that it blindly endorses the ideologies it puts on show. It is a film *about* cultural contestation, where needs, desires and the right to make meaning collide with dominating forces of control and containment. Vicky's mind and body are its conflict zone.

We get a sense of Vicky's enchantment when she accepts Lermontov's summons to his villa outside Monte Carlo. Presumably supposing this to be a romantic overture, she appears decked out as a fairy princess in ball gown and tiara. Travelogue footage chauffeurs her along the coastline to Lermontov's villa, and the camera is clearly enchanted. Powell's film career began along this coast, of course. He and Pressburger would attempt to make it marvellous again in an unfilmed project called 'Undine', which they worked on for some time in 1954. Written with Audrey Hepburn in mind, 'Undine' was to be an updated fantasy legend set in the modern Mediterranean among the Monte Carlo yachting set. It is about a female water sprite who falls in love with a mortal man and leaves the sea for him. As a synopsis for the unfilmed project spells out, 'No mortal man can endure such perfection'. The husband returns to an imperfect mortal woman. The love between the mermaid and the man is defeated by society and she retreats to the Mediterranean, having been torn between two worlds.

Various commentators have noted that Vicky's arrival at Lermontov's villa borrows its magical ambiance from Jean Cocteau, whose *Belle et la Bête* had been released in 1946. The overgrown flight of stairs and extensive gardens do suggest Cocteau's other-worldliness, but the sense of fantasy stems as much from the soundtrack, where the detached aria of an operatic tenor accompanies Vicky's ascent. There are two passages of operatic singing later in the film, and they are both associated with Julian's opera *Cupid and Psyche*. We hear it later when Julian awakes to compose a section of it at his piano, and again on the radio broadcast from Covent Garden during its first performance. Since we know that this is his 'magnum opus' in progress, it seems fitting to think that the tenor voice escorting Vicky through Lermontov's garden also derives from this work. Brian Easdale, who composed the music for the film, also wrote a number of completed operas: one of his unfinished projects was for an opera of the story of Cupid and Psyche. Powell's archives contain Easdale's own notes on 'The Composition of Opera' (1962). Here, he writes that some of what he wrote for his *Cupid and Psyche* opera was used in a film – an allusion, it seems, to *The Red Shoes*. He was drawn to this story because it seemed to express one of his perennial themes: that of being caught alone between two worlds (a theme which is acutely relevant to *The Red Shoes*, the 'Undine' project, and other Archers works). Here, Psyche, the heroine, falls between the worlds of God and Man. Powell and Pressburger draw on this tale to emphasise Vicky's own plight.

Apuleius's classical story of Cupid and Psyche from *The Golden Ass* (AD 160) feeds, then, into the scene of Vicky's arrival at Lermontov's villa. In that tale, Cupid (Eros) is sent by his envious mother to wound the beautiful mortal Psyche. Cupid is so dazzled by Psyche that he shoots himself with his own arrow and secretly falls in love with her. Psyche's father consults an oracle about his daughter's lack of suitors and is told to abandon her at the top of a mountain. He does so, but she is carried by Zephyrus to a neighbouring valley, where she falls asleep. When she wakes, she traces a path through beautiful gardens to a magnificent, uninhabited palace. She enters, and hears a magical voice declare his love for her, as long as she stays in the palace and never tries to see him. Her suitor cares for her invisibly, but she is eventually tempted to look at him, and when she sees it is Cupid, the entire palace, with Cupid, evaporates. Psyche is then required by the gods to undergo a series of trials. Cupid eventually pleads with Zeus to take pity on her, and she is raised to Olympus, where she and Cupid are married. Apuleius's tale – notably the section in the enchanted palace – is the source for *Beauty and the Beast*. This single textual ancestor reinforces the film's kinship to Cocteau, and it signals the love plot which *The Red Shoes* ballet is about to initiate. Tellingly, the first person whom Vicky encounters, curled up against a classical column, is Julian, her future lover and the author of the opera. Psyche's tale is aspirational. Although its heroine defies her lover's injunction, she earns salvation through her labours, and takes her place with him alongside the Gods.

Classical foundations are glimpsed elsewhere through the film's mise-en-scène. Palmer's *Heart of Fire* ballet seems to have an ancient Greek staging; Lermontov's boxes at Covent Garden and Monte Carlo are decorated with winged figures, and through his windows we see apparently divine creatures on the outside of his Monte Carlo offices, all of them peering down on mortals below. Lermontov dwells alongside these plaster gods, suggesting that the elite within his company are in some terpsichorean Valhalla and he is its manipulative Wotan. When, in the film's closing image, he is besieged aloft in his theatre box, undone and bereft of a favourite 'daughter', who chose life among the mortals before killing herself, the loose parallel with the fables of Wagner seem all the stronger.

Cupid and Psyche works to channel or contain desire. When Julian and Vicky have left the Ballet Lermontov, he also seems to be enthralled by the tale. We hear a soprano voice singing as he wakes to look across at Vicky before going to his candlelit piano to continue composing. This is a traditional image of 'inspiration'. (Has Julian dreamt the music before transcribing it? Has it 'possessed' him subconsciously? Do the candles signify the heat of artistic creation?) The candlelight harks back to an earlier Romantic period, and Julian's look at Vicky as she sleeps confirms that his imagination sees her as a passive muse figure. He casts her as Psyche, the soul of his opera. What he does not see as he sits at his piano is that Vicky awakes, opens her drawer and caresses her dancing shoes (nervously, perhaps; she does not pick up the red ones, but they lie there ominously) before walking sadly and silently across their grey bedroom to watch her husband at the keyboard.

The Red Shoes ballet project casts a similar, fateful spell. When Lermontov first tells Julian the ballet's story, the young composer is immediately distracted when the music he has yet to write proleptically overwhelms his consciousness, drowning out Lermontov's voice. Vicky's more intimate connection to the ballet makes her more vulnerable to it. Hans Christian Andersen's story is moralistic. His poor, vain heroine, Karen, aspires to be like a princess she has once seen and covets a pair of red shoes. She wears these to her confirmation and her holy communion, and after an old soldier casts a spell on them she forgets to pray and starts to dance. For days and nights Karen dances, seeing a vision of an angel who rejects her, and she is forsaken by the world. She asks an executioner to chop her feet off, and has wooden feet made for herself. Penitent now, she tries to go to church, but her amputated feet, still in the red shoes, dance in front of her and scare her away. Space is miraculously transmuted in the tale's visionary conclusion, when an angel appears in Karen's room, touching her ceiling with a rose branch to transform it into the sky, causing the walls to spread out and either spiriting the girl to the church or bringing the church magically to her (just as the physical space of the theatre is made magically plastic in the *tour de force Red Shoes* ballet sequence in the film). Bathed in sunshine, Karen's heart breaks and she flies to Heaven.

The centrepiece ballet of *The Red Shoes* revises Andersen's tale substantially: although Hein Heckroth's designs feature a church and Helpmann plays a priest in the ballet's brief concluding scene, the moralising tone is downplayed, and in its more surreal, subjective second half there is a greater sense of salaciousness, until the carnival tone turns darker. Andersen's Karen loses her name, to become the more emblematic 'Girl'. More emphasis is given to the Shoemaker, danced by Ljubov, whose angular, acrobatic and Expressionist-style choreography stands out from the rest of the dancing. Confrontational close-up shots of him point to his devilish importance to the plot. As Lermontov's symbolic substitute in the ballet, it is necessary for Ljubov/the Shoemaker to be a focus of attention. Ivan dances the role of the Boy, and is implicitly Julian's surrogate. At one stage Julian fantastically steps up to the stage from his podium and the two characters dissolve into each other (wishful thinking on Vicky's part). Where Lermontov and Julian reside safely in the frame narrative and are represented in the ballet by surrogates, the situation is more intimately dangerous for Vicky. Dancing the part of the Girl, she plays her own substitute. There is no safe distance between her and her role, and while this doubling of self-on-self intensifies her meaning in the ballet, the sense of excess also makes her image unstable. She has a dangerous over-identification with the image of the dancing Girl.

At the outset of the ballet, a group of young women are buzzing excitedly at the Shoemaker's shop window, enticed by the display of the red shoes, which he is flagrantly polishing. The shop door is ominously shaped like a spider's web, but the women seem selectively blind to this. Consumerism is a form of entrapment. It encourages us to buy back an idealised version of ourselves. Advertising's double bluff is to tell us how or where we are deficient, and then to promise to make good the sense of shortfall it has implanted. Hence, Mary Anne Doane argues that the idea of 'woman as consumer' involves a tautology because, in a marketplace centred on glossy female imagery, 'she is the subject of a transaction in which her own commodification is ultimately the object'.[9] When the Girl/Vicky notices the red shoes, she sees her imaginary double dancing in the window display, prettily clad in a classical tutu. This is her pure ideal; it is what her ego aspires to be. It is also a (window) display of her reflected 'self' as a commodity. The ambiguity here elegantly expresses the wider contradiction which the film explores by drawing on retail imagery to show how, under the consumer aesthetics of capitalism, our sense of ourselves is drawn from processes of identification, and that these social relations are ultimately alienating.

Forces of commodification also underwrite the meaning of traditional glamour close-ups. Both *The Red Shoes* and *Black Narcissus* feature dramatic close-ups of women: Clodagh, Ruth and Vicky/the Girl all memorably face the camera at moments of psychological intensity. Laura Mulvey argues that, as a formal system, close-ups detach objectified characters from the diegesis of the film, and she notes that under the star system in particular, 'the image of woman was conflated with the commodity spectacle'.[10] These images are not innocent: they fetishise what they depict. In the case of the horrified image of the Girl/Vicky, as she realises that by donning the red shoes she has conscripted herself into an invidious regime which robs her of her autonomy, this formal sense of commodification is singularly apt, for a commodity is exactly what Vicky and the Girl have become. She realises in her look of horror that the vision she has of herself dancing in the shop window has led her to misrecognise an ideal for a viable self. She bought that image, and now correctly recognises the iconography to be pernicious.

The Red Shoes sequence was pre-composed, the method of filming which Powell began working towards at the end of *Black Narcissus* and which he achieved most thoroughly in *Hoffmann*. Pre-composition requires that human movement in the filmed performance, and its subsequent editing, are governed by an existing played-back score. One of the possible effects of this technique is to suggest that human elements are guided according to exterior forces, placing autonomous individuals in servitude to a regulated, metered system, encrusted on the living. It is an effect noted by Claudia Gorbman: 'the characters in…narrative film,' she suggests, '…become objects when their movements and speech coincide strictly with the music: for…musical rhythm…can be considered at odds with spontaneous "real" time'.[11] Vicky becomes a pliant mannequin in Lermontov's system and the Girl in the ballet is choreographed to death by supernatural forces: these are re-enactments of the subject's entry into a new space of symbolic order. Since the Ballet Lermontov represents the Archers, this concern with the spectacle and display of commodities, and with the power of iconic imagery, mirrors the film's own processes and reflects on the place of cinema in the late 1940s, just on the cusp of Britain's consumer age. Moira Shearer was marketed boldly as the film's debut star. *The Red Shoes*' affinity with the 'women's picture' genre assumes that it is addressed to a female audience. This is a genre which is typically built around imagery of clothing and cosmetics, constructing its imagined audience as consumers and encouraging viewers to 'buy' the images of women on offer.

After Vicky's death, *The Red Shoes* ballet is performed one more time, in a tribute to her, with the disc of a spotlight marking out her empty space on stage. At face value, the emptiness pathetically expresses the void she has left. The white circle also reminds us, though, that Vicky was erased the moment she decided to dance to Lermontov's (and Julian's) tune. When we simply try to fill in the void with the familiar, imagined shape of Moira Shearer, as we are encouraged to do, we must admit that we are trying guiltily to fetishise the image of the dead ballerina and that we saw her as an ideal sign rather than as a subject in her own right. Imagining Vicky's presence is a fatal exercise in idealism and nostalgia akin to Clive Candy's obsessive replacement of Miss Hunter with two subsequent versions of Deborah Kerr in *Blimp*. The woman in this system can be replaced: in a sense, the vacant circle of light is just that – a vacancy – and in the film's closing image Massine advertises the post by directly offering the red shoes to the camera in a diabolical invitation to the dance.

If the shoes are symbols of an alienating consumerism, they are also, contradictorily, Freudian symbols of female sexuality, and the Girl's drama is a rite of passage into a sphere of adulthood. Ballet's expressive use of the human body can often be coded with sexual meaning. Here, the shoes' shape and colour (the red of viscerality again, as in *Black Narcissus*) intensify the sexual tone. They are like Dorothy's ruby slippers in *The Wizard of Oz* (Victor Fleming, 1939, US): iconic footwear marking a girl's entry into a strange Technicolor world but, ambivalently, also the means of her return home. Vicky has expressed her desire to dance, her dancing shades over into her romantic-sexual life, and the shoes are intimately connected to her (she cannot remove them). The shoes powerfully express what Lesley Stern, in a fascinating comparison between *The Red Shoes* and Scorsese's *Raging Bull* (1980), sees as the obsessive, deathly centre of the film. As with everything we desire, 'to possess these objects is to be possessed by them'.[12]

Once she puts on the red shoes, the Girl/Vicky's debauchery is marked by an energetic jazz riff connoting sexual licence. This section of the ballet features fairground attractions, clowns and side-shows, minstrels and harlequins, so notions of the carnivalesque are foregrounded. The narrative of the ballet, though, is doom-laden and it is during this fairground scene that the Girl's *joie de vivre* pales. The shoes throw her orgiastically from one man to another, and the Boy (a more innocent figure) is kept from her until he is carried off into the blackness. Worn-out men become cellophane, a characteristic material for Heckroth to use – its wrapping-paper connotations implying a world of debasement – and the tone is cheap and gaudy. In Expressionist cinema, the fairground is a place to be feared. Folk-tales have their wild woods; Expressionism has its fair-grounds. For the bourgeoisie, the image of the carnival has always elicited an equivocal mixture of desire and dread. In *The Cabinet of Doctor Caligari* (Robert Weine, 1919, Germany) it brings death. Paul Leni's *Waxworks* (1924, Germany) makes similar dramatic use of fairground attractions and pursuing demons. Particularly in its final tale (a dream-like sequence in which the hero is pursued through a fair by Jack the Ripper), it fulfils Expressionism's defining characteristic, namely the 'objective' depiction of states of psychological disturbance and existential insecurity. *The Red Shoes* ballet seems to invoke directly the memory of Leni's nightmarish fairground pursuit.

The Girl dances through a cemetery and back to the market square, where her efforts to return to her blind mother are hampered by the Shoemaker's grasping shadow (the battle of wills between blind mother and oppressive man prefigures Powell's *Peeping Tom,* 1960). At this point in the ballet, after her horrified close-up, the Girl/Vicky sees Massine, arms outstretched in a threatening gesture. Cued as her subjective point of view, Massine is superimposed by Lermontov and then by Julian, both in the same pose (or possibly in similar gestures of warning?), and she runs towards Julian. Punctuating the images of these men, though, is their black, silhouetted outline, held on screen for as long as the men are depicted, and emphatically synchronised with the beat of the music. It is this black void that the Girl/Vicky is sucked into, and we see her fantastically diminish as she recedes into extreme long shot. There is a similar moment in *Black Narcissus* during one of Clodagh's Irish flashbacks: a cottage door opens, and Clodagh runs excitedly through it to meet her boyfriend Con outside, completely vanishing into the jet black rectangle described by the doorframe. The cut to the next shot is postponed for just long enough for Clodagh's disappearance to register. We know, of course, that the love affair is doomed, that Con will abandon her and that Clodagh will try to erase her early life by escaping to a convent. The way women can be annihilated in an unforgiving or unsatisfactory masculine system is visualised even more powerfully in the ballet sequence, where the black shape of patriarchy is actually figured around the outline of the three dominant men in the film, and where the Girl/Vicky's futile resistance is clear.

In the more surreal, sexually deviant sequence which follows, she falls into a night-town space, where whores wrap themselves round lamp-posts, and where she is haunted by masked, ape-like figures. Crude 'African' figures recast the Girl/Vicky's fear onto racial stereotypes, and as whip-pans show clusters of tribal figures surrounding and approaching her, she is eventually grabbed by them and held aloft in a gesture which resembles the male dancer's customary lifting of a ballerina to an idealised height, but here it is redolent of gang rape. Some recuperation is then allowed. Vicky's sense of Julian seems to become more powerful as she dances through a ballroom and later as she transforms into flowers, birds and clouds (all images planted in her by Julian earlier in the film). After a brief interlude, the ballet ends moralistically with a church scene, where Helpmann, now playing the Priest, is able to untie and remove the shoes from the dying girl. The sense of endless cinematic space contracts again to the theatre stage as the curtain is lowered, but the excessive nature of the ballet (and even its length – it is longer than would be expected for a musical 'number') ensures that complete closure is impossible. The destructive energies animated in the ballet spill out disastrously into Vicky's frame narrative.

Vicky deserts Lermontov to be with Julian, but is eventually tempted back to dance *The Red Shoes* ballet again. Just before her death leap at the film's close, there is a short scene where Julian and Lermontov argue over Vicky, and its awkward construction in a cramped space with sudden cuts and disorienting reflections emphasises the way Vicky is splintered between the competing claims the two men make on her (this hysterical tableau echoes Brian Easdale's comment noted earlier, that Psyche is trapped alone between the worlds of Man and the Gods). Vicky is listening to a radio broadcast from Covent Garden where *Cupid and Psyche* is having its first night. When Julian misses this and arrives unexpectedly at Monte Carlo, he is dressed in black: a funereal black, perhaps, but the smart, reptilian sheen of his coat is sinister. Trevor Howard wears a similar Gestapo-like coat to Harry Lime's funeral in Carol Reed's *The Third Man* (1949). Julian's shock arrival is glimpsed in a dressing table mirror, and just as he begins to plead with her, Lermontov arrives, having heard about Julian's absence from Covent Garden on his own radio. A soprano – presumably playing Psyche – begins to sing as Vicky breaks down to cry, 'I love you, Julian, nobody but you'. The aria is effectively Vicky's own voice, appropriated by Julian, filtered through him, written into myth and transformed into an aria. When it becomes clear Vicky will not abandon her performance, Julian bends stiffly to kiss her on the forehead and leaves. This curiously mechanical piece of histrionics underscores the sequence's unreal, tableau-like feel. Lermontov then manoeuvres himself round Vicky, cradling her like a ventriloquist's dummy while stage-managing the situation to precision. Having successfully coaxed Vicky in the direction of the stage, he suddenly lets his arms fly in an ecstatic eruption. Throughout this action, music from *Cupid and Psyche* has continued, but when Vicky walks into close-up and the red shoes seem to possess her, this music segues perfectly into the familiar overture to the ballet. The soundtrack therefore repeats the cultural conspiracy under which Vicky has suffered: to which of the men's tunes should she dance?

Lermontov's power over his company has been registered cinematically through the use of light. He remains in shadows, and wears sun-glasses. His performers have light directed on them – usually willingly. At one point

Ljubov screeches to an errant electrician, 'Spotlight sur moi! Toujours sur moi!' and here he expresses the principle on which the Lermontovian system works. When Ljubov is celebrating his birthday and Lermontov arrives uninvited, the impresario's headlights dazzle the guests and they cannot see who is coming. Lermontov's power over his 'family' is connected then with a phallic ability to direct light onto them. With Vicky's death, a shattering reversal takes place. He has to appear on stage himself, and is pinned by the beam of a spotlight to the lowered theatre curtains like an insect awaiting dissection. Walbrook's performance quivers with erupting mania. His voice has an inhuman rasp, and his Expressionist mannerisms, excessive, abstract and stylised, are put under all the more pressure by the formal language he has to use to the theatre audience. His regime, like his self-control, is cracking. The last shots of the film show Lermontov alone in his box again, but he survives, and Ljubov (in keeping with the film's cycle of repetitions) offers the red shoes once more to willing debutantes in the cinema audience. This intimate, direct appeal addresses local audiences and recollects Candy's salute to camera in the last shot of *Blimp*. Despite the pathos of the closure, and despite Lermontov's exposure to the light, there is no real sense that his invidious logic of recruitment, repression, displacement and denial has been dealt a fatal blow, or that his power is lost.

'MADE IN ENGLAND'

The Red Shoes ballet anticipates the more sustained, radical, visual fantasy in *The Tales of Hoffmann*. It is important to acknowledge the nature and status of the rhetoric of spectacle Powell and Pressburger are engaged with here. Under the strictures of 1970s and 1980s 'Film Theory' – that nexus of politically modernist 'Lacanian-Althusserian-Barthesian' critique – the word 'spectacle' was often viewed negatively. Spectacle was a sign of objectification, and was one of the dubiously pleasurably mechanisms used by mainstream cinema to stupefy its spectators and to render them politically quiescent. The spectacle in Powell and Pressburger's films underscores or 'performs' its own status as cinema. It is not simply illusionist. Neither is it alienating. Lesley Stern, writing incisively on *Hoffmann*, calls it 'histrionic', by which she means that the amplified actorly codes associated with opera, melodrama and the silent screen are transcribed into a cinematic rhetoric which is 'self-conscious, ostentatious, non-naturalistic, *and* emotionally charged and affective'.[13] There are, though, many shades of discourse which sidestep both the devil of mainstream, empathetic realist illusionism and the deep blue sea of oppositional, intellectual, Brechtian distanciation. Stern's identification of a histrionic mode is one such shade; irony and camp are others. Both draw attention to themselves yet they ask to be entertained, enjoyed and to be received imaginatively. It is certainly possible to read Heckroth's designs as camp, but this fails to account precisely for the nature of the visual rhetoric at work.

The Tales of Hoffmann, Offenbach's posthumous nineteenth-century opera, was first performed in England at Drury Lane in 1910, conducted by Thomas Beecham (who collaborated with Powell and Pressburger on their film version). It centres on the theme of deception as its narrator, Hoffmann (Robert Rounseville), in a frame narrative, tells three bitter tales – each of which relates how love has blighted his vision and led him to disappointment. The structure of external frame narration introducing dramatised 'contained' tales is something Powell and Pressburger tried to resurrect in 1961. Their unfilmed project 'Bouquet' was to have linked English, Welsh, Scottish and Irish tales with David Niven (playing a botany lecturer) directly addressing the audience to introduce each tale. The presence of a diegetic narrator allows familiar themes of artistic creation, romanticised vision and obsessive possession to be explored. International location footage was originally planned for *Hoffmann* (in Germany, France, Venice and London), but eventually it was shot more cheaply at Shepperton, on an old silent stage last used for *Things to Come* in the mid-1930s. Hein Heckroth had worked on numerous productions of the opera before, and his designs are the film's most salient feature. They mark a development of his use of non-naturalistic colour, fabric, costume design and *trompe l'oeil* illusions supplemented by in-camera and post-production effects (as seen in *The Red Shoes* ballet). Designs like these would be seen again when Powell collaborated with Heckroth to make the short ballet film *The Sorcerer's Apprentice* in 1955 and then to film Bartok's opera *Bluebeard's Castle* with him for West German television in 1964. Translucent flats, painted with abstract designs, wafting fabrics, gauzes which appear transparent or opaque according to how they are lit: simple devices such as these play with the viewer's vision. As Raymond Durgnat has observed, in a piece which is otherwise dismissive of Powell's and Heckroth's 'total disdain of plausibility', there is 'an effective simplicity [here]…, drifting pieces of sad, sickly cellophane suggesting gaiety's futility'.[14]

Gelled green filters on the camera lens during Stella's (Moira Shearer's) opening dance make her shimmer and ripple. Unexpected camera angles trick our eyes: a patterned sheet rolled out on the studio floor during Olympia's dance is transformed by a high angle long shot into a magic winding staircase for her to spiral down. In a film about the deceptive nature of appearances, this is all too apt. As if to emphasise our susceptibility to misleading appearances, surprisingly few of the tricks are created by post-production techniques. The integrity of the space before the camera is maintained. Many of the shots during the ballet sequences are surprisingly long takes. Moira Shearer had been irritated by the need to repeat her dance steps many times for the camera in *The Red Shoes* ballet. In part, she was persuaded to return to film for *Hoffmann* with the promise that she would not have to do so again, and certainly quick-cutting is generally avoided. In the early sequence where she dances as Stella, the average duration of each shot is a relatively ponderous 14 seconds. The shots are almost as long in Olympia's main dance during the first of the 'contained tales', while one of the shots during the brief 'Kleinzack' dance sequence in which she is paired with Frederick Ashton lasts as long as 54 seconds.

For *Hoffmann*, which otherwise respects the original opera, Powell and Pressburger transform much of the action into ballet. They filmed it to a pre-recorded soundtrack – effectively making it like a silent film – and grafted the voices of Dorothy Bond, Monica Sinclair, Graham Clifford, Bruce Dargeval, Margherita Grandi and Owen Brannigan to Archers' regulars Moira Shearer, Pamela Brown, Léonide Massine, Ludmilla Tcherina and Robert Helpmann. Stella the prima donna, for example, becomes Stella the prima ballerina. Heckroth's moveable, painterly and ephemeral sets allowed the film crew (already constrained by the need to synchronise shots and action to the recorded soundtrack) to move around the studio stage relatively unhampered. There is a graceful quality to the camera movement. It loosely follows the flow of the music, and explores Heckroth's liquid sets, repeatedly revealing new perspectives (sympathising, in effect, with Hoffmann's romantically deluded narratives).

An unfilmed Anglo-Indian project of Powell's from 1952 entitled 'Lotus of the Moon' shows that *Hoffmann* is a sign of where his artistic ambitions were heading. 'Lotus' was to have been another pre-composed dance and mime spectacular, reuniting Archers regulars such as Brian Easdale and Massine. It would have dispensed with dialogue wherever possible, only adding words where necessary (and in different language versions in the name of internationalism). Described in Powell's handwritten notes as 'an Indian wonder tale', 'Lotus' was adapted from a book by F.W. Bain and was based on Hindu myths. It shows Powell's ongoing interest in Eastern philosophies and religions. Other unfilmed 'Indian' projects show how central the country was in Powell's imagination. As well as the treatments for 'Imperial epics' such as 'Burmese Silver', 'Calcutta' and 'The East and the West' around 1938–39, Powell worked on 'Taj Mahal' in 1953 (with Rudolph Nureyev and Omar Sharif envisaged in key roles). Set in the 1600s, this was to be another complex, masque-like love story, featuring layered flashbacks, 'contained' performances and a diegetic narrator. Both of these studio-based Oriental fantasies are a reminder of *The Thief of Bagdad*, which Powell co-directed for Alexander Korda back in 1940, and they exist alongside *Black Narcissus* as fantastic treatments of the Orient, but the unfilmed projects were set to draw more heavily on *Hoffmann*'s use of ballet and music.

At least one contemporary reviewer, Fred Majdalany of the *Daily Mail* (19 April 1951) associated the illusions in *Hoffmann* with its technique of applying opera singers' voices to ballet dancers' bodies to create something doubly expressive (an audio-visual effect Helpmann had aimed for in the theatre with the *Comus* ballet-masque, as I noted earlier). 'The cinema's edge on its competitors,' he notes, 'is its ability to cheat legally. The screen can, if it chooses, display Betty Grable in a bathing suit singing Wagner with the voice of Kirsten Flagstad while riding the wing of a Flying

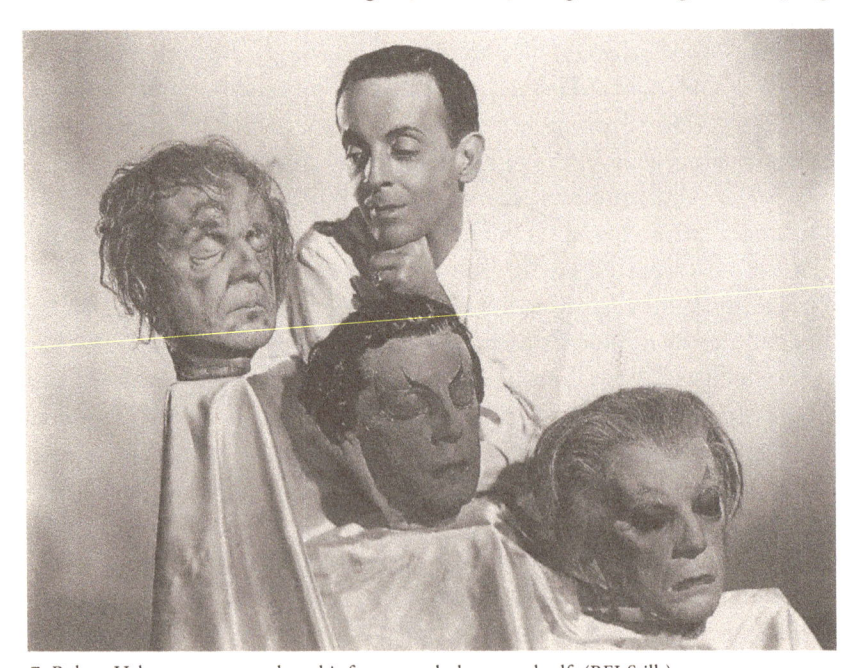

7. Robert Helpmann contemplates his fragmented, de-centred self. (BFI Stills)

Fortress.' His paradoxical phrase 'cheat legally' expresses a partial distrust of the medium and echoes the ambivalence in *The Red Shoes* regarding Lermontov's status as a magician (is he supernatural, or just a trickster?). The same theme is acted out in *Black Narcissus* where Sister Briony impresses a gullible crowd of natives at Mopu by crumbling some powder into a vessel of clear liquid. Her audience goes unanimously agog when the liquid turns a deep violet colour. There is an imperial power-play at work in Briony's performance. To the superstitious natives, she achieves a metaphysical miracle; to Western science, the effect is an inevitable chemical reaction. Cinema is part empirical tool; part a fraudulent set of tricks. Enjoying – and participating in – magic tricks involves a kind of imaginative disavowal: both accepting a sense of wonderment and also wondering *how* the effect is achieved.

Powell and Pressburger repeatedly call for actively imaginative audiences. In notes to accompany the 'Sketch Reel' of *The Red Shoes* ballet (the 'film' of Hein Heckroth's sketches for the ballet which was synchronised and 'edited' to the musical track and then used as a template to help the team to film the ballet itself), Powell decries naturalism and suggests that an 'artist's view… is much more satisfying: to the creator and to the audience. Audiences, who are sick of looking through a plate-glass window at a painstaking reproduction of the workaday world, and who are aching to be asked to use their imagination, have a keen appreciation of this.' Their contract with their audience therefore expects participation and imagination. Given the 'high art' status of ballet and opera, Powell's faith in his post-war audience's cultural competence is socially significant, and the film's relationships to British cinema and to attitudes to the arts are ultimately bound up with public discourses about education, equality of opportunity and universalism.

One obvious point to be made is that models of British cinema emphasising the centrality of 'quality realism' can find no clear place for film-makers who do not see cinema as a 'plate-glass window' on the world. Yet, in the closing joke-shot of *Hoffmann*, Sir Thomas Beecham's score for the opera is snapped shut and is rubber-stamped 'Made in England'. Given the international production team, the French and German genealogies of the opera and its text, and the film's rejection of any of the benchmarks by which 'English' national cinema was labelled, perhaps the directors protest too much. Paradoxically, the explicit act of branding so proudly the film's national identity points to the way it is 'not' English just as much as it claims the opposite. The gesture indicts the stylistic parochialism of British cinema, but is also brusquely patriotic. It is neither vociferous nor bullish, and is made in a comic vein. Its irony therefore raises questions of motivation, and is implicated with wider problems of national identity and culture. The rubber stamp's association with mass production and consumption also points to the tense relationship between commercial cinema and the arts.

This is all a question of the film's cultural standing. It received its world premiere, very prestigiously, at New York's Metropolitan Opera House on 1 April 1951, and was the first film to be screened there. Korda's London Films, with the British Lion Film Corporation, had signed a new Anglo-American deal in 1950 regarding the distribution of British films in the USA, forming a new firm together, the Lopert Film Distributing Company, to deal with this side of their businesses. *The Tales of Hoffmann* was set to be its first beneficiary. It was recognised that there was a drain on traditional mainstream cinema audience figures in the USA (this was attributed to television), and that 'specialist' British and European films had enjoyed longer, profitable runs when shown on a smaller number of select screens such as New York's Bijou Theater, where *The Red Shoes* was a runaway success for two years. The deal arranged for a more focused American distribution of 'mature' British films with artistic merit, rather than mass, blanket distribution – emulating long-running theatre successes rather than commercial cinema. Korda's perception of the 'artistic' status of some British films in the USA chimes with at least one Manhattan commentator, Richard Griffith, the assistant to the director of New York's Museum of Modern Art. Griffith wrote in the *Sunday Review of Literature* (13 January 1951) that, '[b]ecause metropolitan intellectuals are the only articulate audience for foreign films, their taste constitutes the sole yardstick European film-makers can use in aiming at the American market'. *Hoffmann* went on to do good business in the major American cities, so it successfully broke out of its initial coterie audience (by capitalising on both its status as a musical and its high art credentials). Reviews of the first night screening at the Met suggest that the audience then was impressed by the 'Made in England' stamp: it flattered its cosmopolitan, European taste. It also expressed British national pride. At this time, even the popular British magazines and newspaper columns were pervaded by a sense of post-war Britain's financial debt to the USA – a fashion piece about *Hoffmann* in *Housewife* magazine in December 1950 called it a 'first rate dollar earner' – and in the context of its Manhattan premiere, the 'Made in England' insignia explicitly declares the film to be a valuable British export to America.

In Britain, the film's premiere was similarly exclusive. *A Matter of Life and Death* had had a similarly prestigious opening (it was the first Royal Film

Performance). *Hoffmann*'s was at London's Carlton Theatre in the much-publicised presence of Queen Mary, and was shown in aid of the English Opera Group, an organisation founded in 1946 with the Earl and Countess of Harewood as patrons to further the development of English operatic repertory (it was heavily involved with Benjamin Britten's work, and with the Festival of Britain). The Archers' aim, though, was universalistic, not elitist, and the film should be seen as complementing the Labour government's efforts in the arts and in cultural education. In 1940, the Committee for the Encouragement of Music and the Arts (CEMA) had been instigated and its aims broadly carried into the constitution of the post-war Arts Council. These aims were to preserve the highest standards in the arts, to provide opportunities for the people to enjoy the arts, and to encourage participation in the arts.[15] Definitions of art have always been contentious, but noticeably the State never really considered providing support for popular or 'folk' art forms, and the thrust of the campaign was the popularisation of 'high culture'. This accords with the 'universalising' aspirations of government policy, yet this dissemination of values was only ever figured as a *trickle-down* phenomenon (grass roots culture fended for itself, and was not envisaged to enrich the establishment). The Arts Council soon lost the impetus for encouraging artistic activity. Its first priorities were the establishment of the Royal Opera House and the consolidation of the work of Sadler's Wells. Marie Rambert successfully won grants to tour the regions and to take her company to small towns, reaching out to unusual venues. As Alan Sinfield succinctly puts it, 'the traditional conception of "high art" culture persisted, but now with state validation, within the story that it was for all the people'.[16] Coinciding with the establishment of the Arts Council, the BBC opened its high brow Third Programme: again this was meant to make 'high culture' popular, although popularity was something it never achieved. The audience clamouring for good seats in the gods in the opening sequence of *The Red Shoes* were the principal beneficiaries of this state funding: intellectuals and the middle classes.

The Labour government's front bench were, in the main, middle-class custodians of an old order, pursuing a policy of 'welfare capitalism' which was often quite conservative. Welfare capitalism is itself an ideological coalition, a characteristic British compromise. Yoking together two distinct social arrangements, it falls short of a socialist agenda, endorsing wealth production while offering a safety net to ameliorate the effects of capitalism. It was so persuasive a combination that the 1940s mode of consensus politics lasted more or less intact through until the 1980s (although Labour lost the 1951 election, returning Churchill to Downing Street, more people had voted Labour than in 1945; there was no outright rejection of Labour's policies among either the people or the governing classes). The cultural policy of the post-war period was typically conservative. The importance of universal cultural policy suggests a holistic view of society: it is not pluralistic; it is not truly democratic; it remains hierarchical; and what it does not recognise is an emergent consumer society, one which will demand popular culture along mass-produced lines. This new world is one of advertising and Americanisation. Powell and Pressburger resist it – the opening credits of *I Know Where I'm Going!* mock the materialistic way of life, and Dr Reeves in the courtroom sequence of *A Matter of Life and Death* is quick to express his distaste for popular American music.

Released in 1951, *Hoffmann* coincided with what was either a remarkable coda to the war culture and to the first post-war government, or was an auspicious anticipation of the modern Britain to come: the Festival of Britain (inevitably connoted by the film's patriotic rubber stamp). Not surprisingly, the Festival Committee was composed of the cultural elite: R.A. Butler, Sir Kenneth Clark, T.S. Eliot, John Gielgud, Sir Malcolm Sargent and so on; and this group constructed a Festival which in Becky Conekin's eyes disseminated 'education, ideas and tastes, generally held to be the preserve of the elites, to the people of Britain'.[17] Revitalising the South Bank, the Festival created a public space in which groups collected nightly during the summer to dance by the Thames. Events were spread around the country over the summer of 1951 but, as with Arts Council policy, the thrust of its message was middle class and elitist (working-class culture was elided) and the regionalism was an effort to distribute the values of the chattering classes geographically to emphasise national unity by raising national consciousness.

While it was not officially part of the Festival, press coverage of *Hoffmann* and other significant British films in 1951 linked the cinema industry's prestigious work with the aim of the Festival. The British Film Institute sought to secure the widest possible showing of British films throughout the country, and a production company, Festival Film Production, was set up, with Sir Michael Balcon as chair, to make *The Magic Box* (John Boulting, 1951). As a biopic of William Friese-Greene, this film records Britain's role in cinema's invention. It is not persuasive, complacently relying on cameo appearances from British stars and making exaggerated claims for Friese-Greene. Another film was produced specifically for the Festival: Humphrey Jennings' last work, *Family Portrait*.

Echoing his wartime films, he again offers a personal perspective of the nation, again in a romantic tone. It seems part of an earlier world.

Positioned at the century's midpoint, the Festival was genuinely Janus-like. Marking the centenary of the Great Exhibition, and transformed into a celebration of both the 1945 victory and the post-war recovery, it was a gesture of confidence. Opinion was divided, and has been since, as to the Festival's meaning. Despite its emphasis on modern architecture, Michael Frayn's perceptive account situates it squarely within the culture of the 'People's War' and the post-war discourse of unity, tying it to the 'radical middle classes', a sector of society he identifies as the 'Herbivores', as opposed to the Tory 'Carnivores', waiting to retake power in 1951. The Festival, for Frayn, was 'the last, and virtually the posthumous, work of the Herbivore Britain of the BBC News, the Crown Film Unity, the sweet ration, the Ealing comedies, Uncle Mac'.[18] It gave out mixed messages then, with residual wartime sentiments blurring with the emergent tastes for modernisation, new housing, suburbia, television and consumerism.

When Frayn writes of 'radical middle classes' (another British compromise), he unconsciously echoes Peter Carter's qualified claim in *AMOLAD* that he is Conservative by instinct and Labour by experience. While Powell and Pressburger can be allied with the 'People's War' culture, their anti-establishment sympathies write them into a wider cultural tradition of middle-class dissent which is rooted, ultimately, in Romanticism. Trends from across the cultural spectrum – from Fabianism, the Arts and Crafts Movement, Bloomsbury modernism and Cambridge Communism to CND and green politics – variously articulate an educated, middle-class suspicion of industry, mass culture and centralised bureaucracy. The Archers' work consistently rejects consumerism and materialism in favour of transcendental values and social cohesion, even if the society which coheres is a hierarchical one. It is a gentleman culture of squirarchical paternalism.

However, and importantly, the Archers view their art films as universal. 'Will the mind of the audience be able to accept this sudden transition from the objective to the subjective?' asked Monk Gibbon about the potentially confusing shift into a surreal register midway through *The Red Shoes* ballet.[19] Gibbon wrote books to accompany both *The Red Shoes* and *Hoffmann*, offering commentary and background information.[20] His rhetoric is explanatory and didactic, a little precious and balletomaniac, but his books lubricate the universalising purpose of the films. Powell similarly remembered that the Archers initially mooted some form of coda for *Hoffmann*, to 'explain to them [the audience] what they had seen. A sort of summing up'.[21] Powell's repeated faith in his audience's cultural competence should be in the light of his frequently repeated motto, 'All art is one!' His refusal to differentiate between the arts (high/middle/low brow) complements and reformulates one of the chief reasons he favoured silent cinema. Synchronised sound parochialised the art form, where it had once been international. Powell's non-hierarchical view of art goes hand in hand with his internationalism: both express a wish to break boundaries. Original plans for *Hoffmann* suggested it would probably be recorded in three different languages (the soundtrack was recorded separately, and careful synchronisation between three different tracks would mean that one image print could illustrate all three language versions). The clear foreign marketing opportunities here undo neither Powell's genuine democratic-internationalism, nor his faith that by pitching *Hoffmann*'s red-haired star and its spectacle, viewers would rise to his challenge.

Connoisseurship, the possession of an aesthetic disposition, is, as Pierre Bourdieu has pointed out, an expression of taste, and therefore of class. It is bound up with education and with the possession of 'codes' which enable difficult works to be unpacked and consumed. Cultural tastes, for Bourdieu, are primarily divisive. He argues that they are 'first and foremost distastes, disgust provoked by horror and visceral intolerance...of the tastes of others'.[22] The Archers' art films work to cement over that rift by mediating between the worlds of high and popular art, and *The Red Shoes* at least contributed to affecting popular attitudes by causing a popular rush of enthusiasm for ballet (the successful stage careers of Fonteyn and Shearer doubtless played their part too). Powell and Pressburger's later updating and translation of *Die Fledermaus* into *Oh...Rosalinda!!* can be seen in the same universalising light. Yet the Archers were, by this time, losing favour with their producers. They had only ever been truly central when their particular line of romantic international nationalism had accorded with the culture of the early and mid-1940s. Their attempts to incorporate elite art forms into a popular medium met halfway the State's wish to popularise 'high culture' for the masses (and to emphasise the unifying, universalising rhetoric which had seen the Labour government sweep into power). The film industry, though, never met with full State support, and it suffered from vagaries of government legislation such as the Entertainment Tax (much despised by Pressburger) and the post-war protectionist policies aiming to shore up the domestic economy. *Hoffmann*'s eradication of external reality is the mark of a Hoffmann-like detachment from post-war economics, politics and taste; its gossamer appearance is a sign of how fragile that Romantic denial was.

Notes

Introduction

1 Charles Barr, 'In a Strange Land: the Collaboration of Michael Powell and Emeric Pressburger', *La Lettre de la Maison française d'Oxford* 11 (Trinity-Michaelmas, 1999).
2 Andrew Higson (ed.), *Dissolving Views: Key Writings on British Cinema* (London, Cassell, 1996).
3 Michael Powell, *A Life in Movies* (London, Faber and Faber, 2000), p.109.
4 Kevin Macdonald, *Emeric Pressburger: The Life and Death of a Screenwriter* (London, Faber and Faber, 1994), p.8.
5 Gerhard Hirschfeld (ed.), *Exile in Great Britain* (Leamington Spa, Berg Publishers, 1984), p.301.
6 John Russell Taylor (ed.), *The Pleasure Dome: Graham Greene: The Collected Film Criticism 1935–40* (Oxford, Oxford University Press, 1980), p.78.
7 Taylor (ed.): *Pleasure Dome*, p.80.
8 Taylor (ed.): *Pleasure Dome*, p.80.
9 Homi K. Bhaba (ed.), *Nation and Narration* (London, Routledge, 1990), p.4.
10 Sarah Street, *British National Cinema* (London, Routledge, 1997).
11 Tom Ryall, *Alfred Hitchcock and the British Cinema* (London, Athlone Press Ltd, 1996).
12 See Pam Cook (ed.), *Gainsborough Pictures* (London, Cassell, 1997) and Andrew Higson, 'Film Europe: a Transitional Challenge to the Idea of British Cinema', *La Lettre de la Maison française d'Oxford* 11 (Trinity-Michaelmas, 1999).
13 Cook (ed.): *Gainsborough Pictures*, p.75.
14 Michael Powell, *A Life in Movies* (London, Faber and Faber, 2000), p.182.

15 Michael Powell, *Million Dollar Movie* (London, Mandarin, 1993), p.541.
16 Hamid Naficy (ed.), *Home, Exile, Homeland: Film, Media and the Politics of Place* (London, Routledge, 1999), p.19.
17 Naficy (ed.): *Home, Exile, Homeland*, p.31.
18 Terry Eagleton, *Exiles and Émigrés: Studies in Modern Literature* (London, Chatto and Windus, 1970), p.9.
19 Joseph Brodsky, 'The Condition We Call Exile', *New York Review of Books*, vol. 34, no. 21 (21 January 1988).
20 Hamid Naficy, *An Accented Cinema: Exilic and Diasporic Filmmaking* (Princeton, Princeton University Press, 2001).
21 Naficy: *An Accented Cinema*, p.13.
22 Anthony D. Smith, *National Identity* (London, Penguin, 1991), p.17.
23 Chantal Mouffe (ed.), *Gramsci and Marxist Theory* (London, Routledge and Kegan Paul, 1979), p.181.
24 Powell: *Million Dollar Movie*, p.16.
25 Quoted in Macdonald: *Emeric Pressburger*, p.189.
26 Geoffrey Macnab, *J. Arthur Rank and the British Film Industry* (London, Routledge, 1993), p.96.
27 Powell: *Million Dollar Movie*, p.78.
28 Powell: *A Life in Movies*, p.93.
29 Powell: *Million Dollar Movie*, p.546.
30 Powell: *A Life in Movies*, p.48.
31 Raymond Williams, *Culture and Society 1780–1950* (Harmondsworth, Penguin, 1961), p.56.
32 Antonio Gramsci (Quintin Hoare and Geoffrey Nowell-Smith trans. and eds), *Selections from the Prison Notebooks* (London, Lawrence and Wishart, 1971), p.12.
33 Bhaba (ed.): *Nation and Narration*, pp.4–5.
34 Andrew Higson, *Waving the Flag: Constructing a National Cinema in Britain* (Oxford, Clarendon Press, 1995), p.275.
35 Duncan Petrie (ed.), *New Questions in British Cinema* (London, BFI, 1982), p.15.
36 Petrie (ed.): *New Questions*, p.18.
37 Alan Sinfield, *Faultlines: Cultural Materialism and the Politics of Dissident Reading* (Oxford, Clarendon Press, 1992).

Chapter 1

1 Michael Powell, *A Life in Movies* (London, Faber and Faber, 2000), p.305.
2 Jeffrey Richards (ed.), *The Unknown 1930s: An Alternative History of the British Cinema, 1929–39* (London, Athlone Press, 1998), p.93.
3 Michael Denning, *Cover Stories: Narrative and Ideology in the British Spy Thriller* (London, Routledge, 1987), p.39.

4   For an account of the processes of the masquerade, and its original use, see Joan Riviere, 'Womanliness and the Masquerade', in Victor Burgin et al. (eds), *Formations of Fantasy* (London, Routledge, 1986).
5   Tom Ryall, *Alfred Hitchcock and the British Cinema* (London, Athlone Press, 1996), p.124.
6   John G. Cawelti and Bruce A. Rosenberg, *The Spy Story* (Chicago, University of Chicago Press, 1987), p.17.
7   Rosemary Jackson, *Fantasy: The Literature of Subversion* (London, Methuen, 1981), p.178.
8   Jerry Palmer, *Thrillers: Genesis and Structure of a Popular Genre* (London, Edward Arnold, 1978), p.127.
9   Powell: *A Life in Movies*, p.303.
10 Lotte Eisner, *The Haunted Screen: Expressionism in the German Cinema and the Influence of Max Reinhardt* (London, Secker & Warburg, 1973), p.100.
11 Richards (ed.): *The Unknown 1930s*, p.135.
12 Richards (ed.): *The Unknown 1930s*, p.123.
13 Christine Gledhill (ed.), *Stardom: Industry of Desire* (London, Routledge, 1991), p.211.
14 Quoted in Michael Patterson, *The Revolution in German Theatre, 1900–33* (London, Routledge & Kegan Paul, 1981), p.57.
15 Tony Williams, 'Michael Powell', *Films and Filming* (no. 326, November 1981), p.12.
16 Andrew Higson (ed.), *Dissolving Views: Key Writings on British Cinema* (London, Cassell, 1996), p.36.
17 James Chapman, *The British at War: Cinema, State and Propaganda* (London, I.B. Tauris, 1998), p.70.
18 Chapman: *The British at War*, p.72.

Chapter 2

1   Reprinted in Ian Christie (ed.), *The Life and Death of Colonel Blimp* (London, Faber and Faber, 1994), p.28.
2   Kevin Macdonald, *Emeric Pressburger: The Life and Death of a Screenwriter* (London, Faber and Faber, 1994), p.228.
3   Quoted in Colin Seymour-Ure and Jim Schoff, *David Low* (London, Secker & Warburg, 1985), p.136.
4   George Orwell, *The Penguin Essays of George Orwell* (London, Penguin, 1984), p.157.
5   Orwell: *Penguin Essays*, p.159.
6   Orwell: *Penguin Essays*, p.162.
7   David Low, *Ye Madde Designer* (London, The Studio Ltd, 1935), p.10.
8   Low: *Ye Madde Designer*, p.16.
9   Seymour-Ure and Schoff: *David Low*, p.45.

10 Peter Mellini, 'Colonel Blimp's England', *History Today* (vol. 34, October 1984), p.30.
11 Robert Graves, *Occupation Writer* (New York, Creative Age Press, 1942), p.222.
12 Raymond Williams, *Marxism and Literature* (Oxford, Oxford University Press, 1977), p.122.
13 Quintin Hoare and Geoffrey Nowell-Smith (trans. and eds), Antonio Gramsci, *Selections from the Prison Notebooks* (London, Lawrence and Wishart, 1971), p.267.
14 Sue Harper, *Picturing the Past: The Rise and Fall of the British Costume Film* (London, BFI, 1994), pp.105–6 and 185.
15 Marcia Landy, *British Genres: Cinema and Society 1930–60* (London, Princeton University Press, 1991), p.150.
16 Raymond Durgnat, *A Mirror for England: British Movies from Austerity to Affluence* (London, Faber and Faber, 1970), p.83.
17 See Karel Kulik, *Alexander Korda: The Man Who Could Work Miracles* (London, W.H. Allen, 1975), p.97.
18 Graham Dawson, *Soldier Heroes: British Adventure, Empire and the Imagining of Masculinity* (London, Routledge, 1994), p.1.
19 Michael Powell, *A Life in Movies* (London, Faber and Faber, 2000), p.499.
20 Powell: *A Life in Movies*, pp.536 and 582.
21 Steve Cohen and Ina Rae Hark (eds), *Screening the Male: Exploring Masculinities in Hollywood Cinema* (London, Routledge, 1993), p.17.
22 J.A. Mangan and James Walvin (eds), *Manliness and Morality: Middle Class Masculinity in Britain and America, 1800–1940* (Manchester, Manchester University Press, 1987), p.179.
23 Ian Christie (ed.), *The Life and Death of Colonel Blimp* (London, Faber and Faber, 1994), p.183.
24 Robert Murphy, *British Cinema and the Second World War* (London, Continuum, 2000), p.72.
25 Andrew Higson (ed.), *Dissolving Views: Key Writings on British Cinema* (London, Cassell, 1996), p.54.
26 E.W. Robson and M.M. Robson, *The Shame and Disgrace of Colonel Blimp: The True Story of The Film* (London, The Sidneyan Society, 1943), p.4.
27 Robson and Robson: *Shame and Disgrace of Colonel Blimp*, pp.14–15.
28 Fredric Jameson, *Signatures of the Visible* (London, Routledge, 1990), p.33.
29 Williams: *Marxism and Literature*, p.125.
30 Williams: *Marxism and Literature*, p.125.

Chapter 3

1. Alan Burton et al. (eds), *Liberal Directions: Basil Dearden and Postwar British Film Culture* (Trowbridge, London, 1997), p.19.
2. Benedict Anderson, *Imagined Communities: Reflections on the Origins and Spread of Nationalism* (London, Verso, 1983).
3. Martin J. Wiener, *English Culture and the Decline of the English Spirit, 1885–1980* (Cambridge, Cambridge University Press, 1981), p.74.
4. Homi K. Bhaba (ed.), *Nation and Narration* (London, Routledge, 1990), p.4.
5. Wiener: *English Culture*, p.98.
6. E. J. Hobsbawm, *Industry and Empire: An Economic History of Britain Since 1750* (London, Weidenfield and Nicolson, 1968), p.141.
7. Michael Powell, *A Life in Movies* (London, Faber and Faber, 2000), pp.53–9.
8. See, for example, Alain Frogley (ed.), *Vaughan Williams Studies* (New York, Cambridge University Press, 1996).
9. David Mellor (ed.), *A Paradise Lost: The Neo-Romantic Imagination in Britain, 1935–1955* (London, Lund and Humphries, 1987), p.7.
10. Kevin Macdonald, *Emeric Pressburger: The Life and Death of a Screenwriter* (London, Faber and Faber, 1994), p.233.
11. David Gervais, *Literary Englands: Versions of 'Englishness' in Modern Writing* (Cambridge, Cambridge University Press, 1993), p.26.
12. Jeffrey Richards and Anthony Aldgate, *Best of British: Cinema and Society* (Oxford, Basil Blackwell, 1983), p.55.
13. Raymond Williams, *The Country and the City* (St Albans, Paladin, 1975), p.347.
14. Antonia Lant, *Blackout: Reinventing Women for Wartime British Cinema* (Princeton, Princeton University Press, 1991), p.219.
15. Wiener: *English Culture*, p.77.
16. Powell: *A Life in Movies*, p.437.
17. Ian Christie, *Arrows of Desire: The Films of Michael Powell and Emeric Pressburger* (London, Faber and Faber, 1994), p.6.
18. Powell: *A Life in Movies*, p.70.
19. Phillip Mallett (ed.), *Kipling Considered* (London, Macmillan, 1989), p.59.
20. Raphael Samuel (ed.), *Patriotism: The Making and Unmaking of British National Identity: Volume Three: National Fictions* (London, Routledge, 1989), p.208.
21. Macdonald: *Emeric Pressburger*, p.237.
22. Douglas McVay, 'Michael Powell: Three Neglected Films', *Films and Filming* no. 328 (1982), p.19.
23. Alan Sinfield, *Faultlines: Cultural Materialism and the Politics of Dissident Reading* (Oxford, Clarendon Press, 1992).
24. Macdonald: *Emeric Pressburger*, p.233.
25. Richards and Aldgate: *Best of British*, p.55.
26. Pam Cook, *I Know Where I'm Going!* (London, BFI Classics, 2002), p.33.

Chapter 4

1. Alex J. Robertson, *The Bleak Midwinter: 1947* (Manchester, Manchester University Press, 1987).
2. Robertson: *The Bleak Midwinter*, p.6.
3. Geoffrey Macnab, *J. Arthur Rank and the British Film Industry* (London, Routledge, 1993), p.164.
4. George Perry, *The Great British Picture Show: From the 90s to the 70s* (London, Hart-Davis MacGibbon Ltd, 1974), p.124.
5. Macnab, *J. Arthur Rank*, p.174.
6. Robert Murphy, *Realism and Tinsel: Cinema and Society in Britain 1939–49* (London, Routledge, 1989; reprinted 1992), pp.241–47.
7. Kaja Silverman, *Male Subjectivity at the Margins* (London, Routledge, 1992).
8. Reprinted in David Lazar (ed.), *Michael Powell Interviews* (Jackson MS, Mississippi University Press, 2003), p.57.
9. Andrew Spicer, *Typical Men: The Representation of Masculinity in Popular British Cinema* (London, I.B. Tauris, 2001).
10. Murphy: *Realism and Tinsel*, p.174.
11. Silverman: *Male Subjectivity*, p.52.
12. Silverman: *Male Subjectivity*, p.60.
13. Ian Christie, *A Matter of Life and Death* (London, BFI Classics, 2000), pp.64–5.
14. Christie: *A Matter of Life and Death*, p.72.
15. Raymond Durgnat, *A Mirror for England: British Movies from Austerity to Affluence* (London, Faber and Faber, 1970), p.29.
16. Reprinted in Ian Christie (ed.), *The Life and Death of Colonel Blimp* (London, Faber and Faber, 1994), p.28.
17. Christie: *A Matter of Life and Death*, p.14.
18. Sue Harper and Vincent Porter, 'A Matter of Life and Death – The View from Moscow', *Historical Journal of Film, Radio and Television*, vol. 9, no. 2 (1989).
19. Harper and Porter: 'A Matter of Life and Death', p.181.
20. Ian Christie (ed.), *Powell, Pressburger and Others* (London, BFI, 1978), p.91.
21. Rudolf Arnheim, *Film Art* (London, Faber and Faber, 1957; reprinted in 1983).
22. Durgnat: *A Mirror for England*, p.215.
23. Robert Murphy, *British Cinema and the Second World War* (London, Continuum, 2000), p.200.
24. Murphy: *British Cinema and the Second World War*, p.190.
25. John Ellis, 'Alien Insight', *New Statesman and Society*, vol. 7 (27 May 1994), p.46.
26. Printed in Lazar (ed.): *Michael Powell Interviews*, p.17.
27. Murphy: *British Cinema and the Second World War*, p.190.
28. Brian McFarlane, *Novel into Film: An Introductory Theory of Adaptation* (Oxford, Clarendon Press, 1996), p.9.
29. McFarlane: *Novel into Film*, p.13.

30 Christie (ed.): *Powell, Pressburger and Others*, p.75.
31 Christie (ed.): *Powell, Pressburger and Others*, p.75.
32 Geoff Hurd (ed.), *National Fictions: World War Two in British Films and Television* (London, BFI, 1984), p.35.
33 James Chapman, 'Our Finest Hour Revisited: The Second World War in British Feature Films Since 1945', *Journal of Popular British Cinema*, no. 1 (1998), p.65.
34 Hurd (ed.): *National Fictions*; Christine Geraghty, *British Cinema in the Fifties: Gender, Genre and the 'New Look'* (London, Routledge, 2000).
35 Winston Wheeler Dixon (ed.), *Re-Viewing British Cinema, 1900–92* (Albany NY, State University of New York Press, 1994).
36 Durgnat: *A Mirror for England*, p.83.
37 Geraghty: *British Cinema in the Fifties*, p.179.
38 Ian Christie, *Arrows of Desire: The Films of Michael Powell and Emeric Pressburger* (London, Faber and Faber, 1994), p.78.
39 Michael Powell, *Million Dollar Movie* (London, Mandarin, 1993), p.267.
40 Michael Powell, *Graf Spee* (London, Hodder and Stoughton, 1956), p.224.
41 Hurd (ed.): *National Fictions*, p.35.

Chapter 5

1 Jane Lewis, *Women in Britain since 1945* (Oxford, Blackwell, 1992), p.21.
2 Elizabeth Wilson, *Only Halfway to Paradise: Women in Post-war Britain, 1945–68* (London, Tavistock Publications, 1980), p.189.
3 Sue Aspinall and Robert Murphy (eds), *Gainsborough Melodrama* (London, BFI, 1983), p.14.
4 Andrew Higson (ed.), *Dissolving Views: Key Writings on British Cinema* (London, Cassell, 1996), p.62.
5 Higson (ed.): *Dissolving Views*, p.104.
6 Richard Dyer, *Brief Encounter* (London, BFI Classics, 1993), p.49.
7 First published in 1969, the article is reprinted in Bill Nichols (ed.), *Movies and Methods: An Anthology* (London, University of California Press, 1976).
8 Nichols (ed.): *Movies and Methods*, p.27.
9 Ian Christie (ed.), *Powell, Pressburger and Others* (London, BFI, 1978), p.70.
10 Michael Powell, *A Life in Movies* (London, Faber and Faber, 2000), p.583
11 Powell: *A Life in Movies*, p.581.
12 Quoted in Norman King, *Abel Gance* (London, BFI, 1984), p.72.
13 Richard Abel (ed.), *Silent Film* (London, The Athlone Press, 1996), p.35.
14 Quoted in King: *Abel Gance*, p.75.
15 Powell: *A Life in Movies*, p.343.
16 Powell: *A Life in Movies*, p.158.
17 Sergei Eisenstein (Jay Leyda trans. and ed.), *The Film Sense* (London, Faber and Faber, 1968), pp.14–18.

18   Powell: *A Life in Movies*, p.581.
19   Eisenstein (Leyda trans. and ed.): *The Film Sense*, p.66.
20   Eisenstein (Leyda trans. and ed.): *The Film Sense*, p.74.
21   Eisenstein (Leyda trans. and ed.): *The Film Sense*, p.77.
22   Eisenstein (Leyda trans. and ed.): *The Film Sense*, p.119.
23   Powell: *A Life in Movies*, p.582.
24   Powell: *A Life in Movies*, p.583.
25   Powell: *A Life in Movies*, p.561.
26   Powell: *A Life in Movies*, p.560.
27   Joseph Breuer and Sigmund Freud, *Studies in Hysteria* (London, Penguin, 1974), p.571.
28   Breuer and Freud: *Studies in Hysteria*, p.74.
29   Victor Burgin et al. (eds), *Formations of Fantasy* (London, Routledge, 1986), p.2.
30   Eisenstein (Leyda trans. and ed.): *The Film Sense*, p.122.
31   Rumer Godden, *Black Narcissus* (London, Pan Books, 1994), p.46.
32   Sigmund Freud, *The Essentials of Psycho-Analysis* (London, Penguin, 1986), p.306.
33   Breuer and Freud: *Studies in Hysteria*, p.74.
34   Christine Gledhill (ed.), *Home is Where the Heart is* (London, BFI, 1987), p.73.
35   Teresa de Lauretis and Stephen Heath (eds), *The Cinematic Apparatus* (London, Macmillan, 1980), p.47.
36   Reprinted in Sergei Eisenstein, *Eisenstein on Disney* (London, Methuen, 1988), p.28.
37   Toril Moi (ed.), *The Kristeva Reader* (London, Basil Blackwell, 1986), p.92.
38   Powell: *A Life in Movies*, p.168.
39   Edward Said, *Orientalism* (London, Pelican Books, 1985), p.40.
40   Sarah Street, *Transatlantic Crossings: British Feature Films in the USA* (London, Continuum, 2002), p.130.

Chapter 6

1   Raymond Williams, *Culture and Society 1780–1950* (Harmondsworth, Penguin, 1961), p.55.
2   Dyer Richard, *Only Entertainment* (London, Routledge, 1992).
3   Michael Powell, *A Life in Movies* (London, Faber and Faber, 2000), p.653.
4   Powell: *A Life in Movies*, p.549.
5   André Aciman (ed.), *Letters of Transit: Reflections on Exile, Identity and Loss* (New York, The New York Public Library, 1999), p.11.
6   Ellis Hanson (ed.), *Out Takes: Essays on Queer Theory and Film* (London, Duke University Press, 1999), p.51.
7   Arnold Haskell et al., *Since 1939: Ballet, Films, Music, Painting* (London, Phoenix Houses, 1948), p.18.

8   Winston Wheeler Dixon (ed.), *Re-Viewing British Cinema*, 1900–92 (Albany NY, State University of New York Press, 1994), p.108.
9   John Belton (ed.), *Movies and Mass Culture* (London, The Athlone Press, 1996), p.128.
10 Laura Mulvey, *Fetishism and Curiosity* (London, BFI, 1996), p.41.
11 Claudia Gorbman, *Unheard Melodies: Narrative Film Music* (London, BFI, 1987), p.24.
12 Lesley Stern, *The Scorsese Connection* (London, BFI, 1995), p.20.
13 Jeongwon Joe and Rose Theresa (eds), *Between Opera and Cinema* (London, Routledge, 2002), p.41.
14 Ian Christie (ed.), *Powell, Pressburger and Others* (London, BFI, 1978), p.69.
15 Harold Baldry, *The Case for the Arts* (London, Secker and Warburg, 1981), p.13.
16 Alan Sinfield, *Literature, Politics and Culture in Postwar Britain* (Oxford, Blackwell, 1989), p.53.
17 Becky Conekin, Frank Mort and Chris Waters (eds), *Moments of Modernity: Reconstructing Britain, 1945–64* (London, Rivers Oram Press, 1990), p.234.
18 Michael Sissons and Philip French (eds), *Age of Austerity* (London, Hodder and Stoughton, 1963), pp.319–20.
19 Monk Gibbon, *The Red Shoes Ballet: A Critical Study* (London, Saturn Press, 1948), p.25.
20 Gibbon: *The Red Shoes Ballet* and Monk Gibbon, *The Tales of Hoffmann: A Study of the Film* (London, Saturn Press, 1951).
21 Michael Powell, *Million Dollar Movie* (London, Mandarin, 1993), p.92.
22 Pierre Bourdieu, *Distinction: A Social Critique of the Judgement of Taste* (Cambridge MA, Harvard University Press, 1984), p.56.

Bibliography

Abel, Richard (ed.) (1996). *Silent Film* (London, The Athlone Press)
Aciman, André (ed.) (1999). *Letters of Transit: Reflections on Exile, Identity and Loss* (New York, The New York Public Library)
Allen, Richard (1995). *Projecting Illusion: Film Spectatorship and the Impression of Reality* (Cambridge, Cambridge University Press)
Anderson, Benedict (1983). *Imagined Communities: Reflections on the Origins and Spread of Nationalism* (London, Verso)
Arnheim, Rudolf (1983). *Film Art* (London, Faber and Faber)
Aspinall, Sue and Murphy, Robert (eds) (1983). *Gainsborough Melodrama* (London, BFI)
Babington, Bruce (ed.) (2001). *British Stars and Stardom* (Manchester, Manchester University Press)
Baldry, Harold (1981). *The Case for the Arts* (London, Secker and Warburg)
Barr, Charles (1999). 'In a Strange Land: the Collaboration of Michael Powell and Emeric Pressburger', *La Lettre de la Maison française d'Oxford* (no. 11, Trinity-Michaelmas)
Belton, John (ed.) (1996). *Movies and Mass Culture* (London, The Athlone Press)
Bhaba, Homi K. (ed.) (1990). *Nation and Narration* (London, Routledge)
Bordwell, David et al (1985). *The Classical Hollywood Cinema: Film Style and Mode of Production to 1960* (London, Routledge and Kegan Paul)
Bourdieu, Pierre (1984). *Distinction: A Social Critique of the Judgement of Taste* (Cambridge MA, Harvard University Press)
Breuer, Joseph and Freud, Sigmund (1974). *Studies in Hysteria* (London, Penguin)
Brodsky, Joseph (1988). 'The Condition We Call Exile', *New York Review of Books* (vol. 34, no. 21, 21 January)
Burgin, Victor et al (eds) (1986). *Formations of Fantasy* (London, Routledge)

Burton, Alan et al (eds) (1997). *Liberal Directions: Basil Dearden and Postwar British Film Culture* (Trowbridge, London)

Cawelti, John G. and Rosenberg, Bruce A. (1987). *The Spy Story* (Chicago, University of Chicago Press)

Chapman, James (1998). *The British at War: Cinema, State and Propaganda* (London, I. B. Tauris)

Chapman, James (1998). 'Our Finest Hour Revisited: The Second World War in British Feature Films Since 1945', *Journal of Popular British Cinema* (no. 1)

Christie, Ian (ed.) (1978). *Powell, Pressburger and Others* (London, BFI)

Christie, Ian (1994). *Arrows of Desire: The Films of Michael Powell and Emeric Pressburger* (London, Faber and Faber)

Christie, Ian (ed.) (1994). *The Life and Death of Colonel Blimp* (London, Faber and Faber)

Christie, Ian (2000). *A Matter of Life and Death* (London, BFI Classics)

Christie, Ian and Moor, Andrew (eds) (2005) *Michael Powell: International Perspectives on an English Film-Maker* (London: British Film Institute)

Cohen, Steve and Hark, Ina Rae (eds) (1993). *Screening the Male: Exploring Masculinities in Hollywood Cinema* (London, Routledge)

Conekin, Becky, Mort, Frank and Waters, Chris (eds) (1990). *Moments of Modernity: Reconstructing Britain, 1945–64* (London, Rivers Oram Press)

Connelly, Mark (2005). *The Red Shoes* (London, I.B.Tauris)

Cook, Pam (ed.) (1997). *Gainsborough Pictures* (London: Cassell)

Cook, Pam (2002). *I Know Where I'm Going!* (London, BFI Classics)

Dawson, Graham (1994). *Soldier Heroes: British Adventure, Empire and the Imagining of Masculinity* (London, Routledge)

de Lauretis, Teresa and Heath, Stephen (eds) (1980). *The Cinematic Apparatus* (London, Macmillan)

Denning, Michael (1987). *Cover Stories: Narrative and Ideology in the British Spy Thriller* (London, Routledge)

Dixon, Winston Wheeler (ed.) (1994). *Re-Viewing British Cinema, 1900–92* (Albany NY, State University of New York Press)

Durgnat, Raymond (1970). *A Mirror for England: British Movies from Austerity to Affluence* (London, Faber and Faber)

Dyer, Richard (1992). *Only Entertainment* (London, Routledge)

Dyer, Richard (1993). *Brief Encounter* (London, BFI Classics)

Eagleton, Terry (1970). *Exiles and Émigrés: Studies in Modern Literature* (London, Chatto and Windus)

Eisenstein, Sergei (Jay Leyda trans. and ed.) (1968). *The Film Sense* (London, Faber and Faber)

Eisenstein, Sergei (1988). *Eisenstein on Disney* (London, Methuen)

Eisner, Lotte (1973). *The Haunted Screen: Expressionism in the German Cinema and the Influence of Max Reinhardt* (London, Secker & Warburg)

Ellis, John (1994). 'Alien Insight', *New Statesman and Society* (vol. 7, 27 May)

Bibliography 241

Freud, Sigmund (1955). *The Standard Edition of the Complete Psychological Works, Vol. XCII* (London, Hogarth Press)
Freud, Sigmund (1986). *The Essentials of Psycho-Analysis* (London, Penguin)
Frogley, Alain (ed.) (1996). *Vaughan Williams Studies* (New York, Cambridge University Press)
Geraghty, Christine (2000). *British Cinema in the Fifties: Gender, Genre and the 'New Look'* (London, Routledge)
Gervais, David (1993). *Literary Englands: Versions of 'Englishness' in Modern Writing* (Cambridge, Cambridge University Press)
Gibbon, Monk (1948). *The Red Shoes Ballet: A Critical Study* (London, Saturn Press)
Gibbon, Monk (1951). *The Tales of Hoffmann: A Study of the Film* (London, Saturn Press)
Gilbert, Eliot L. (ed.) (1966). *Kipling and the Critics* (London, Peter Owen)
Gledhill, Christine (ed.) (1987). *Home is Where the Heart is* (London, BFI)
Gledhill, Christine (ed.) (1991). *Stardom: Industry of Desire* (London, Routledge)
Godden, Rumer (1994). *Black Narcissus* (London, Pan Books)
Gorbman, Claudia (1987). *Unheard Melodies: Narrative Film Music* (London, BFI)
Gramsci, Antonio (Quintin Hoare and Geoffrey Nowell-Smith trans. and eds) (1971). *Selections from the Prison Notebooks* (London, Lawrence and Wishart)
Graves, Robert (1942). *Occupation Writer* (New York, Creative Age Press)
Hanson, Ellis (ed.) (1999). *Out Takes: Essays on Queer Theory and Film* (London, Duke University Press)
Harper, Sue (1994). *Picturing the Past: The Rise and Fall of the British Costume Film* (London, BFI)
Harper, Sue and Porter, Vincent (1989). '*A Matter of Life and Death* – The View from Moscow', *Historical Journal of Film, Radio and Television* (vol. 9, no. 2)
Haskell, Arnold et al (1948). *Since 1939: Ballet, Films, Music, Painting* (London, Phoenix House)
Higson, Andrew (1995). *Waving the Flag: Constructing a National Cinema in Britain* (Oxford, Clarendon Press)
Higson, Andrew (ed.) (1996). *Dissolving Views: Key Writings on British Cinema* (London, Cassell)
Higson, Andrew (1999). 'Film Europe: a Transitional Challenge to the Idea of British Cinema', *La Lettre de la Maison française d'Oxford* (No. 11, Trinity-Michaelmas)
Hirschfeld, Gerhard (ed.) 1984. *Exile in Great Britain* (Leamington Spa, Berg Publishers)
Hobsbawm, E.J. (1968). *Industry and Empire: An Economic History of Britain Since 1750* (London, Weidenfield and Nicolson)
Hurd, Geoff (ed.) (1984). *National Fictions: World War Two in British Films and Television* (London, BFI)

Jackson, Rosemary (1981). *Fantasy: The Literature of Subversion* (London, Methuen)
Jameson, Fredric (1990). *Signatures of the Visible* (London, Routledge)
Joe, Jeongwon and Theresa, Rose (eds) (2002). *Between Opera and Cinema* (London, Routledge)
King, Norman (1984). *Abel Gance* (London, BFI)
Kulik, Karel (1975). *Alexander Korda: The Man Who Could Work Miracles* (London, W.H. Allen)
Landy, Marcia (1991). *British Genres: Cinema and Society 1930–60* (London, Princeton University Press)
Lant, Antonia (1991). *Blackout: Reinventing Women for Wartime British Cinema* (Princeton, Princeton University Press)
Lazar, David (ed.) (2003). *Michael Powell Interviews* (Jackson MS, Mississippi University Press)
Lewis, Jane (1992). *Women in Britain since 1945* (Oxford, Blackwell)
Low, David (1935). *Ye Madde Designer* (London, The Studio Ltd)
Macdonald, Kevin (1994). *Emeric Pressburger: The Life and Death of a Screenwriter* (London, Faber and Faber)
Macnab, Geoffrey (1993). *J. Arthur Rank and the British Film Industry* (London, Routledge)
Mallett, Phillip (ed.) (1989). *Kipling Considered* (London, Macmillan)
Mangan, J.A. and Walvin, James (eds) (1987). *Manliness and Morality: Middle Class Masculinity in Britain and America, 1800–1940* (Manchester, Manchester University Press)
McFarlane, Brian (1996). *Novel into Film: An Introductory Theory of Adaptation* (Oxford, Clarendon Press)
McVay, Douglas (1982). 'Michael Powell: Three Neglected Films', *Films and Filming* (no. 328)
Mellini, Peter (1984). 'Colonel Blimp's England', *History Today* (vol. 34, October)
Mellor, David (ed.) (1987). *A Paradise Lost: The Neo-Romantic Imagination in Britain, 1935–55* (London, Lund and Humphries)
Moi, Toril (ed.) (1986). *The Kristeva Reader* (London, Basil Blackwell Ltd)
Mouffe, Chantal (ed.) (1979). *Gramsci and Marxist Theory* (London: Routledge and Kegan Paul)
Mulvey, Laura (1989). *Visual and Other Pleasures* (Basingstoke, Macmillan)
Mulvey, Laura (1996). *Fetishism and Curiosity* (London, BFI)
Murphy, Robert, (1989, reprinted 1992). *Realism and Tinsel: Cinema and Society in Britain 1939–49* (London, Routledge)
Murphy, Robert (2000). *British Cinema and the Second World War* (London, Continuum)
Naficy, Hamid (ed.) (1999). *Home, Exile, Homeland: Film, Media and the Politics of Place* (London, Routledge)
Naficy, Hamid (2001). *An Accented Cinema: Exilic and Diasporic Filmmaking* (Princeton, Princeton University Press)

Nichols, Bill (ed.) (1976). *Movies and Methods: An Anthology* (London, University of California Press)
Orwell, George (1984). *The Penguin Essays of George Orwell* (London, Penguin)
Palmer, Jerry (1978). *Thrillers: Genesis and Structure of a Popular Genre* (London, Edward Arnold)
Patterson, Michael (1981). *The Revolution in German Theatre, 1900–33* (London, Routledge & Kegan Paul)
Perry, George (1974). *The Great British Picture Show: From the 90s to the 70s* (London, Hart-Davis MacGibbon Ltd)
Petrie, Duncan (ed.) (1982). *New Questions in British Cinema* (London, BFI)
Powell, Michael (1956). *Graf Spee* (London, Hodder and Stoughton)
Powell, Michael (1990). *Edge of the World* (London, Faber and Faber)
Powell, Michael (1993). *Million Dollar Movie* (London, Mandarin)
Powell, Michael (2000). *A Life in Movies* (London, Faber and Faber)
Richards, Jeffrey (1997). *Films and British National Identity: From Dickens to Dad's Army* (Manchester, Manchester University Press)
Richards, Jeffrey (ed.) (1998). *The Unknown 1930s: An Alternative History of the British Cinema, 1929–39* (London, The Athlone Press)
Richards, Jeffrey and Aldgate, Anthony (1983). *Best of British: Cinema and Society* (Oxford, Basil Blackwell)
Robertson, Alex J. (1987). *The Bleak Midwinter: 1947* (Manchester, Manchester University Press)
Robson, E.W. and Robson, M.M. (1943). *The Shame and Disgrace of Colonel Blimp: The True Story of The Film* (London, The Sidneyan Society)
Ryall, Tom (1996). *Alfred Hitchcock and the British Cinema* (London, The Athlone Press)
Said, Edward (1985). *Orientalism* (London, Pelican Books)
Samuel, Raphael (ed.) (1989). *Patriotism: The Making and Unmaking of British National Identity: Volume Three: National Fictions* (London, Routledge)
Seymour-Ure, Colin and Schoff, Jim (1985). *David Low* (London, Secker & Warburg)
Showalter, Elaine (1985). *The Female Malady: Women, Madness and English Culture, 1830–1980* (London, Virago Press)
Silverman, Kaja (1992). *Male Subjectivity at the Margins* (London, Routledge)
Sinfield, Alan (1989). *Literature, Politics and Culture in Postwar Britain* (Oxford, Blackwell)
Sinfield, Alan (1992). *Faultlines: Cultural Materialism and the Politics of Dissident Reading* (Oxford, Clarendon Press)
Sissons, Michael and French, Philip (eds) (1963). *Age of Austerity* (London, Hodder and Stoughton)
Smith, Anthony D. (1991). *National Identity* (London, Penguin)
Spicer, Andrew (2001). *Typical Men: The Representation of Masculinity in Popular British Cinema* (London, I. B. Tauris)
Stern, Lesley (1995). *The Scorsese Connection* (London, BFI)

Street, Sarah (1997). *British National Cinema* (London, Routledge)
Street, Sarah (2002). *Transatlantic Crossings: British Feature Films in the USA* (London, Continuum)
Street, Sarah (2005). *Black Narcissus* (London, I.B.Tauris)
Taylor, John Russell (1978). 'Michael Powell: Myths and Supermen', *Sight and Sound* (vol. 47. no. 4)
Taylor, John Russell (ed.) (1980). *The Pleasure Dome: Graham Greene: The Collected Film Criticism 1935–40* (Oxford: Oxford University Press).
Tonnies, Ferdinand (reprinted 1963). *Community and Society* (New York, Harper and Row)
Wiener, Martin J. (1981). *English Culture and the Decline of the English Spirit, 1885–1980* (Cambridge, Cambridge University Press)
Williams, Raymond (1961). *Culture and Society 1780–1950* (Harmondsworth, Penguin)
Williams, Raymond (1975). *The Country and the City* (St Albans, Paladin)
Williams, Raymond (1977). *Marxism and Literature* (Oxford, Oxford University Press)
Williams, Tony (1981). 'Michael Powell', *Films and Filming* (no. 326, November)
Wilson, Elizabeth (1980). *Only Halfway to Paradise: Women in Post-war Britain, 1945–68* (London, Tavistock Publications)

Index

Films are listed by title and are by Powell and Pressburger unless specified. Their uncompleted and unrealised film projects are listed under 'unfilmed works'.

accented cinema 12–14
   see also exile and émigrés
Age of Consent (1969) 14, 204
Airman's Letter to his Mother, An
   (M. Powell, 1941) 111
Andersen, Hans Christian 200, 210
Arnheim, Rudolf 151–52
Around the World in Eighty Days
   (M. Anderson, 1956) 139
art films 196–200
Arts and Crafts Movement 101
Arts Council, the 225, 226
As You Like It (W. Shakespeare) 108
Auden, W.H. 92

Baden-Powell, Robert 74
Balchin, Nigel 154
Bassermann, Albert 9
Battle of the River Plate, The (1956) 4, 133, 164–67
Beecham, Thomas 220
Belle et la Bête (J. Cocteau, 1946) 211
Bells Go Down, The (B. Dearden, 1943) 151

Best Years of Our Lives, The (W. Wyler, 1948) 131
Bhaba, Homi K. 9, 90
Black Narcissus (1947) 4, 11, 13, 171–72, 176, 179, 214, 217
Blackmail (A. Hitchcock, 1929) 11
Blue Lamp, The (B. Dearden, 1949) 131
Bluebeard's Castle (M. Powell, 1964) 220
Boer War 72, 76
Bourdieu, Pierre 228
Breuer, Joseph 181, 187
Brideshead Revisited (E. Waugh) 133–34
Brief Encounter (D. Lean, 1945) 130, 174–76
Brighton Rock (J. Boulting, 1947) 131
Brooke, Rupert 85, 86
Byron, Kathleen 121, 195

Cabinet of Doctor Caligari, The
   (R. Weine, 1919) 28, 38, 179, 216
Canterbury Tale, A (1944) 3, 4, 14, 17, 85–118, 120
Captive Heart, The (B. Dearden, 1946) 85–87, 131

Cardiff, Jack 181
Challenge, The (M. Rosmer and L. Trenker, 1938) 2–3
Chesterton, G.K. 108
Coal Face (A. Cavalcanti, 1935) 111
Committee for the Encouragement of Music and the Arts 225
Comolli, Jean-Luc 175
Contraband (1940) 4, 28, 43–47, 165
Courtneys of Curzon Street, The (H. Wilcox, 1947) 131
Craig, Edward Gordon 42–43
Cruel Sea, The (C. Frend, 1952) 162
Culpeper, Nicholas (1616–54) 104
'Cupid and Psyche' (Apuleius) 212

Dam Busters, The (M. Anderson, 1954) 152–54, 156, 163
Demi-Paradise, The (A. Asquith, 1943) 88
Denham Studios 180
Diaghilev, Sergei 205, 206, 207
diaspora *see* exile and émigrés
documentary 51, 110–11, 115–16, 146, 151, 191–92, 226
Dracula (B. Stoker) 37–38
Drum, The (Z. Korda, 1938) 27, 28, 68, 70
Duel in the Sun (K. Vidor, 1946) 131

Ealing Studios 86, 132–33
Easdale, Brian 66, 120, 182, 211
Edge of the World, The (1937) 2, 19, 118

Eisenstein, Sergei 177–78, 189
Elusive Pimpernel, The (1950) 13, 129, 139, 176
English Opera Group 225
exile and émigrés 7, 9, 11–13
Expressionism 28–29, 35, 40, 46–47, 204, 213

Farrar, David 140–41, 157, 190
Festival of Britain 226, 227
Film Europe 10
Film Society (London) 9
Fires Were Started (H. Jennings, 1943) 111, 151
First a Girl (V. Saville, 1935) 10
Flaherty, Robert 2
Four Feathers, The (Z. Korda, 1939) 6, 68, 70–71
49th Parallel (1941) 2, 4, 14, 19, 47–50, 206
Freud, Sigmund 181, 186

Gainsborough Studios 172–76
Gance, Abel 177
Gaslight (T. Dickinson, 1940) 205
Gemeinschaft (Ferdinand Tonnies) 98–100
Gentle Sex, The (L. Howard, 1943) 171
Georgian poetry 91
Gesamtkunstwerk (Richard Wagner) 178
Gesellschaft (Ferdinand Tonnies) 98–100

Index   247

Godden, Rumer 179
Golden Ass, The (Apuleius) 212
Goldwyn, Samuel 129
Gone to Earth (1950) 4, 119, 129, 171, 176, 201
Gramsci, Antonio 16, 22, 23, 65
Gray, Allan 66, 70, 120, 143, 182
Great Expectations (D. Lean, 1946) 148
Greene, Graham 7–8

Hamlet (L. Olivier, 1948) 130
Heart of Britain (H. Jennings, 1941) 110
Heaven Can Wait (E. Lubitsch, 1943) 161
Heckroth, Hein 9, 207, 213, 220, 223
Helpmann, Robert 200, 205, 207
Henry V (W. Shakespeare) 62, 78
Hiller, Wendy 18, 121
Hillier, Erwin 9, 123
Hitchcock, Alfred 30, 45
Hoffmann, E.T.A. 46
  see also *The Tales of Hoffmann*
Home 11, 15–16, 155
  see also exile and émigrés
Home from the Hill (V. Minnelli, 1959) 170
homoeroticism 73, 208–9
hybridity 8, 9, 10–11
hysteria 137, 183, 185–87

I Know Where I'm Going! (1945) 2, 4, 17, 118–25, 171, 225

I was Monty's Double (J. Guillermin, 1958) 162
Ice Cold In Alex (J.L. Thompson, 1958) 163
Ill Met by Moonlight (1957) 4, 133, 164
Imitation of Life (D. Sirk, 1959) 175
imperial epics 67–71, 222
incorporation 78–82
Independent Producers 19
Ingram, Rex 2
It Always Rains on Sunday (R. Hamer, 1947) 132
It's a Wonderful Life (F. Capra, 1946) 142

Jameson, Fredric (on utopia) 83–84
Jennings, Humphrey 110–11, 115–16, 146, 151, 226
Jolson Story, The (A.E. Green, 1946) 131
Jooss, Kurt 200, 207
Junge, Alfred 9, 59, 76, 143, 147

Kerr, Deborah 4, 79–80, 121, 194–95
Kipling, Rudyard 102–6
  Rewards and Fairies 20, 103, 105–6
  and *A Canterbury Tale* 20
  Kim 30
  Puck of Pook's Hill 103–4, 110
  Actions and Reactions 103
Korda, Alexander 2, 6, 11, 19, 27, 68–69, 129, 180, 193, 200, 205, 224

Kristeva, Julia 189
Kurwille (Ferdinand Tonnies) 99

Life and Death of Colonel Blimp, The
    (1943) 3, 11, 14, 17, 30, 31,
    54–84, 165, 166
Listen to Britain (H. Jennings and S.
    McAllister, 1942) 110, 115–16,
    146
literary adaptation 157–61, 183
London Films 6, 224
Low, David 54, 57, 58–59

Madonna of the Seven Moons (A.
    Crabtree, 1944) 172, 173
Magic Box, The (J. Boulting, 1951) 226
magic spaces 3–5
  and fantasy 35–36
Man in the White Suit, The (A.
    MacKendrick, 1951) 153
Marriage of Corbal, The (K. Grune) 7
masculinity 72–74
  and hunting 75, 133–67, 134
masquerade 33, 51–52
Massine, Léonide 205, 207
Matter of Life and Death, A (1946) 12,
    14, 51, 126, 133–52
Meet Me In St Louis (V. Minnelli, 1944)
    131
melodrama 170–77, 187
Metropolis (F. Lang, 1926) 193
Michel Strogoff (J. de Baroncelli and
    R. Eichberg, 1935) 10

Midsummer Night's Dream, A
    (W. Shakespeare) 4, 104, 146–47
Millions Like Us (F. Launder and S.
    Gilliat, 1943) 170
Mrs Miniver (W. Wyler, 1942) 89

Narboni, Jean 175
Nash, Paul 76, 92, 158
national cinema, British 5–6, 7–9,
    15–16, 21–26, 55, 78–82, 85–87
neo-Romanticism 92–93, 158
neurosis 181
Nibelungen, Die (F. Lang, 1924) 177
Nijinsky, Vaslav 205, 207
Niven, David 139, 220
nomadism *see* exile and émigrés
Nosferatu, Eine Symphonie des Grauens
    (F.W. Murnau, 1922) 30, 37, 40

Odd Man Out (C. Reed, 1947) 131
Oh… Rosalinda!! (1955) 4, 228
'… *one of our aircraft is missing'* (1942)
    4, 13, 14, 47, 50–53, 165, 206
Orientalism 192–93, 222
Orwell, George 57, 102

Passport to Pimlico (H. Cornelius, 1948)
    132
pastoralism 88–93, 94–98
Pavlova, Anna 205
Peeping Tom (M. Powell, 1960) 5, 14,
    204, 217
Perinal, Georges 70, 181

Index

Pinewood Studios 180
Powell, Michael
  early life and career 1–2
  publications
    Graf Spee 166
    A Life in Movies 204
    The Red Shoes (novel) 201–2
pre-composition 11, 179
Pressburger, Emeric
  early life and career 2
  and exile 6–7
  publications
    The Red Shoes (novel) 201–2
Private Life of Henry VIII, The
  (A. Korda, 1933) 6
psychosis 181

quality realism 5, 85, 130, 223
Queen of Spades, The (T. Dickinson, 1949) 205
Queen's Guards, The (1961) 167
queerness 208

Rambert, Marie 199, 205, 225
Rank, J. Arthur 18, 54, 128
Rebel without a Cause (N. Ray, 1955) 170
Red Ensign, The (1934) 204
Red Shoes, The (1948) 4, 11, 13, 171, 198–219
Richard II (W. Shakespeare) 88
Richardson, Ralph 4, 112–13
Riviere, Joan 33
  see also masquerade 33

Robber Symphony, The (F. Feher, 1937) 179
Robson, E.W. and M.M., *The Shame and Disgrace of Colonel Blimp* (1943) 55, 81
Royal Ballet 207

Sabotage (A. Hitchcock, 1936) 45
Sadler's Wells 225
Said, Edward 192
Selznick, David 129
Seventh Veil, The (C. Bennett, 1945) 131
Shearer, Moira 205
Small Back Room, The (1949) 37, 126, 133–38, 152–62
Soldier and the Lady, The (G. Nicholls Jr, 1937) 10
Sorcerer's Apprentice, The (1955) 220
spectacle 17, 72, 151–52, 219–20
Spy in Black, The (1939) 4, 13, 27–43, 45, 165
spy thrillers 30
Student of Prague, The (A. Robinson, 1935) 205
synaesthesia 151, 178

Tales of Hoffmann, The (1951) 4, 7, 11, 14, 198, 219–29
Tawny Pipit (B. Miles and C. Saunders, 1944) 89
Tempest, The (W. Shakespeare) 146
Third Man, The (C. Reed, 1949) 129, 131, 135

This England (D. Macdonald, 1941) 88
This Happy Breed (D. Lean, 1944) 88
Tonnies, Ferdinand 98–100
2000 Women (F. Launder and S. Gilliat, 1944) 171

unfilmed works (Powell and Pressburger)
  'Bouquet' 220
  'Burmese Silver' 193, 222
  'Calcutta' 222
  'East and the West, The' 27, 193, 222
  'Lotus of the Moon' 221
  'South East Frontier' 27, 193
  'Taj Mahal' 222
  'Undine' 211

Valois, Ninette de 207
Veidt, Conrad 9, 28, 204
Viktor und Viktoria (R. Schünzel, 1933) 10
Volunteer, The (1943) 4, 14, 51, 111–13

Wagner, Richard 178, 197, 203
Walbrook, Anton 9, 42, 81, 204–5, 206
war film (1950s) 152–54, 156, 162–67
Waxworks (P. Leni, 1924) 28, 38, 216
Way Ahead, The (C. Reed, 1944) 140
Way to the Stars, The (A. Asquith, 1945) 133
Webb, Mary 91
Welfare State 16, 126, 127, 132, 144–45, 168–70
Went the Day Well? (A. Cavalcanti, 1942) 88
Wesenwille (Ferdinand Tonnies) 99, 107
Wicked Lady, The (L. Arliss, 1945) 131, 172–76
Williams, Raymond
  on Romanticism 21
  residual, dominant and emergent 64, 84
  on the countryside 95
  on 'Art' 197
Williams, Vaughan 92
Wizard of Oz, The (V. Fleming, 1939) 116–17, 146, 216
Words for Battle (H. Jennings, 1941) 110